Communications
in Computer and Information Science 2035

Editorial Board Members

Rationale

The CCIS series is devoted to the publication of proceedings of computer science conferences. Its aim is to efficiently disseminate original research results in informatics in printed and electronic form. While the focus is on publication of peer-reviewed full papers presenting mature work, inclusion of reviewed short papers reporting on work in progress is welcome, too. Besides globally relevant meetings with internationally representative program committees guaranteeing a strict peer-reviewing and paper selection process, conferences run by societies or of high regional or national relevance are also considered for publication.

Topics

The topical scope of CCIS spans the entire spectrum of informatics ranging from foundational topics in the theory of computing to information and communications science and technology and a broad variety of interdisciplinary application fields.

Information for Volume Editors and Authors

Publication in CCIS is free of charge. No royalties are paid, however, we offer registered conference participants temporary free access to the online version of the conference proceedings on SpringerLink (http://link.springer.com) by means of an http referrer from the conference website and/or a number of complimentary printed copies, as specified in the official acceptance email of the event.

CCIS proceedings can be published in time for distribution at conferences or as post-proceedings, and delivered in the form of printed books and/or electronically as USBs and/or e-content licenses for accessing proceedings at SpringerLink. Furthermore, CCIS proceedings are included in the CCIS electronic book series hosted in the SpringerLink digital library at http://link.springer.com/bookseries/7899. Conferences publishing in CCIS are allowed to use Online Conference Service (OCS) for managing the whole proceedings lifecycle (from submission and reviewing to preparing for publication) free of charge.

Publication process

The language of publication is exclusively English. Authors publishing in CCIS have to sign the Springer CCIS copyright transfer form, however, they are free to use their material published in CCIS for substantially changed, more elaborate subsequent publications elsewhere. For the preparation of the camera-ready papers/files, authors have to strictly adhere to the Springer CCIS Authors' Instructions and are strongly encouraged to use the CCIS LaTeX style files or templates.

Abstracting/Indexing

CCIS is abstracted/indexed in DBLP, Google Scholar, EI-Compendex, Mathematical Reviews, SCImago, Scopus. CCIS volumes are also submitted for the inclusion in ISI Proceedings.

How to start

To start the evaluation of your proposal for inclusion in the CCIS series, please send an e-mail to ccis@springer.com.

Ulf Brefeld · Jesse Davis · Jan Van Haaren ·
Albrecht Zimmermann
Editors

Machine Learning and Data Mining for Sports Analytics

10th International Workshop, MLSA 2023
Turin, Italy, September 18, 2023
Revised Selected Papers

 Springer

Editors
Ulf Brefeld
Leuphana Universität Lüneburg
Lüneburg, Germany

Jesse Davis ⓘ
KU Leuven
Leuven, Belgium

Jan Van Haaren
KU Leuven
Leuven, Belgium

Albrecht Zimmermann ⓘ
University of Caen Normandy
Caen CEDEX 5, France

ISSN 1865-0929   ISSN 1865-0937 (electronic)
Communications in Computer and Information Science
ISBN 978-3-031-53832-2   ISBN 978-3-031-53833-9 (eBook)
https://doi.org/10.1007/978-3-031-53833-9

This Springer imprint is published by the registered company Springer Nature Switzerland AG
The registered company address is: Gewerbestrasse 11, 6330 Cham, Switzerland

Paper in this product is recyclable.

Preface

The Machine Learning and Data Mining for Sports Analytics workshop aims to bring together a diverse set of researchers working on Sports Analytics in a broad sense. In particular, it aims to attract interest from researchers working on sports from outside of machine learning and data mining. The 10th edition of the workshop was co-located with the European Conference on Machine Learning and Principles and Practice of Knowledge Discovery 2023.

Sports Analytics has been a steadily growing and rapidly evolving area over the last decade, both in US professional sports leagues and in European football leagues. The recent implementation of strict financial fair-play regulations in European football will definitely increase the importance of Sports Analytics in the coming years. In addition, there is the popularity of sports betting. The developed techniques are being used for decision support in all aspects of professional sports, including but not limited to:

- Match strategy, tactics, and analysis
- Player acquisition, player valuation, and team spending
- Training regimens and focus
- Injury prediction and prevention
- Performance management and prediction
- Match outcome and league table prediction
  Tournament design and scheduling
- Betting odds calculation

The interest in the topic has grown so much that there is now an annual conference on Sports Analytics at the MIT Sloan School of Management, which has been attended by representatives from over 70 professional sports teams in eminent leagues such as Major League Baseball, National Basketball Association, National Football League, National Hockey League, Major League Soccer, English Premier League, and the German Bundesliga. Furthermore, sports data providers such as Statsbomb, Stats Perform, and Wyscout have started making performance data publicly available to stimulate researchers who have the skills and vision to make a difference in the sports analytics community. Moreover, the National Football League has been sponsoring a Big Data Bowl where they release data and a concrete question to try to engage the analytics community.

There has been growing interest in the Machine Learning and Data Mining community about this topic, and the 2023 edition of MLSA built on the success of prior editions at ECML PKDD 2013 and, ECML PKDD 2015 – ECML/PKDD 2022.

Both the community's on-going interest in submitting to and participating in the MLSA workshop series, and the fact that you are reading the fifth volume of MLSA proceedings show that our workshop has become a vital venue for publishing and presenting sports analytics results. In fact, as participants, many of whom had submitted before, expressed during the workshop itself, venues for presenting machine learning and data mining-based sports analytics work remain rare, motivating us to continue to organize the workshop in future years.

In 2023, the workshop received a record 31 submissions of which 18 were selected after a single-blind reviewing process involving at least three program committee members per paper. One of the accepted papers was withdrawn from publication in the proceedings; two more were extended abstracts based on journal publications. In terms of the sports represented, soccer was less dominant than in past years, and, notably, a paper on sailing analysis was presented for the first time. Topics included tactical analysis, outcome predictions, data acquisition, performance optimization, and player evaluation, both physical and mental.

The workshop featured an invited presentation by Martin Rumo of OYM AG, University of Applied Sciences of Lucerne, and the Swiss Association of Computer Science in Sport on "Sports Data Analytics: A Science and an Art".

Further information about the workshop can be found on the workshop's website at https://dtai.cs.kuleuven.be/events/MLSA23/.

October 2023

Ulf Brefeld
Jesse Davis
Jan Van Haaren
Albrecht Zimmermann

Organization

Workshop Co-chairs

Ulf Brefeld   Leuphana University Lüneburg, Germany
Jesse Davis   KU Leuven, Belgium
Jan Van Haaren   Club Brugge, Belgium & KU Leuven, Belgium
Albrecht Zimmermann   Université de Caen Normandie, France

Program Committee

Gennady Andrienko   Fraunhofer, Germany
Adrià Arbués Sangüesa   Zelus Analytics, Spain
Gabriel Anzer   Universität Tübingen, Germany
Harish S. Bhat   University of California, Merced, USA
Lotte Bransen   SciSports, The Netherlands
Arie-Willem de Leeuw   Universiteit Leiden, Belgium
Kilian Hendrickx   KU Leuven/Siemens Digital Industries Software,
                               Belgium
Mehdi Kaytoue   Infologic, France
Leonid Kholkine   University of Antwerp, Belgium
John Komar   Nanyang Technological University, Singapore
Patrick Lambrix   Linköping University, Sweden
Etienne Lehembre   Université de Caen Normandie, France
Wannes Meert   KU Leuven, Belgium
Alexis Mortelier   Université de Caen Normandie, France
Konstantinos Pelechrinis   University of Pittsburgh, USA
François Rioult   GREYC CNRS UMR6072 - Université de Caen
                               Normandie, France
Pieter Robberechts   KU Leuven, Belgium
Robert Seidl   StatsPerform, Germany
Laszlo Toka   Budapest University of Technology and
                               Economics, Hungary
Maaike Van Roy   KU Leuven, Belgium
Nicolas Vergne   Université de Rouen Normandie, France
Steven Verstockt   University of Ghent, Belgium
Josh Weissbock   Carleton University, Canada

Contents

Keynote

Sports Data Analytics: An Art and a Science

Martin Rumo[✉]

University of Applied Sciences of Lucerne, Luzern, Switzerland
`martin.rumo@hslu.ch`

Abstract. This short paper highlights the role of sports data analytics in providing credible metrics for complex skills, aiding managers and coaches in decision-making processes. While Sport Science has been successful in contributing to exercise physiology and theories of training adaptions, it is less successful in explaining success in complex sports such as invasion sports. We propose a framework to deal with this complexity and providing meaningful metrices for individual and team performances. We demonstrate its utility by providing an example for individual and an example for team performance.

Keywords: Sports Data Analytics · Analytics Translation · Skill Representation

1 Definition of Sports and Its Consequencies for Sports Data Analytics

Sports must involve competition with winners determined by clear rules, emphasizing victory as the primary goal [1]. A rule-based process determining binary outcomes aligns with the principles of computer science. However, there are occasions where we presume the winner did not earn the victory but rather achieved it through luck. We define `skill` as the ability to do something well and we define `luck` as success or failure apparently brought about by chance. So, our perception of `success` in Sport is expressed by Eq. 1, with $0 \leq x \leq 1$:

$$\texttt{success} = \texttt{skill} \cdot x + \texttt{luck} \cdot (1 - x) \tag{1}$$

The ratio defined by x constitutes a distinctive attribute within a specific sport. Notably, an large value of x is observable through a reduced rate of regression to the mean in repeated competitions. This observation implies that in sports characterized by a larger x proficient athletes demonstrate the ability to consistently outperform their rivals, because their success relies less on chance. Consequently, strategic decisions within these sports tend to emphasize training methodologies and the application of sports science.

When x is small however, there is a faster regression to the mean and one can observe that `success` in these more `luck`-based sports rely more on good tactical decisions and coordinated team efforts.

U. Brefeld et al. (Eds.): MLSA 2023, CCIS 2035, pp. 3–7, 2024.
https://doi.org/10.1007/978-3-031-53833-9_1

1.1   It's All About Skill

What distinguishes sports from games is that success in sport should by definition not rely on any "luck" element (i.e. dices, shuffling of cards) specifically designed into the sport [1]. When we attribute success to chance, it might be because the skills involved are not quite understood. Complex skills are difficult to predict, and this difficulty often makes the situation seem more random to us. Therefore we propose that the luck part of success is rather due to unknown or not yet understood skills. Managers and Coaches try to understand skills in order to develop them and use them as selection criteria. Sports Data Analytics provides them with credible metrics for particulars skills in order to help them in their decision process.

1.2   What Contributes to Complexity?

In team sports, complexity arises from the interaction between players [3]. The dynamic interplay between teammates and opponents adds layers of complexity. Additionally, sports where offensive and defensive phases are enforced by strict rules on the number of possible scoring attempts, such as Baseball or American Football to a certain extend, tend to lower complexity in contrast to sports like Ice Hockey or European Football where both teams can enforce a phase shifts, introducing strategic options. Moreover, the average number of plausible points each team can score influences complexity, as scoring then can prompt strategic shifts during the game. Overall, the level of complexity in team sports is influenced by player interactions, rule structures, and strategic adaptations based on scoring dynamics.

2   How Do We Develop Meaningful Skill Metrics in Complex Sports?

Apart from basic physical requirements for football players, sport science still has little impact on practice in the day-to-day activity of football organisations [2]. We argue that this is mainly because the data do not adequately represent the technical and tactical concepts used in the reasoning of coaches and managers. In order to fill this semantic gap, we propose a process of reducing complexity along the concepts around skill and performance in specific sport related tasks [4]. In a sport science approach skills are usually broken down into basic skills that can be tested in a more standardized way. As an example, agility is seen as a combination of Change of Direction (COD) speed and the capability to quickly react to stimulus. Both can be tested separately. But for the coach, agility is a the capacity to solve a task, which is creating space in on-ball actions through quick and short accelerations. We propose that for the coach or manager it is more valuable to be able to evaluate to what extent a player is able to solve a task relevant for in-game performance.

2.1 How We Deal with Complexity?

Humans create concepts that chunk and generalize observations in order to understand complex processes. Data are raw facts about observations. In order to make data useful for a decision maker we need to align them with the shared concepts of the decision maker (e.g. coaches, managers and others.). Therefore, we propose the framework depicted in Fig. 1 for extracting information about in-game performance that is meaningful to coaches and managers. In the following sections, we will demonstrate its use for the concept of offensive agility as an individual skill and coordinated actions to regain possession of the ball as a team level skill.

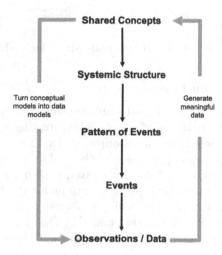

Fig. 1. Framework to create more meaningful data through Analytics Translation

2.2 Skills on the Individual Level

As mentioned in Sect. 2, agility is a complex skill that requires the optimal interplay of fast and accurate decision making, reactive strength and effective biomechanics. But on the pitch agility is required to complete specific tactical tasks, such as creating enough space for on-ball actions in offensive play. We propose to measure agility as the capacity to create oneself space for on-ball actions in game situation using tracking data. In Fig. 2, we show how the mentioned framework can be used for it.

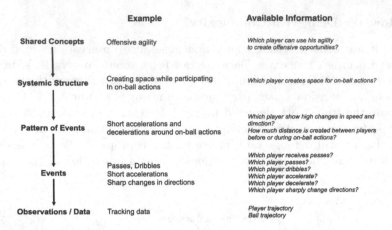

Fig. 2. Agility as the capacity to create space for on-ball actions

2.3   Skills on the Team Level

This framework further allows to model team coordination as systemic structure, that can be reduced to patterns of events, thus making it possible to create metrics for team coordination. In this example, we examine the shared concept of how a team can actively regain possession of the ball through coordinated player actions. The players involved in this coordinated task must either put pressure on the ball carrying player, or close passing options for the ball carrying player. A metric for the amount of pressure a single player exerts on the ball carrying player was proposed by Seidenschwarz et al. [5]. One can objectively measure how well a player closes passing options by counting the number of players in his cover shadow (Fig. 3).

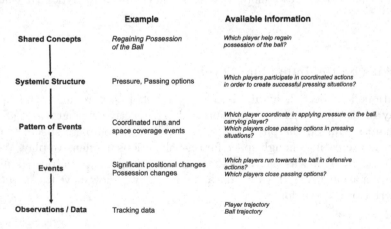

Fig. 3. Team coordination is required to effectively regain possession of the ball

3 Conclusion

Recognizing the existing semantic gap between traditional sport science concepts and the practical reasoning of coaches and managers, we proposed a framework aimed at aligning data with the shared concepts of decision makers in the sports industry. Our suggested framework, illustrated in Fig. 1, offers a structured approach to extracting meaningful information about in-game performance. In order to demonstrate its utility, we applied this framework to the evaluation of offensive agility at individual level and extended its applicability to the modeling of team coordination as a systemic structure, allowing for the reduction of complex coordination patterns into measurable metrics. In essence, this paper advocates for a paradigm shift in sports data analytics, urging to focus on concepts that matter most to coaches and managers. By bridging the gap between raw data and the technical and tactical reasoning of decision makers, our proposed framework aims to enhance the effectiveness of sports analytics in providing valuable insights for performance improvement and strategic decision-making in team sports.

References

1. Definition of sport - services - sportaccord - international sports federation. https://web.archive.org/web/20111028112912/. http://www.sportaccord.com/en/members/index.php?idIndex=32&idContent=14881. Accessed 12 Sept 2023
2. Drust, B., Green, M.: Science and football: evaluating the influence of science on performance. J. Sports Sci. **31**(13), 1377–1382 (2013). https://doi.org/10.1080/02640414.2013.828544, pMID: 23978109
3. Lames, M., McGarry, T.: On the search for reliable performance indicators in game sports. Int. J. Perform. Anal. Sport **7**(1), 62–79 (2007)
4. Seidenschwarz, P., Rumo, M., Probst, L., Schuldt, H.: A flexible approach to football analytics: assessment, modeling and implementation. In: Lames, M., Danilov, A., Timme, E., Vassilevski, Y. (eds.) IACSS 2019. AISC, vol. 1028, pp. 19–27. Springer, Cham (2020). https://doi.org/10.1007/978-3-030-35048-2_3
5. Seidenschwarz, P., Rumo, M., Probst, L., Schuldt, H.: High-level tactical performance analysis with sportsense. In: Proceedings of the 3rd International Workshop on Multimedia Content Analysis in Sports, pp. 45–52 (2020)

Football/Soccer

ETSY: A Rule-Based Approach to Event and Tracking Data SYnchronization

Maaike Van Roy[(✉)] [iD], Lorenzo Cascioli [iD], and Jesse Davis [iD]

Department of Computer Science, KU Leuven and Leuven.AI, Leuven, Belgium
{maaike.vanroy,lorenzo.cascioli,jesse.davis}@kuleuven.be

Abstract. Event data, which records high-level semantic events (e.g., passes), and tracking data, which records positional information for all players, are the two main types of advanced data streams used for analyses in soccer. While both streams when analyzed separately can yield relevant insights, combining them allows us to capture the entirety of the game. However, doing so is complicated by the fact that the two data streams are often not synchronized with each other. That is, the timestamp associated with an event in the event data does not correspond to the analogous frame in the tracking data. Thus, a key problem is to align these sources. However, few papers explicitly describe approaches for doing so. In this paper, we propose a rule-based approach ETSY for synchronizing event and tracking data, evaluate it, and compare experimentally and conceptually with the few state-of-the-art approaches available.

1 Introduction

Over the past years, there has been a dramatic increase in the amount of in-game data being collected about soccer matches. Until a few years ago, clubs that were using data mostly only had access to event data that describes all on-the-ball actions but does not include any information about what is happening off the ball. Hence, the configurations and movements of players, both during actions and in between, are missing. For example, it is impossible to distinguish between a pass from midfield with 5 defenders vs. 1 defender in front of the ball. Nonetheless, event data on its own can help address crucial tasks such as valuing on-the-ball actions [1, 6–10, 13] and assessing in-game decisions [4, 5, 11, 12].

More recently, top-level clubs have installed in-stadium optical tracking systems that are able to record the locations of all players and the ball multiple times per second. Thus, tracking data provides the necessary context that is missing in event data. However, it is not straightforward to perform tactical and technical analyses solely based on tracking data as it does not contain information about events such as passes, carries, and shots which are crucial to make sense of a match since they contain semantic information.

Consequently, the richest analyses require integrating both data streams. Unfortunately, these streams are often not time synchronized. That is, the event

U. Brefeld et al. (Eds.): MLSA 2023, CCIS 2035, pp. 11–23, 2024.
https://doi.org/10.1007/978-3-031-53833-9_2

at a specific timestamp does not correspond to the tracking frame with the same timestamp. Two main factors can create such misalignment. First, the clocks used in event and tracking data collection might start at slightly different times, introducing a constant bias. Second, because event data are manually annotated, the timestamp of an event can occasionally be inaccurate due to human reaction time or mistakes. Unfortunately, there are few approaches described in the literature for synchronizing these data types and the relative merits of existing approaches are unclear. In this paper, we propose a rule-based approach for accomplishing this. Then, this paper attempts to answer the following questions:

Q1 What are the current state-of-the-art synchronization approaches?
Q2 Is a simple rule-based approach sufficient to synchronize event and tracking data, or is a more complex approach needed?
Q3 What are the advantages and disadvantages of each approach?

Additionally, we provide a publicly available implementation of ETSY[1].

2   Problem Statement and Existing Approaches

Formally, the task of synchronizing event and tracking data from the same game is defined as follows:

Given:

1. Event data of a game, which contains for each on-the-ball action its location on the pitch (i.e., the x and y coordinate), the type (e.g., pass, shot, interception), the time of the action, the result, the body part used, the player that performed the action and the team he plays for.
2. Tracking data of the same game, which typically contains 10 or 25 frames per second (FPS), and includes in each frame all x,y-coordinates of all players and the x, y, z-coordinates of the ball at that moment in time.

Do: Assign each event a matching tracking frame such that it corresponds to the match situation at the moment of the event (i.e., the ball is at the same location in the event and tracking data, the player that performs the action in the event data is the same player that is in possession of the ball in the frame, and this player performs the same action as recorded in the event data).

There are few publicly described synchronization approaches. The approach by Anzer & Bauer [2,3] uses two steps to synchronize the data streams. First, it matches the kickoff event with its analogous tracking frame and computes the offset in time between them. It then uses this offset to shift all timestamps in the tracking data to remove the constant bias. To match the kickoff event with its analogous tracking frame, they use the movement of the ball to identify the kickoff frame within the first frames of the tracking data when the game has started. Second, for each event, it determines windows of possession where the

---

[1] https://github.com/ML-KULeuven/ETSY.

player is within two meters of the ball and uses a weighted sum of features (e.g., time difference between the event and the tracking frame, distance between ball and player, distance between ball coordinates in the event and tracking data) to determine the best frame. Grid search on a manually labeled test set is used to optimize the weights. Currently, their approach has only been evaluated on the most relevant actions, passes and shots, and yields satisfactory results for both.

Alternatively, `sync.soccer` is a bio-informatics-inspired approach by Clark & Kwiatkowski[2]. Their method is based upon the Needleman-Wunsch algorithm (similar to Dynamic Time Warping) that can synchronize any two sequences of data. In a nutshell, this approach compares every event with every tracking frame and uses a self-defined scoring function (i.e., a weighted combination of time difference between the event and the tracking frame, distance between ball and player, distance between ball coordinates in the event and tracking data, and whether the ball is in play) to measure the fit between them. Next, it constructs the synchronized sequence with the best overall fit. This approach is more general than that of Anzer & Bauer as it allows to synchronize any event type instead of only passes and shots, and without the need for manually labeled examples. However, the weights of the scoring function need to be tuned separately for each game, which is not straightforward and time intensive.

3   ETSY

We now outline our rule-based synchronization approach ETSY. To represent the event data, we use SPADL [6] which is a unified format to represent all on-the-ball actions in soccer matches. Therefore, any event stream that can be transformed to SPADL can be used. Next, we outline the necessary preprocessing steps to prepare the data and describe our algorithm.

3.1   Preprocessing

Before aligning the two data streams, four preprocessing steps are performed.

1. Event and tracking data often use different coordinate systems to represent the pitch, with event data often using the intervals $[0, 100] \times [0, 100]$ and tracking data the IFAB coordinate system (i.e., $[0, 105] \times [0, 68]$). Therefore, the event coordinates are transformed to match the coordinate system of the tracking data.[3]
2. The event data of each team is transformed to match the playing direction of the tracking data.
3. Only the tracking frames in which the game is not officially paused are kept. This removes e.g., frames before the start, VAR checks, and pauses due to injury. This ensures that events are matched with open-play frames only.
4. The velocity and acceleration of the ball are computed and added to each tracking frame.

---

[2] https://github.com/huffyhenry/sync.soccer.
[3] The following package provides such a transformation: https://mplsoccer. readthedocs.io/en/latest/gallery/pitch_plots/plot_standardize.html.

3.2   Synchronization

The event and tracking data of each game are divided into the first and second period. The synchronization is run for each period separately. Our rule-based algorithm consists of the following two steps:

Step 1. Synchronize kickoff. Similar to Anzer & Bauer, we remove the constant bias between the timestamps in the event and tracking data by aligning the kickoffs. We determine which frame best matches the kickoff event by identifying, in the first five seconds of the game, the frame in which the ball is within two meters from the acting player and where the acceleration of the ball is the highest. The tracking data timestamps are then corrected for this offset.

Step 2. Synchronize remaining events. We synchronize all remaining SPADL events except "non_action", which is not an action, and "dribbles", which are imputed in the SPADL conversion but not present in the original data. Algorithm 1.1 summarizes the two steps needed: (1) identify the qualifying window of frames, and (2) score each frame in this window to find the best one.

```
1  For each action:
2      window = get_window_of_frames_around(action, t_a)
3      frame, score = get_matching_frame(action, window)
```
Algorithm 1.1. Core synchronization approach of ETSY.

`get_window_of_frames_around(action, $t_a$)` identifies a qualifying window of frames in which the matching frame is most likely to be found. It retrieves all tracking frames within a time window of $2*t_a$ seconds around the tracking frame with the same (adjusted) timestamp as the event's timestamp.

`get_matching_frame(action, window)` assigns a score to each frame in the window based on how well it matches the action. First, it filters out all frames within the window that cannot be considered due to general and event-specific consistency rules. As a general rule, the timestamp of the frame should be later than the last matched frame. Other filters are action specific and we provide an overview in Sect. 3.3. Second, it scores each remaining frame using the (unweighted) sum of three linear functions with the same range of output values. These functions are (1) a function that maps the distance between the ball and the acting player in the tracking frame to a score $\in [0, 33.33]$, (2) a function that maps the distance between the acting player's location in the event data and the tracking data to a score $\in [0, 33.33]$, and (3) a function that maps the distance between the ball's location in the event data and the tracking data to a score $\in [0, 33.33]$. This yields a minimum score of 0 and a maximum score of 100. The frame with the highest total score is returned as the best matching frame.

3.3   Action-Specific Filters

Table 1 provides a summary of the employed action-specific filters. First, we group all SPADL actions into five categories, depending on their semantics:

- "Set-piece" denotes all possible actions performed during a set-piece.
- "Pass-like in open-play" denotes actions performed during open-play that move the ball away from the acting player.
- "Incoming" denotes actions where the acting player is receiving the ball.
- "Bad touch" simply denotes a bad touch.
- "Fault-like" denotes either a foul or tackle.

Next, we define for each category the time window parameter t_a. For all categories but set-pieces, we choose t_a equal to five seconds. Set-pieces typically require some set-up time and their annotated timestamps might be more off with respect to other actions. Hence, we extend t_a to 10 s to increase the chances that the matching frame is contained in the window.

Finally, we define the action-specific filters. We want the ball to be sufficiently close to the acting player. Thus, we enforce a maximum threshold on the distance between the two, allowing for some measurement error in the data. The distance for bad touches is set a bit larger as those typically already move the ball further away from the player. Similarly, fault-like actions do not need to be in close proximity to the ball. Filters on ball height aim at excluding frames where the ball height is not coherent with the body part used to perform the action. When the ball is up in the air, players typically do not use their feet to kick it; vice versa, a low ball is rarely hit with the head. Actions performed with hands (e.g., throw-ins, keeper saves) can happen at higher heights, as the players can jump and use their arms. In some cases, we add an extra limitation on whether the ball should be accelerating or decelerating. The ball should clearly be accelerating when a set-piece or pass-like action is performed with a player's feet. Similarly, the ball should be decelerating when the acting player is receiving the ball.

4   Evaluation

We evaluate our approach on one season of a European first-division league. After removing games where one data source had too many errors (e.g., ball location was not recorded), we have 313 games. We compare the proposed approach to the existing approaches, both experimentally and conceptually. The approach of Anzer & Bauer is left out of the experimental comparison, as we do not have access to matching video footage nor experts to label a part of our data set.

Table 1. Action-specific filters and time window parameters.

Type	Actions	t_a	Distance	Height	Extra
Set-piece	throw_in, freekick, corner, goalkick, penalty	10s	$\leq$ 2.5m	$\leq$ 1.5m (with foot), $\leq$ 3m (other)	accelerate (with foot)
Pass-like in open-play	pass, cross, shot, take_on, clearance, keeper_punch	5s	$\leq$ 2.5m	$\leq$ 1.5m (with foot), $\geq$ 1m (with head), $\leq$ 3m (other)	accelerate (with foot)
Incoming	interception, keeper_save, keeper_claim, keeper_pickup	5s	$\leq$ 2m	$\leq$ 3m	decelerate
Bad touch	bad_touch	5s	$\leq$ 3m	$\leq$ 1.5m (with foot), $\geq$ 1m (with head), $\leq$ 3m (other)	/
Fault-like	foul, tackle	5s	$\leq$ 3m	$\leq$ 4m	/

4.1   Experimental Setup

It must be noted that the original implementation of `sync.soccer` is written in Haskell and only accepts StatsPerform's F24 event feeds and ChyronHego's Tracab files. As these formats are different from the data we have available, we have created a Python implementation of the same algorithm that can use our data set and compare against our implementation.

The original `sync.soccer` implementation does not remove the constant bias between the event and tracking data timestamps. Therefore, this method relies entirely on the weights of the score function, which need to be tuned separately for each game. This is not straightforward and requires one to trade off the time difference between the events and tracking frames with the different distance metrics used. Including the kickoff synchronization step outlined in our approach to remove the constant time-bias mitigates this problem and improves the quality of the synchronization. In the comparison, we have included both `sync.soccer` approaches and used equal weights for all parts of the score function.

4.2   Experimental Comparison

It is not straightforward to measure the quality of the resulting synchronization as we do not have access to ground truth labels. Even when one has access to video footage of the game to validate with, it is unlikely that the video's timestamps will perfectly align with the extracted tracking data. Consequently, it is difficult to link the tracking frames to the snapshots in the video and determine the exact moment of an event. Thus, it is hard to report an accuracy-like metric. Therefore, we propose to look at two alternative metrics: the coverage (i.e., the

percent of events for which a matching frame can be found), and the agreement
with ETSY within s seconds (i.e., the percent of events for which the found frame
is within a range of s seconds from the one identified by ETSY). Additionally, we
compare the runtime of the different approaches.

Coverage and Runtime. Table 2 summarizes the coverage and runtime of
ETSY, sync.soccer and a naive timestamp-based approach, both with and without the time-bias adjustment using the kickoff alignment step.

Table 2. Experimental comparison of ETSY, sync.soccer, and a timestamp-based
approach on runtime and coverage. A * indicates the time-bias adjusted version.

Approach	Average time/game	Coverage
ETSY	2.7 min ($\pm$ 17 s)	91.61 %
timestamp	21 s ($\pm$ 2 s)	95.90%
timestamp (*)	21 s ($\pm$ 2 s)	99.83%
sync.soccer	8.6 min ($\pm$ 38 s)	100%
sync.soccer (*)	8.6 min ($\pm$ 38 s)	100%

By construction, sync.soccer pairs every event with a tracking frame and
hence achieves a coverage of 100%, regardless of how bad the resulting match is.
The timestamp-based approach finds a matching frame for an event as long as
a corresponding timestamp exists among the tracking data. When misalignment
due to clock bias is present, some events at the beginning or end of a period
might not be covered because the tracking frames have either not started yet or
are already finished. In contrast, when no suitable frame can be found according
to the rule base, ETSY does not return a match. Over all considered events, ETSY
yields a coverage of 91.61%. We perform an analysis on ETSY's missed events in
Sect. 4.3. Additionally, the score given to each match by our algorithm can be
used as a threshold during a subsequent analysis process. For example, one could
retrieve all passes with a matched frame and a score >95% (i.e., the method is
quite certain that this is the exact frame that matches the event) to ensure only
perfectly synchronized data is used in the analysis.

Naturally, using a timestamp-based approach is the fastest as this involves
only a retrieval of the frames with the matching timestamps. Compared to our
implementation of sync.soccer, ETSY performs its synchronization roughly six
minutes per game faster. The runtime of our sync.soccer implementation is
consistent with that reported by Clark & Kwiatkowski. Note that including the
time-bias adjustment step only incurs a negligible amount of extra runtime.

Agreement. Figure 1 shows the agreement with ETSY for both sync.soccer
and timestamp-based approaches. Without time-bias adjustment, most of the

found frames lie more than five seconds apart and hence no longer correspond to the same match context. In contrast, the time-bias adjusted versions perform much better. Most of the frames lie within one second of the frame found by ETSY. This indicates the need for a time-bias adjustment in the existing approaches.

Additionally, we inspect the agreement for each of the defined action categories in Fig. 2. This gives us an indication of which actions are easier to match than others. We only compare with the time-bias adjusted versions as the kickoff alignment step was shown to be necessary. For bad touches, open-play, incoming, and fault-like actions, the distributions are quite similar. The majority of the found frames are within one second from the frame identified by ETSY, indicating a rather strong agreement. However, for set-pieces, we see an increase in the number of events with a frame that is further off from the one identified by ETSY. This could possibly indicate that the fixed time window used for set-pieces is not ideal and might need adjusting in the future.

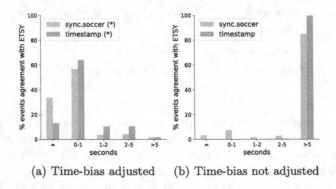

(a) Time-bias adjusted   (b) Time-bias not adjusted

Fig. 1. Agreement with ETSY for (a) the time-bias adjusted and (b) the non-adjusted versions of `sync.soccer` and the timestamp-based approach. All action types are included and the agreement is computed over five disjunct windows.

4.3   Missed Events Analysis

Next, we look at what happens in those cases where ETSY does not find a suitable match. The method does not find a matching frame when all the frames in the selected window are filtered out by the rules presented in Sects. 3.2 and 3.3. Thus, we take the events where no matching frame is found and in turn drop one of the filters to verify if without it a matching frame would have been found. This allows us to analyze whether some of the imposed rules are largely responsible for the misses. Table 3 shows the results for each action category.

Note that the row values do not sum to 100%. As long as there is at least one frame left after filtering, a matching frame is identified by the algorithm. However, different filters might exclude different frames. Thus, it is possible (and likely), that multiple filters are concurrently responsible for not returning a match, and removing each filter could "free" a different frame in the window.

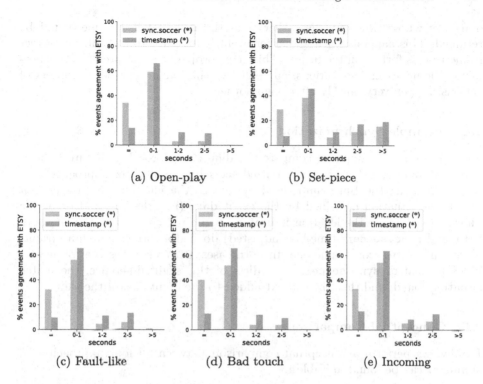

Fig. 2. Agreement with ETSY for the time-bias adjusted versions of `sync.soccer` and the timestamp-based approach. The agreement is calculated for each action category.

Table 3. ETSY missed events analysis. The percentages indicate how many of the unmatched events would have a matching frame if each filter was dropped.

Action type	Total misses	Distance	Height	Time	Acceleration
Set-piece	982	100%	1%	10%	8%
Pass-like in open-play	24783	91%	17%	42%	25%
Incoming	4718	98%	3%	41%	22%
Bad touch	309	89%	19%	58%	/
Fault-like	883	98%	1%	69%	/

In most cases, removing the distance filter would yield a matching frame. However, the associated frame would probably be wrong, as the ball would be far away from the acting player. It is possible that these are cases where either a slight error exists in the tracked locations, thus stretching distances between player and ball, or in the annotated timestamps, meaning that the window of selected frames does not include the correct frame. While filters on ball height and acceleration show a minor influence, the filter on timestamps also has a consistent effect. Except for set-pieces, roughly half of the misses would be avoided if frames whose timestamp is earlier than the last matched frame would be retained. This happens when an earlier event is matched to a slightly incorrect frame that is further in the future. This error propagates and prevents synchronizing the next couple of actions. For example, this can occur when a number of actions happen very quickly after one another.

4.4   Example Synchronization

Next, we use an example to compare the different approaches. Figure 3 shows two random events that are synchronized according to all three approaches.

When using the timestamp-based approach, the identified frames do not match the situation described by the event data (i.e., the ball and/or acting player are not near the location indicated by the red cross). In contrast, both ETSY and sync.soccer (time-bias adjusted) do find a correct matching frame, although not the exact same one. In both cases, ETSY identifies the frame previous to that of sync.soccer. Regardless of this slight difference, the match situation found, and thus the context added to the event, is still the same.

4.5   Conceptual Comparison

Finally, we perform a conceptual comparison between all four approaches. A summary can be found in Table 4.

Table 4. Conceptual comparison of ETSY, sync.soccer, the timestamp-based approach, and Anzer & Bauer's approach. A − means a property is only partially present.

Approach	Automated	All actions	No extra data	Bias solved	Code
ETSY	X	X	X	X	X
timestamp	X	X	X	−	
sync.soccer	−	X	X	−	X
Anzer & Bauer	−			X	

Both sync.soccer and ETSY are a general open-source approach to synchronize *all actions* in event data with their matching tracking frame. In contrast, the approach by Anzer & Bauer has so far only been applied to and proven to work for passes and shots. Additionally, it requires an expert to manually label a set of training data and thus relies on more information than is available in the event and tracking data. As neither the video footage nor experts are always available, both sync.soccer (especially when augmented with a time-bias adjustment) and ETSY provide a more general approach to synchronize event and tracking data. The original sync.soccer approach is not entirely automated as it still requires one to fine-tune the weights of the scoring function for each game. This

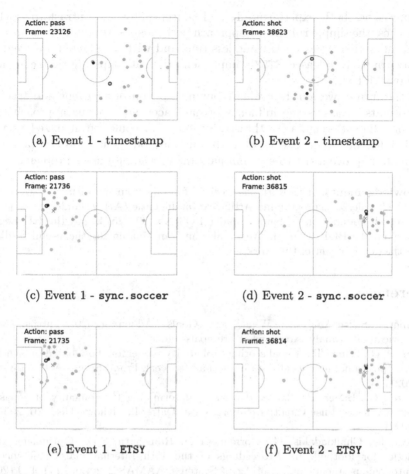

Fig. 3. Illustration of two random events synchronized by three approaches. The red cross indicates where the event takes place in the event data, the black encircled player is the acting player according to the event data. All player positions are shown according to the matched frame and the ball is shown in black. (Color figure online)

can be mitigated by adding a time-bias adjustment step, after which the approach produces an automated and satisfactory synchronization. Naturally, the timestamp-based approach is automated and can be applied to synchronize all actions. However, its performance is unacceptable.

5   Conclusion

This paper addresses the task of synchronizing soccer event data with tracking data of the same game, which is a problem that is not often explicitly mentioned in the literature. This paper provides an overview of the current state-of-the-art approaches, introduces a simple rule-based approach ETSY, and compares the approaches both experimentally and conceptually. In contrast to existing approaches, the simple rule-based approach performs a satisfactory synchronization for all action types while using less time and without manual intervention. We have publicly released ETSY's implementation at https://github.com/ML-KULeuven/ETSY.

In the future, we aim to evaluate our method on other event and tracking data formats to assess the influence of data accuracy on our approach. The effect of different weights for the scoring function could be analyzed as well. Additionally, we would like to evaluate our method using video footage, and investigate improvements to e.g., mitigate the cascading misses problem.

Acknowledgements. This work has received funding from the Flemish Government under the "Onderzoeksprogramma Artificiële Intelligentie (AI) Vlaanderen" program, the Research Foundation - Flanders under EOS No. 30992574, and the KU Leuven Research Fund (iBOF/21/075). We thank Jan Van Haaren for the useful feedback during the development of this work.

References

1. AmericanSoccerAnalysis: What are Goals Added (2020). https://www.americansocceranalysis.com/what-are-goals-added
2. Anzer, G., Bauer, P.: A goal scoring probability model for shots based on synchronized positional and event data in football (soccer). Front. Sports Active Living **3** (2021)
3. Anzer, G., Bauer, P.: Expected passes - determining the difficulty of a pass in football (soccer) using spatio-temporal data. Data Min. Knowl. Disc. **36**, 295–317 (2022)
4. Beal, R., Chalkiadakis, G., Norman, T.J., Ramchurn, S.D.: Optimising game tactics for football. In: Proceedings of the 19th International Conference on Autonomous Agents and MultiAgent Systems, AAMAS 2020, pp. 141–149 (2020)
5. Beal, R., Changder, N., Norman, T., Ramchurn, S.: Learning the value of teamwork to form efficient teams. In: Proceedings of the AAAI Conference on Artificial Intelligence, vol. 34, pp. 7063–7070 (2020)
6. Decroos, T., Bransen, L., Van Haaren, J., Davis, J.: Actions speak louder than goals: valuing player actions in soccer. In: Proceedings of the 25th ACM SIGKDD International Conference on Knowledge Discovery & Data Mining, KDD 2019, pp. 1851–1861 (2019)
7. Merhej, C., Beal, R.J., Matthews, T., Ramchurn, S.: What happened next? Using deep learning to value defensive actions in football event-data. In: Proceedings of the 27th ACM SIGKDD Conference on Knowledge Discovery & Data Mining, KDD 2021, pp. 3394–3403 (2021)
8. Rudd, S.: A framework for tactical analysis and individual offensive production assessment in soccer using Markov chains. In: New England Symposium on Statistics in Sports (2011)
9. Singh, K.: Introducing Expected Threat (2019). https://karun.in/blog/expected-threat.html
10. StatsBomb: Introducing On-Ball Value (OBV) (2021). https://statsbomb.com/articles/soccer/introducing-on-ball-value-obv/

11. Van Roy, M., Robberechts, P., Yang, W.C., De Raedt, L., Davis, J.: Leaving goals on the pitch: evaluating decision making in soccer. In: Proceedings of the 15th MIT Sloan Sports Analytics Conference, pp. 1–25 (2021)
12. Van Roy, M., Robberechts, P., Yang, W.C., De Raedt, L., Davis, J.: A Markov framework for learning and reasoning about strategies in professional soccer. J. Artif. Intell. Res. **77**, 517–562 (2023)
13. Yam, D.: Attacking Contributions: Markov Models for Football (2019). https:// statsbomb.com/2019/02/attacking-contributions-markov-models-for-football/

Masked Autoencoder Pretraining for Event Classification in Elite Soccer

Yannick Rudolph[✉] and Ulf Brefeld

Leuphana University of Lüneburg, Lüneburg, Germany
yannick.rudolph@leuphana.de

Abstract. We show that pretraining transformer models improves the performance on supervised classification of tracking data from elite soccer. Specifically, we propose a novel self-supervised masked autoencoder for multiagent trajectories. In contrast to related work, our approach is significantly simpler, has no necessity for handcrafted features and inherently allows for permutation invariance in downstream tasks.

Keywords: Self-supervised learning · Multiagent trajectories · Masked autoencoder · Factorized transformer architecture · Tracking data · Soccer

1 Introduction

Automatically labeling instances of multiagent tracking data from team sports regarding the occurrence of selected in-game events (such as on-ball actions) is an important topic for sports analytics. While supervised learning for this task is conceptually straightforward, contemporary deep learning models may require a substantial amount of manually annotated labels, even when exploiting inherent data symmetries.

To date, supervised models for multiagent trajectories involve training on either handcrafted or static features [1,5,11] or make use of self-supervised and semi-supervised methods incorporating autoregressive reconstruction tasks [7,13]. Although autoregressive models have demonstrated impressive performance in certain generative tasks [3,14], recent research in language and vision domains suggests that data denoising techniques might be more suitable for pretraining models for downstream tasks [6,9]. Moreover, some self-supervised approaches for multiagent trajectory data fail to account for apparent symmetries in the data. Specifically, models and objectives may not exhibit permutation equivariance or permutation invariance concerning the ordering of agents.

In this paper, we introduce a novel self-supervised pretraining method designed for the classification of multiagent trajectory instances. We refer to this method as trajectory masked autoencoder (T-MAE). In our approach, we

---

Y. Rudolph—Work in large part performed while at SAP SE, Machine Learning R&D, Berlin.

reconstruct randomly masked segments within trajectories, integrating a novel masking scheme into a transformer architecture that factorizes over both time and agent dimensions. The factorization endows the encoder, which serves as the feature extractor, with permutation equivariance concerning the ordering of trajectories. Empirically, our approach enables modeling capacities of highly over-parameterized modern transformer architectures for downstream tasks even when provided with only a limited number of labeled instances. At the same time, the approach enhances performance for scenarios with lots of training data. Our experiments demonstrate that pretrained models consistently outperform their un-pretrained counterparts on the task of classifying instances of multiagent trajectories concerning events in professional soccer matches.

2   Preliminaries and Problem Formulation

In this paper, we focus on trajectories with a consistent length of T timesteps that involve a fixed number of K agents across all instances of multiagent trajectories. Notably, we refrain from assuming any partial or total order on the set of agents. The observations collected for agent $1 \leq k \leq K$ at timestep $1 \leq t \leq T$ are represented as $\mathbf{x}_k^t$. The observations may encompass various features, including but not limited to two-dimensional positions in space as well as the speed or/and rotation angles of agents or parts of agents. A comprehensive trajectory for a specific agent, denoted as k, can be expressed as $\mathbf{x}_k^{1:T}$, while a single timestep t for the entire *set* of agents is represented as $\{\mathbf{x}_1^t, \ldots, \mathbf{x}_K^t\}$. Given that each instance comprises a *set* of trajectories, we denote a complete multiagent trajectory instance as $\mathbf{x} = \{\mathbf{x}_1^{1:T}, \ldots, \mathbf{x}_K^{1:T}\}$.

Let $\mathcal{X}$ be the space of possible multiagent trajectories. Our objective is to address the following multi-label classification problem: Given a set of N labeled instances of multiagent trajectories denoted as $\mathcal{D} = \{(\mathbf{x}^{(n)}, \mathbf{y}^{(n)})\}_{n=1}^{N}$, where $\mathbf{x}^{(n)}$ belongs to $\mathcal{X}$ and $\mathbf{y}^{(n)}$ are binary label vectors in $\mathbb{Z}_2^L$, with L denoting the number of classes, our aim is to learn a function $f : \mathcal{X} \to \mathbb{Z}_2^L$ that can effectively generalize when applied to unseen data.

Because we need to introduce a certain (potentially random) arrangement of agents and their respective trajectories within our model's input, the direct application of conventional supervised classification networks is rendered suboptimal. In light of this, we require that the function f possesses the property of being *permutation invariant* with respect to the ordering of trajectories. To be precise: Let π denote a K-tuple representing permutations of integers from 1 to K. If we have $f\left([\mathbf{x}_1^{1:T}, \ldots, \mathbf{x}_K^{1:T}]\right) = \hat{\mathbf{y}}$, it is essential that for any permutation π, we also achieve $f\left([\mathbf{x}^{1:T}\pi_1, \ldots, \mathbf{x}^{1:T}\pi_K]\right) = \hat{\mathbf{y}}$.

Furthermore, considering that obtaining labels for multiagent trajectories is often resource-intensive, it becomes desirable for our classifier f to make efficient use of labeled data. Thus, we focus on applying the classifier f to a pretrained representation denoted as $\phi(\mathbf{x})$, which can be acquired solely from unlabeled data. Regarding permutation invariance, we make the following observation: If the learned representation $\phi(\mathbf{x})$ satisfies the property of *permutation equivariance*, we can still consider the classifier to be permutation invariant. Assuming that we can decompose $\phi(\mathbf{x})$ into components corresponding to individual trajectories $\left[\phi\left(\mathbf{x}_1^{1:T}\right), \ldots, \phi\left(\mathbf{x}_K^{1:T}\right)\right]$, permutation equivariance concerning the ordering of trajectories implies that for any permutation π of our K-tuple, it is essential that $\phi\left(\left[\mathbf{x}_{\pi_1}^{1:T}, \ldots, \mathbf{x}_{\pi_K}^{1:T}\right]\right) = \left[\phi\left(\mathbf{x}_{\pi_1}^{1:T}\right), \ldots, \phi\left(\mathbf{x}_{\pi_K}^{1:T}\right)\right]$. It is worth noting that permutation equivariance within the encoder ensures that the set $\phi(\mathbf{x})$ remains unaffected by the permutation of $\mathbf{x}$. Consequently, any permutation-invariant classifier applied to $\phi(\mathbf{x})$ will also exhibit permutation invariance regarding $\mathbf{x}$.

3 Trajectory Masked Autoencoder

In this section, we propose a novel self-supervised pretraining approach for multiagent trajectory data. Our proposition centers on training a model tasked with reconstructing multiagent trajectory instances, under the condition that segments of the individual trajectories are randomly masked out. The model comprises an encoder and a decoder and thus can be regarded as a denoising autoencoder [16,17]. The approach shares similarities with the recently introduced masked autoencoder [9], which was designed for image data.

For both the encoder and decoder constituting the architecture of our pretraining process, we propose the use of a *factorized* transformer architecture. Our choice is driven by the fact that we directly apply and finetune the encoder for downstream tasks, allowing us to leverage the modeling capabilities of the transformer for our classification task. In the *factorized* transformer architecture, we factorize self-attention across both time and agents: The transformer architecture essentially comprises stacks of two standard transformer encoder layers [15]. One layer operates across temporal segments and is independently applied to each trajectory, while the other layer operates across segments per agent and is independently applied to all temporal positions. The explicit separation of model components working along the temporal and agent dimensions has played a pivotal role in recent developments in multiagent trajectory models [4,18]. Most recently, [8] suggested to implement both operations with factorized transformer encoder layers.

3.1 Masked Autoencoder for Multiagent Trajectories

In this section, we will provide an overview of our masked autoencoder. We want to emphasize, that each stage of the autoencoder exhibits permutation equivariance concerning the order of the trajectories. Since a composition of permutation equivariant functions is also permutation equivariant [19], the trajectory masked autoencoder is thus permutation equivariant. For a visual representation of our approach, we refer to Fig. 1.

Encoder. We begin by describing the encoder, denoted as $\phi_{\text{enc}}(\mathbf{x})$, within the architecture of the proposed trajectory masked autoencoder (T-MAE). The

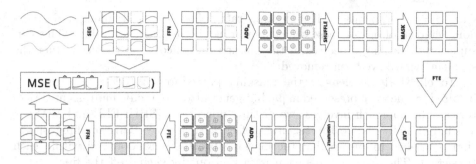

Fig. 1. Sketch of the proposed trajectory masked autoencoder (T-MAE). Notation and details are provided in the text. In the encoder section at the top, segments that will be subjected to masking in subsequent steps are highlighted using dotted lines. This highlighting is intended for illustrative purposes only.

encoder operates on a multiagent trajectory instance, $\mathbf{x} = \{\mathbf{x}_1^{1:T}, \ldots, \mathbf{x}_K^{1:T}\}$. We first split each individual trajectory $\mathbf{x}_k^{1:T}$ into S segments $\bar{\mathbf{x}}_k^s$. These segments are of equal length and encompass a fixed number of timesteps, referred to as l_S. Consequently, each segment comprises a specific set of timesteps. It is noteworthy that when $l_S = 1$, each timestep corresponds to one segment, resulting in a total of $S = T$ segments. This segmentation operation is formally represented as $\mathrm{SEG}_{l_S}(\mathbf{x}_k^{1:T}) = \bar{\mathbf{x}}_k^{1:S}$, where the segmentation process is applied individually to each trajectory.

Each of the created segments is separately embedded with a shared fully-connected feed-forward network (FFN), which projects the segments into a common model dimension denoted as d. Subsequently, we enhance the representation of each segment by incorporating positional encodings (PE) and, optionally, trajectory embeddings (TE). This augmentation operation is denoted as ADD_{emb}, where the term "emb" signifies the embeddings added to each trajectory segment. To encode the temporal position of each segment, we employ sinusoidal positional encodings (PE), following [15]. This technique has also been utilized in previous work by [8] for multiagent trajectories. Alternatively, it is possible to employ learnable embeddings for positional encoding. The positional encodings have a dimensionality of d and are added element-wise to each segment. Mathematically, this operation can be expressed as $\mathrm{ADD}_{PE}(\bar{\mathbf{x}}_k^s) = \mathrm{PE}^s \oplus \bar{\mathbf{x}}_k^s$. Furthermore, we introduce trajectory embeddings (TE), which are learnable embeddings also with a dimensionality of d. These embeddings encode specific properties of individual trajectories and are also added to segments element-wise. In this case, the same trajectory embedding is added to each segment of any given individual trajectory. Mathematically, this process can be represented as $\mathrm{ADD}_{TE}(\bar{\mathbf{x}}_k^s) = \mathrm{TE}_k \oplus \bar{\mathbf{x}}_k^s$.

For each segmented, embedded and enriched trajectory, we uniformly chose random segments to be masked out, following a predetermined masking ratio denoted as r. *Masking out* refers to the process of removing segments from the current representation of the trajectory. For example, a trajectory representation with $S = 3$ segments and a masking ratio of $r = \frac{1}{3}$ will undergo the random removal of one of these segments during the masking procedure. The self-supervised learning objective of the masked autoencoder is to reconstruct the segments that have been removed.

To efficiently implement the masking procedure, we adopt an approach inspired by the work presented in [9], but generalized to handle multiagent trajectories. The approach involves two distinct operations: SHUFFLE and MASK_r. We individually shuffle the segments of each trajectory. This shuffling operation is applied to ensure that the masking process is randomized within each trajectory. The masking operation is carried out by slicing off the final $\lfloor S \cdot r \rfloor$ shuffled segments from all trajectories. This step effectively removes the selected segments, while the number of segments to remove is determined by the masking ratio r. The combined application of SHUFFLE and MASK_r operations results in uniform masking of each individual trajectory. It is important to note that the removal of segments is particularly efficient, as it reduces the input to a transformer model, which exhibits quadratic computational cost relative to the number of segments in each trajectory.

As the final step in the encoding process, the resulting segments are updated by a factorized transformer architecture (FTE). The architecture consists of multi-head self-attention that is factorized over both the agent and the time dimensions: Notably, these operations distribute information across time and interactions among trajectories (i.e. agents) within the representation. See Sect. 3.2 on details regarding the architecture and its properties. Importantly, the application of the FTE maintains permutation equivariance concerning the order of the trajectories. In summary, the encoder ϕ_{enc} is defined as follows:

$$\phi_{\text{enc}}(\mathbf{x}) = \text{FTE} \circ \underset{r}{\text{MASK}} \circ \text{SHUFFLE} \circ \underset{\text{PE,TE}}{\text{ADD}} \circ \text{FFN} \circ \underset{l_S}{\text{SEG}}(\mathbf{x}).$$

Since the encoder is a composition of permutation equivariant functions with respect to the ordering of the trajectories it is itself permutation equivariant. The encoder generates a set of representations per trajectory, where each segment could theoretically have been updated with respect to all other segment representations that remain after masking, due to the application of the FTE.

Decoder. In our pretraining approach, we apply a decoder denoted as θ_{dec} to the representation $\phi_{\text{enc}}(\mathbf{x})$. The initial step in this process involves concatenating $\lfloor S \cdot r \rfloor$ query tokens Q to the end of each trajectory. This concatenation is denoted as CAT_Q. As a result of this operation, the query tokens occupy the positions that were previously held by the removed segments. The query tokens will subsequently be trained to reconstruct just these segments.

Next, we perform an operation denoted as UNSHUFFLE on all segments. This operation entails applying the inverse of the encoder shuffle function to all trajectories. Consequently, the resulting representation consists of ordered segments and query tokens, preserving the original segment shape, with dimensions corresponding to the number of agents K by the number of segments per trajectory S. To this representation, we add an additional positional encoding denoted as PE. This encoding is added element-wise to each segment, analogously to the positional encoding employed in the encoder, as described in the ADD_{PE} operation. Notably, this positional encoding informs each query token Q about its position within a trajectory.

In the subsequent step, we employ another factorized transformer architecture (FTE) to update the query tokens, taking into account all other information present within the instance. Similar to the encoder, these updates occur iteratively within the FTE, involving every input segment and query token along the trajectory and time dimensions. We refer to Sect. 3.2 for detailed information on the FTE. Finally, a fully-connected feed-forward network (FFN) is used to project the updated query tokens back into input space. Each of these tokens is tasked with reconstructing the features of the respective masked trajectory segments. We arrive at

$$\theta_{\text{dec}}\left(\phi_{\text{enc}}(\mathbf{x})\right) = \text{FFN} \circ \text{FTE} \circ \underset{\text{PE}}{\text{ADD}} \circ \text{UNSHUFFLE} \circ \underset{\text{Q}}{\text{CAT}}\left(\phi_{\text{enc}}(\mathbf{x})\right).$$

Reconstruction Objective and Downstream Tasks. To ensure the reconstruction of the masked segments by their corresponding query tokens, we implement a training objective based on the mean squared error (MSE). Specifically, we aim to minimize the MSE between the predicted features of the query tokens and the actual features of the masked segments in the input space. Although minimizing the MSE is a straightforward reconstruction objective, it has been shown to be very effective for pretraining [9].

If, after pretraining, we aim to apply the encoder for a downstream task, we simply set the masking ratio r to zero, ensuring that all the information in the multiagent trajectory instance is encoded. In most cases, it will be sensible to unshuffle the extracted representation following the procedure described in the section on the decoder. Subsequently, we can train a downstream model, denoted as $f\left(\phi_{\text{enc}}(\mathbf{x})\right)$, using the encoded representation as input. Here, we can choose whether to keep the weights in ϕ_{enc} fixed or finetune them during downstream task training.

3.2 Factorized Transformer Encoder (FTE)

To update both the segment and query token representations within the T-MAE, we employ a factorized transformer architecture. We will refer to this model as *factorized transformer encoder* (FTE), for reasons that will soon become clear.

The FTE, which we use within the T-MAE, was initially introduced as part of the encoder in a variational autoencoder for trajectory generation in [8], where it is referred to as a *multi-head attention block* (MAB). While the FTE and the MAB are architecturally identical, they operate on different representations. Most importantly, the FTE that is employed in the encoder of the T-MAE operates on shuffled segments per trajectory. This results in segments not being temporally aligned for updates along the agent dimension. Consequently, the model relies on the positional encoding to determine which other segments to

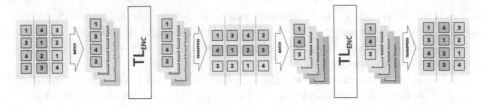

Fig. 2. Sketch of one layer within the factorized transformer encoder (FTE) applied to input which is shuffled along the temporal dimension (1–4, agent dimension is color-coded). TL$_{enc}$ represents a standard transformer encoder layer.

attend to. For a visualization of one layer of the FTE applied to shuffled segment representations, please refer to Fig. 2.

For simplicity, we will use the term $\tilde{\mathbf{x}}$ to refer to both segment and query token representations throughout the remainder of this section. The architecture of the FTE consists of two distinct types of standard transformer encoder layers, as proposed in [15]. These layers include multi-head self-attention layers, residual connections, dropout [12], layer normalization [2], and feed-forward neural networks. For more detailed information on these layers, we refer to either [15] or [8]. In the context of the FTE, one of these layers operates over segments in time and is separately applied to each trajectory. The other layer operates over segments per agent and is applied independently to all temporal positions. To clarify, in the first operation, we effectively extend the batch dimension to encompass individual trajectories, while in the second operation, we extend the batch dimension to encompass temporal positions: Temporal self-attention is applied to $\tilde{\mathbf{x}}_k^{1:\tilde{S}}$ for all $k \in [1, \dots, K]$, where $\tilde{S} = S$ in the T-MAE decoder and T-MAE encoder during testing, and $\tilde{S} = S - \lfloor S \cdot r \rfloor$ in the T-MAE encoder during self-supervised pretraining. Self-attention with respect to trajectory interactions is applied to $\tilde{\mathbf{x}}_{1:K}^s$, for all $s \in \tilde{S}$. Combining these two operations, the encoder layer with temporal self-attention and the encoder layer with self-attention concerning trajectory interactions constitute a single FTE layer. This FTE layer can be applied repeatedly to the input. In our experiment in Sect. 4 we use three FTE layers both in the encoder and decoder of T-MAEs, as well as for the baseline transformer models.

The application of FTE on $\tilde{\mathbf{x}}$ exhibits permutation equivariance concerning the arrangement of trajectories. This property of FTE follows directly from the fact that the standard transformer encoder is permutation equivariant with respect to its input, and that the temporal self-attention (which is provided with positional information through encodings) is separately applied to each trajectory. For a formal proof of FTE's permutation equivariance, we refer to [8].

Fig. 3. Visualization of T-MAE masking (middle) and reconstruction (right) for a validation multiagent trajectory instance (ground truth left). The reconstruction combines ground truth timesteps provided to the model (i.e. dots in the middle column with l_S, $r = 5, 0.8$) and masked timesteps predicted by the model.

Note on Shuffling. In Sect. 4, we provide empirical evidence that rearranging segments along the temporal dimension, as implemented in the trajectory masked autoencoder, yields favorable performance outcomes in subsequent tasks. Due to the random removal of segments prior to FTE, the model cannot depend on the sequential order of segments in terms of their temporal positions. While the shuffling is no issue for the temporal self-attention, self-attention along the agent dimension has to rely on the positional encoding to decide to which other segments to attend to. We intentionally choose not to unshuffle the segments before applying the FTE to avoid spurious alignments and we shuffle the input during downstream tasks for consistency with pretraining.

4 Event Classification in Elite Soccer

We evaluate our trajectory masked autoencoder (T-MAE) on event classification in proprietary trajectory data from professional soccer matches[1], investigating the effect of pretraining transformer architectures on four different data regimes, with 5, 10, 50 and 100% of the labeled training data respectively. We evaluate the classification according to mean average precision (mAP), which is suited to unbalanced datasets.

In our dataset, features are the xy-coordinates of agents on the soccer pitch, along with their current speed in kilometers per hour (km\h) for all players and the ball. The features are recorded at a rate of 25 Hz (frames per second). We create multiagent trajectory instances by considering five-second intervals with a one-second overlap between consecutive instances. To simplify our analysis, we exclusively focus on intervals in which all 22 players and the ball are consistently tracked. We use data of 54 games (totaling 280,000 instances). We experiment with respect to four data folds over halftimes, training the classification always on 54 halftimes and validating and testing on 27 each. Pretraining is performed over different data splits without access to the labels.

---

[1] All data is from the German Bundesliga (2017/18) and can be acquired from DFL.

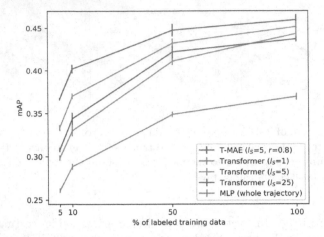

Fig. 4. Comparing T-MAE (with segment length $l_S = 5$ and mask ratio $r = 0.8$) to un-pretrained transformer models with similar architecture and MLP baseline. Metric is mean average precision (mAP, higher is better), SE = standard error.

We transform the data so that the home team always plays from left to right and provide type embeddings which encode whether a trajectory belongs to (i) the ball, (ii) the home keeper, (iii) a home field player, (iv) the guest keeper or (v) a guest field player. We work with minimal data augmentation, mirroring the instances along horizontal and vertical lines going through the middle point of the pitch. Instances are labeled with an event, if it occurs within the 75 central frames. We consider ten labels, of which the label *pass* occurs most frequently and *corner kick* least frequently. Sparsity in positive labels results in an mAP of only 0.067 for random guessing. In Fig. 3, we provide visualizations of a ground truth, masked and reconstructed instance (from the validation data). Even though large parts of the input data is masked, the model apparently learned to account for turns, twists and possibly interactions in the players movements.

The main results of our experiment are presented in Fig. 4, where we compare the classification performance of a factorized transformer model pretrained with T-MAE to models of similar architecture without pretraining. We conducted experiments involving both pretrained and un-pretrained models using three distinct segment lengths $l_S \in 1, 5, 25$ and a linear classifier on top of the factorized transformer architecture. The feature representation, obtained from the encoder of T-MAE, remains unshuffled and is aggregated across agents. This aggregated representation is then concatenated along the segment dimension within the classifier. While the factorized transformer architecture is maintained for both pretrained and un-pretrained models, we opted not to shuffle segments within trajectories for the latter, as it is not necessary. Optimization is performed with Adam [10] and *early stopping* on validation performance. During classification training, we finetune the weights of the pretrained model. While we use a standard learning rate of 0.001 and no dropout in the FTEs for the pretrained models, un-pretrained models are additionally trained with learning rate 0.0001 and dropout 0.2 to provide for stability and regularization in absence of pretraining. Regarding these additional runs, we choose the hyperparameter configuration according to validation mAP separately for each data regime. A multi-layer perceptron (MLP) simply operating on raw features of the whole instance (with ordered agents) is provided as a further baseline. For the MLP baseline, we evaluate models with varying modeling capacities and select the one with the best performance on the validation set. Mean and standard error of the mean are calculated with respect to the four data splits.

Table 1. Results of T-MAE pretraining model variations for downstream classification task on soccer data for different fractions of classification training data. Metric is mean average precision (mAP, higher is better), SE = standard error.

Model	0.05		0.1		0.5		1.0	
	Mean	SE	Mean	SE	Mean	SE	Mean	SE
Variations in r								
T-MAE (l_S, $r = 5$, 0.2)	0.367	±0.006	0.395	±0.004	0.441	±0.006	0.453	±0.006
T-MAE (l_S, $r = 5$, 0.4)	**0.370**	±0.004	0.400	±0.006	0.445	±0.006	0.456	±0.004
T-MAE (l_S, $r = 5$, 0.6)	0.362	±0.004	0.394	±0.007	0.446	±0.007	0.458	±0.009
T-MAE (l_S, $r = 5$, 0.8)	0.367	±0.001	**0.402**	±0.005	**0.447**	±0.007	**0.459**	±0.007
Variations in l_S								
T-MAE (l_S, $r = 1$, 0.8)	0.371	±0.004	0.399	±0.002	0.442	±0.007	0.456	±0.007
T-MAE (l_S, $r = 5$, 0.8)	0.367	±0.001	**0.402**	±0.005	**0.447**	±0.007	**0.459**	±0.007
T-MAE (l_S, $r = 25$, 0.8)	**0.348**	±0.003	0.382	±0.002	0.438	±0.007	0.453	±0.004

The results clearly demonstrate that the model pretrained with the trajectory masked autoencoder consistently outperforms the models without pretraining across all four data regimes. This indicates that the pretrained model is more data-efficient, achieving the same level of performance with less labeled data. Furthermore, it is worth highlighting that the pretraining approach yields the best overall performance even when 100% of the labeled data is available. This suggests that the trajectory masked autoencoder is not only useful in scenarios with limited labeled data but also beneficial when abundant labeled data is accessible. Additionally, we observe that pretrained models are robust to variations in hyperparameter l_S and r as indicated in Table 1. The relatively poor performance of the MLP baseline underscores the significance of permutation invariance concerning agents and emphasizes the need for increased modeling capacity.

5   Conclusion

We proposed a novel self-supervised approach for multiagent trajectories. We introduced a masking scheme that rendered masking of individual trajectories independent of one another and made novel use of a transformer architecture that is factorized over time and agents. This makes the encoder of our pretraining model permutation equivariant with respect to the order of trajectories and naturally lends itself to downstream tasks that require permutation invariance with respect to agent order. Empirically, pretraining with our approach improved the performance of classifying multiagent trajectory instances with respect to in-game events for tracking data from professional soccer matches.

Acknowledgements. We would like to thank Eraldo Rezende Fernandes, Marius Lehne and Marco Spinaci for their input and support while writing this paper.

References

1. Anzer, G., Bauer, P.: Expected passes: determining the difficulty of a pass in football (soccer) using spatio-temporal data. Data Min. Knowl. Discov. **36**, 295–317 (2022)
2. Ba, J.L., Kiros, J.R., Hinton, G.E.: Layer normalization. arXiv preprint arXiv:1607.06450 (2016)
3. Brown, T., et al.: Language models are few-shot learners. In: Advances in Neural Information Processing Systems, vol. 33, pp. 1877–1901 (2020)
4. Casas, S., Gulino, C., Suo, S., Luo, K., Liao, R., Urtasun, R.: Implicit latent variable model for scene-consistent motion forecasting. In: Vedaldi, A., Bischof, H., Brox, T., Frahm, J.M. (eds.) ECCV 2020. LNCS, vol. 12368, pp. 624–641. Springer, Cham (2020). https://doi.org/10.1007/978-3-030-58592-1_37
5. Chawla, S., Estephan, J., Gudmundsson, J., Horton, M.: Classification of passes in football matches using spatiotemporal data. ACM Trans. Spat. Algorithms Syst. **3**(2), 1–30 (2017)
6. Devlin, J., Chang, M.W., Lee, K., Toutanova, K.: BERT: pre-training of deep bidirectional transformers for language understanding. arXiv preprint arXiv:1810.04805 (2018)
7. Fassmeyer, D., Anzer, G., Bauer, P., Brefeld, U.: Toward automatically labeling situations in soccer. Front. Sports Active Living **3** (2021)
8. Girgis, R., et al.: Latent variable sequential set transformers for joint multi-agent motion prediction. In: International Conference on Learning Representations (2022)
9. He, K., Chen, X., Xie, S., Li, Y., Dollár, P., Girshick, R.: Masked autoencoders are scalable vision learners. In: IEEE Conference on Computer Vision and Pattern Recognition (2022)
10. Kingma, D.P., Ba, J.L.: Adam: a method for stochastic optimization. arXiv preprint arXiv:1412.6980 (2014)
11. Power, P., Ruiz, H., Wei, X., Lucey, P.: Not all passes are created equal: objectively measuring the risk and reward of passes in soccer from tracking data. In: SIGKDD International Conference on Knowledge Discovery and Data Mining, pp. 1605–1613 (2017)
12. Srivastava, N., Hinton, G., Krizhevsky, A., Sutskever, I., Salakhutdinov, R.: Dropout: a simple way to prevent neural networks from overfitting. J. Mach. Learn. Res. **15**(1), 1929–1958 (2014)

13. Sun, J.J., Kennedy, A., Zhan, E., Anderson, D.J., Yue, Y., Perona, P.: Task programming: learning data efficient behavior representations. In: IEEE Conference on Computer Vision and Pattern Recognition (2021)
14. van den Oord, A., et al.: WaveNet: a generative model for raw audio. arXiv preprint arXiv:1609.03499 (2016)
15. Vaswani, A., et al.: Attention is all you need. In: Advances in Neural Information Processing Systems, pp. 5998–6008 (2017)
16. Vincent, P., Larochelle, H., Bengio, Y., Manzagol, P.A.: Extracting and composing robust features with denoising autoencoders. In: International Conference on Machine Learning, pp. 1096–1103. ACM (2008)
17. Vincent, P., Larochelle, H., Lajoie, I., Bengio, Y., Manzagol, P.A.: Stacked denoising autoencoders: learning useful representations in a deep network with a local denoising criterion. J. Mach. Learn. Res. **11**, 3371–3408 (2010)
18. Yeh, R.A., Schwing, A.G., Huang, J., Murphy, K.: Diverse generation for multi-agent sports games. In: IEEE Conference on Computer Vision and Pattern Recognition (2019)
19. Zaheer, M., Kottur, S., Ravanbakhsh, S., Poczós, B., Salakhutdinov, R.R., Smola, A.J.: Deep sets. In: Advances in Neural Information Processing Systems, pp. 3391–3401 (2017)

Quantification of Turnover Danger
with xCounter

Henrik Biermann[1]([✉])[iD], Weiran Yang[1,5][iD], Franz-Georg Wieland[2,3][iD],
Jens Timmer[2,3,4][iD], and Daniel Memmert[1][iD]

[1] Institute of Exercise Training and Sport Informatics, German Sport University of
Cologne, 50933 Cologne, Germany
h.biermann@dshs-koeln.de
[2] Institute of Physics, University of Freiburg, Freiburg, Germany
[3] Freiburg Center for Data Analysis and Modelling (FDM), University of Freiburg,
Freiburg, Germany
[4] Germany Centre for Integrative Biological Signalling Studies (CIBSS), University
of Freiburg, Freiburg, Germany
[5] Department of Computer Science, RWTH Aachen University, Aachen, Germany

Abstract. Counterattacks in soccer are an important strategical component for goal scoring. Previous work in the literature has described their impact and has formulated descriptive advice on successful actions *during* a *counterattack*. In contrast, in this work, we propose the notion of expected counter, i.e., quantifying forward progress by the ball-winning team *at the moment of the turnover*. Therefore, we apply a previously proposed framework for understanding complex sequences in soccer. Using this framework, we perform a novel feature-specific assessment that yields (a) critical feature values, (b) relevant feature pitch zones, and (c) feature prediction capabilities. The insights from this assessment step allow for creating concrete guidelines for optimal behavior in and out of possession. Thus, we find that preparing horizontally spaced pass options facilitates an own *counterattack* in case of a ball win while moving as a compact unit prevents an opposing *counterattack* in case of a ball loss. As a final step, we generalize our results by creating a predictive XGBoost model that outperforms a location-based baseline but still shows room for improvement.

Keywords: Soccer Analytics · Position Data · Event Data ·
Interpretable features · Machine Learning

1 Introduction

There are various strategies for scoring goals in soccer, such as set pieces or build-up play. One particular strategy that attracts attention are so-called *counterattacks*, i.e., quick transition attacks executed immediately after winning the ball [2,11,16]. Previous studies have examined the defensive team's tactical behavior *at the moment of a turnover* [2], while others have focused on the offensive behavior *during a counterattack* [16,18]. In contrast, this study focuses on understanding the situation *at the moment of the turnover*. To achieve this, we propose the concept of expected counter (xCounter), in analogy to expected goals (xGoals) [17], that quantifies for every turnover the danger of a counterattack in terms of the forward progress of the ball-winning team.

In the process of creating an xCounter model, we pay respect to the fact that practitioners often value interpretability over predictive performance [20]. Therefore, we do not use a black box architecture but follow our recently published framework for understanding complex sequences [5]. Using the framework, we identify *sequences of interest* and employ a continuous labelling approach with *temporal* and *spatial success criteria*. We further implement a systematic strategy to compute 47 *comprehensible features* and assess each feature's prediction capability using a novel, position-aware assessment that identifies critical feature values and provides the most relevant pitch locations. As a final step, we integrate previous insights to implement predictive xCounter.

The outcomes derived from our assessment strategy offer a substantial advancement to the operational procedures followed by practitioners. We are able to identify advantageous defensive behaviors that effectively mitigate counterattack threats, as well as promising offensive behaviors that maximize such threats. Our models encompass the overarching concept of xCounter, enabling independent analysis of player performance irrespective of factors like team strength.

2   Dataset

We conduct our analysis on StatsPerform position and event data for 289 matches of elite men's soccer. All matches took place within the 20/21 season of a top-five European league. The position data is automatically collected and comprises all players and the ball while the event data is manually annotated and contains information about the event type, player identity, and a timestamp. To ensure consistency, we exclude situations with fewer than 22 players due to reasons such as red cards or injuries. To address missing frames, we employ linear interpolation between the last previous and first following player positions. Additionally, we normalize the direction of play, ensuring that the team in possession always plays from left to right.

3   Application of the Framework for Understanding Complex Sequences

The game of soccer has been identified as one of the most challenging sports to analyze, due to its low-scoring nature, comparably spacious pitch, large number of players, and low degree of structure [12]. These inherent properties often complicate the statistical examination of individual game situations. Consequently, there has been a recent surge of predictive (black box) machine learning algorithms in various scenarios [2,3,12,18]. While these approaches demonstrate high

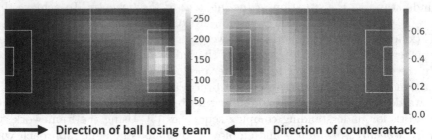

Fig. 1. Heatmap of *open play turnover* frequencies (left) and location average *continuous labels* (right). Both heatmaps are smoothed with gaussian smoothing [9]. Design choices for the involved parameters are listed in Sect. 3.6.

predictive capability, they often lack the desired degree of interpretability sought by domain experts [20]. In the light of this, we have previously proposed a framework for understanding complex sequences in soccer.

3.1 Sequences of Interest

The concept of xCounter encompasses the situation *at the moment of the turnover*. Therefore, we find turnovers in the data as a pair of temporally adjacent events from opposite teams in the stream of event data. We define the timestamp of the latter of the two events (ball win event) to be the turnover moment. Thus, we result with $N = 144\,158$ total turnovers (497 per match).

Based on the type of the two events, we further group turnovers into (i) *dead ball* ($N_{\text{dead}} = 56\,721$): one of the two events includes a stoppage of play [4], (ii) *set piece originated* ($N = \text{setpiece} = 21\,871$): there is a previous set piece event (corner, freekick, throw-in, goalkick, penalty) within a range of t_{setpiece}, and (iii) *open play* ($N_{\text{open}} = 65\,566$): the remaining turnovers. In this work, we decide to analyze *open play turnovers* and exclude the remaining types.

3.2 Success Criteria

Given the sparsity of scores in soccer, it becomes necessary to adopt alternative criteria to effectively assess the danger of *counterattacks* resulting from *open play turnovers*. In this context, a *counterattack* has been described as a fast attack after a turnover that results with ball possession close to the opposing teams goal [10,13,19]. To incorporate the *temporal component* of this definition, we examine all events assigned to the ball-winning team within a time window t^i_{counter} after the turnover. By focusing solely on events, we ensure that only deliberate offensive actions are considered, while disregarding other actions like clearances. Additionally, we exclude 8,332 possibly ambiguous sequences that involve a (tactical) foul committed by the ball-losing team. To address the *spatial*

Table 1. *Comprehensible features* comprising a *metric* and *team subgroup*.

	All Field Players	Behind Ball	Infront Ball	Around Ball
Vertical Centroid-to-Ball	yes	yes	yes	yes
Horizontal Centroid-to-Ball	yes	yes	yes	yes
Vertical Compactness	yes	yes	yes	yes
Horizontal Compactness	yes	yes	yes	yes
Player-Count	non-varying	yes	yes	yes
Free Player-Count$^{1.5}$	only off.	only off.	only off.	only off.
Free Player-Count^{3}	only off.	only off.	only off.	only off.
Free Player-Count^{5}	only off.	only off	only off.	only off.

component of the definition, we identify the event closest to the goal of the ball-losing team. Subsequently, we apply a function $f_{success} : \mathbf{x} \mapsto y^i \in [0,1]$ which maps a pitch location $\mathbf{x}$ onto a *continuous label* y representing the danger of the *counterattack* following the turnover. The resulting dataset, consisting of *open play turnovers* and their *continuous labels* are plotted in Fig. 1.

3.3 Comprehensible Features

To better understand tactical behavior, a common approach is to segment a team into various *team subgroups* [1,2]. In this study, we define the initial subgroup as *all field players* by excluding the goalkeepers from the analysis. From this group, we create additional subgroups using specific criteria. Previous research on turnover analysis has introduced subgroups *players behind ball* (distance to their own goal smaller than the ball's), *players around ball* (vice versa), and *players direct to ball* [2]. In this study, we create these subgroups for both teams. Therefore, we avoid a distance-based definition of the *players direct to ball* which may not accurately capture players who are potential direct pass options despite being farther from the ball. Thus, we construct this subgroup using a Delaunay triangulation [6] from the direct links to the player in possession for both teams.

As a next step, we identify *metrics* that describe team positioning from a tactical perspective. In our previous work [5] we found *player-count* (for *players behind ball*) and *vertical compactness* to be predictive metrics for *counterattacks*. In this study, we aim to expand our set of features by incorporating the commonly used team centroids [8]. However, considering the correlation between turnover location and *counterattack* success that we established previously [5], we normalize this feature by measuring the distance from the *centroid-to-ball*. Additionally, we introduce a metric to measure man-marking, an essential defensive component [19]. Thus, we incorporate the *free-player-count*^{r} which indicates the number of players without an opposing player within a given radius r. For choice of the critical radius, we follow Tenga et al. [19] that propose $r_1 = 1.5\,\mathrm{m}$, but also introduce two broader features using $r_2 = 3\,\mathrm{m}$ and $r_3 = 5\,\mathrm{m}$.

Finally, we systematically combine the aforementioned *team subgroups* with each *metric*, separately for both teams, to create a set of *comprehensive features*.

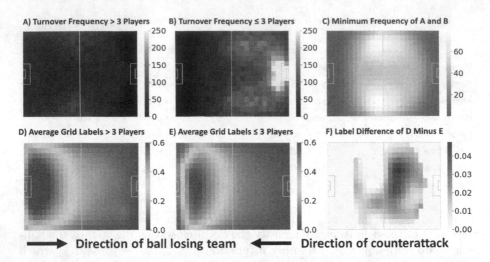

Fig. 2. Prediction capability assessment of feature *Infront ball Player-Count* for the *ball losing team*. Panels A and D represent the turnover frequencies and average continuous labels for the "above" group. Panels B and E represent the corresponding information for the "below" group. Panel C illustrates the reliable pitch regions where the minimum threshold $N_{\text{sample, min}}$ is met by both groups. Panel F shows the difference of label values between the "above" and "below" groups. For example, at the darkest pitch grid in midfield (left half space of ball-losing team), the "above" subgroup has a 0.04 higher xCounter value than the "below" group. The resulting aggregation of pitch differences is provided in Table 2, bottom row, second column.

However, certain combinations do not contain relevant information. For example, the *player-count* of *all field players* is always ten, as described in Sect. 2, and the *free player-count* only describes player marking when measured for offensive players. Consequently, we exclude these combinations from the analysis. An overview of the selected combinations is provided in Table 1.

3.4   Feature-Specific Prediction Capability

The location of turnovers has a significant impact on the success of counterattacks, as shown in Fig. 1. Consequently, a feature that coincides with the turnover position possesses inherent predictive capability, regardless of the feature itself. To address this issue, we propose a novel approach for the position-aware assessment of individual features using feature quantiles and label heatmaps.

First, we select a (quantile-based) threshold value for a specific feature. This threshold divides all turnovers into two groups. For example, consider the feature of *Infront Ball Player-Count* of the ball-losing team. Given that the 60% quantile for this feature corresponds to a *Infront Ball Player-Count* of three, turnovers with feature values below the threshold are assigned to the "below" group, while the remaining turnovers are assigned to the "above" group. Next, we create two heatmaps for each turnover group: one displaying turnover frequencies and another showing the average continuous labels. To ensure a reliable comparison and minimize the influence of outliers, we set a minimum turnover frequency of $N_{\text{sample, min}}$ in each grid, which must be met by both the "above" and the "below" group. Grids that do not meet this frequency threshold are discarded. Consequently, the remaining pitch grids describe the pitch regions where both groups can be reliably compared (pitch regions in Panel C of Fig. 2).

For the reliable pitch regions, we compute the label differences between the heatmaps on a grid-by-grid basis. This heatmap can be aggregated into a single value, which we use as a position-agnostic proxy for prediction capability of the examined feature. The computation of the label differences and the resulting heatmap are visualized in the bottom row of Fig. 2. The top features with most predictive capability are presented in Sect. 4.1.

3.5 Predictive Model

Finally, we proceed to build regression models based on the insights gained in the previous four steps of the framework. All models, including the baselines, are trained on a 70% of the available data (randomly selected from all matches) and evaluated on the remaining 30%. Our analysis is conducted using Python 3.10 and the *scikit-learn* library [15].

Feature- and Location-Based Baselines. As a first simple baseline, we create a location-based model that assigns an xCounter value to a turnover based on the respective pitch grid label (refer to Fig. 1). In addition, we extend the location-based approach using the results of the feature assessment. Specifically, we choose the top N_{top} features and modify the location-based value by aggregating the pitch grid differences for all features with sufficient turnover grid frequency.

Machine Learning (XGBoost). To address the limitation of the baseline models that only consider the features independently and do not account for interaction effects, we employ machine learning techniques.

Specifically, we utilize XGBoost, which has been chosen for a similar turnover prediction task in related studies [2]. We optimize the XGBoost algorithm, on a set of hyperparameters, detailed in the Appendix. Each model is trained using a long feature vector that includes the turnover position as well as the top N_{top} features (for both teams).

3.6 Design Choices

In this section, we introduce our design choices for the previously introduced parameters and discuss potential implications.

Sequences of Interest. We decide if a turnover is *set piece originated* by searching for set pieces within a time window t_{setpiece} after the execution [18]. Yet, choosing on a concrete value for t_{setpiece} is generally difficult since are no established guidelines to determine the end of a set piece. In our case, as we focus on *open play turnovers* we aim for a relatively long duration to ensure that the remaining turnovers have minimal residual set piece originated positioning. After discussions and careful inspections of individual situations we choose $t_{\text{setpiece}} = 30\,\text{s}$.

Success Criteria. We define the success of a *counterattack* using both a *temporal criterion* and a *spatial criterion*. The *temporal criterion* aims to label only immediate, fast progress after a turnover as a *counterattack*. Since the distance that needs to be covered in an attack varies between turnovers, we choose a location-dependent turnover duration. To calculate this duration, we determine the amount of time needed to go from the turnover location to the losing team's goal. Following Sahasrabudhe and Bekkers [18], who label attacks progressing with a speed of $5\,\text{ms}^{-1}$ as *counterattacks*, we use the formula

$$t_{\text{counter}}^{i}(\|\mathbf{x}^{i}\|) = 5\,\text{s} + \frac{\|\mathbf{x}^{i}\|}{5\,\text{ms}^{-1}}, \tag{1}$$

where $\mathbf{x}^{i}$ is the turnover location and $\|\cdot\|$ denotes the Euclidean distance to the losing team's goal. We incorporate the fixed time offset of five seconds to account for synchronization errors and *counterattacks* initiated after a few initial backward or sideways actions. As a result, our analysis time varies between a maximum of 32 s at the corner flag and 10 s for ball losses close to the losing team's goal.

For the *spatial criterion* we evaluate pitch locations reached after a *counterattack*. While various concepts have been proposed for this purpose, such as expected possession value [7], expected goals [3], or expected threat [14], they all share the idea that pitch value generally increases with decreasing goal distance. To provide a flexible and simple solution that is not dependent on a specific concept, we choose a linear relation between goal distance and pitch value. We define the label function $f_{\text{success}}(\|\mathbf{x}_{\text{off}}^{i}\|)$ as follows:

$$y^{i} = f_{\text{success}}(\|\mathbf{x}_{\text{max}}^{i}\|) = \begin{cases} \frac{\|\mathbf{x}_{\text{center}}\| - \|\mathbf{x}_{\text{off}}^{i}\|}{\|\mathbf{x}_{\text{center}}\|} & \text{if } \|\mathbf{x}^{i}\| \leq \|\mathbf{x}_{\text{center}}\|, \\ 0 & \text{else} \end{cases} \tag{2}$$

where $\mathbf{x}_{\text{max}}^{i}$ denotes the position of the ball-winning team's closest event to the ball-losing goal within t_{counter}^{i} after the turnover and $\mathbf{x}_{\text{center}}$ denotes the position of the center mark.

Feature Assessment. To assess the prediction capability of our *comprehensible features* and account for the influence of turnover location on *counterattack* success, we use heatmaps. We discretize the pitch into equal-sized grids and compare turnovers with different feature values grid by grid. However, to reduce the influence of outliers, we only consider differences within a grid if there is a minimum turnover frequency of $N_{\text{sample, min}} = 30$ in both feature subgroup grids. Since the number of open play turnovers in our dataset is limited ($N_{\text{open}} = 65566$), we need to choose a sufficiently large grid size to obtain reliable results. Since we require at least 60 turnovers per grid (30 each) to compare two feature subgroups, after

Table 2. The four most predictive features with critical feature values, most relevant pitch zones, and aggregated prediction capability, separately listed for both teams.

◄— Direction of counterattack	▨ xC Higher than Average	▨ xC Lower than Average

Ball-winning Team				
Feature				
Team Subgroup	*Infront Ball*	*All Players*	*Around Ball*	*Around Ball*
Metric	*Compactness*	*Compactness*	*Compactness*	*Free Pl.-Count*[5]
Direction	*Horizontal*	*Horizontal*	*Horizontal*	
Feature Value Above	16.35m	14.75m	13.74m	2 Players
Pitch Zones w/ increased xCounter				
Aggregate	**3.82**	**3.66**	**3.59**	**2.87**

Ball-losing Team				
Feature				
Team Subgroup	*Around Ball*	*Infront Ball*	*All Players*	*Behind Ball*
Metric	*Compactness*	*Player-Count*	*Compactness*	*Centroid to Ball*
Direction	*Vertical*		*Vertical*	*Vertical*
Feature Value Below or Equal	10.89m	3 Players	12.54m	19.95m
Pitch Zones w/ decreased xCounter				
Aggregate	**5.68**	**3.46**	**2.83**	**2.40**

experimentation, we find that a grid size of four by four meters satisfies this criterion in most cases. Thus, each grid has a frequency of $N_{\text{grid}} = 132 \pm 66$ turnovers on average. We further enhance the quality of the heatmaps and reduce the influence of grid outliers, by application of Gaussian smoothing [9] with a smoothing factor of $s = 2$. This smoothing helps to create more visually interpretable and robust heatmaps.

4 Results and Discussion

4.1 Prediction Capability of Features

In the assessment, various features were evaluated to determine their predictive power for xCounter (with quantiles from 15% to 90% and 5% step width). The most influential features are summarized in Table 2, and a comprehensive list of ranked features can be found in the Appendix.

For the ball-losing team, the analysis revealed that compactness is the most prolific *metric* for xCounter. Specifically, a vertical compactness of less than 10 m for players around the ball significantly reduces the danger of a counterattack.

Table 3. Evaluation results of baselines and XGBoost with varying top N_{top} features being used. Results are presented in terms of mean absolute error (MAE), mean squared error (MSE), mean squared logarithmic error (MLE), and R^2. The superscripts for XGBoost describe different hyperparameter configurations, listed in the Appendix.

Model	N_{top}	MAE	MSE	MLE	R^2	Model	N_{top}	MAE	MSE	MLE	R^2
Location BL	-	.129	**.186**	**.020**	**.448**	XGBoost[A]	1	.133	.185	**.020**	**.463**
Feat.- & Loc. BL	1	.138	.196	.022	.379	XGBoost[B]	1	.122	.186	**.020**	.454
	5	.133	.199	.023	.373	XGBoost[C]	6	**.101**	.204	.025	.249
	10	.131	.201	.024	.362	XGBoost[D]	9	.133	**.184**	**.020**	.391
	30	**.128**	.207	.025	.327						

Moreover, maintaining a team-wide compactness below 12 m also shows beneficial effects. When the ball is lost at the sidelines, in addition to compactness, it is important for players behind the ball to maintain a distance of 20 m. Additionally, for ball losses in the opposing third, it is advantageous for the ball-losing team to have no more than three players positioned in front of the ball. These findings align with the tactical notion of counterpressing, where a compact team unit aims to quickly regain possession after losing the ball [2]. The indication that no more than three should participate in the attack in front of the ball provides further strategic guidance.

On the other hand, for the ball-winning team, a large horizontal compactness emerged as a crucial factor. Having a horizontal compactness above 15 m for all players and 14 m for players around the ball increases xCounter for ball wins in the center. In the team's own third, a compactness in front of the ball of 17 m or more, combined with having at least three players without opponents within a five-meter radius, positively affects xCounter. These findings suggest that, in addition to their defensive responsibilities, players in the defending team should also focus on anticipating ball wins and positioning themselves horizontally as open passing options if their team gains possession.

4.2 Predictive Models for Expected Counter

After training regression models using the top predictive features, as described in Sect. 3.5, the evaluation results are presented in Table 3.

The results indicate that the influence of introducing features to predictive models is ambiguous and depends on the specific evaluation metric. In the feature-based baseline, incorporating more features leads to a reduction in MAE, yet, to an inferior performance in R^2, MLE, and MSE. In contrast, different configurations of XGBoost are able to outperform the baselines in each individual metric. However, no single model can perform superior in all evaluation metrics. This could also be due to the non-linear influence of the features on xCounter. The best-performing XGBoost models use a relatively small amount of features (the best R^2 score is achieved using a single feature). This indicates that the models struggle to effectively incorporate the additional information provided by the features beyond the already strong predictive capability of the location. Thus, a more refined algorithm is needed to effectively leverage the predictive potential of the features in conjunction with the location data.

5   Related Work

Various studies in literature have dealt with the subject of *counterattacks*. Bauer and Anzer [2] have used XGBoost to classify defensive team behavior after a turnover into passive and aggressive ball regain attempts. They found that counterpressing (aggressive) attempts are more effective at the sidelines and demonstrated that successful teams generate more shots when counterpressing. Raudonius et al. [16] isolated players contribution to a *counterattack* using four types of performance indicators and identified outstanding performers. Sahasrabudhe and Bekkers [18] developed a graph neural network that predicts the outcome of individual frames during a *counterattack*. They found that player speed, ball-, and goal angles are most predictive for the success of a *counterattack*.

This work, to the best of our knowledge, is first to predict *counterattack* danger *at the moment of the turnover*. It complements existing literature and can be combined with other approaches, e.g. to find the best counterpressing strategy in high xCounter situations [2] or to analyze systematic over/underperformance at different stages of the *counterattack* [16, 18].

6   Application

To demonstrate the practical applicability of our approach, we applied xCounter to analyze an additional match from another European league of the 22/23 season, separate from our original dataset. Therefore, we leveraged the location-based baseline, given its high capability in the previous experiment. We evaluated the execution of counterattacks by comparing the actual forward progress of the ball-winning team to the xCounter value. This allowed us to assess the effectiveness of teams after a ball win, relative to the league average observed in our dataset, and identify instances of over/under-performance during counters. The results of this team-wide analysis are presented in Table 4.

For a more detailed analysis, we examined ball wins and losses for each player. Thus, for each player, we aggregated the respective labels of ball wins/losses to describe the created/allowed counter danger by that player (see Table 5). Although we observed a strong bias based on playing positions, meaningful comparisons between similar positions and across teams were possible. Moreover, by integrating our algorithm, we were able to provide a more meaningful extension of the turnover +/- value. For example, we found that the RCM (Right Central Midfielder) of the away team created the most danger despite having an even number of ball wins and ball losses.

Table 4. Counter effectiveness of both teams in our example match. High values of over-performance were expected, due to the high number of goals scored by both teams.

Team	Score	Turnovers	xCounter Sum	Real Counter Danger	+/-
Home	5	252	53.55	62.88	**+9.33**
Away	5	252	60.60	71.57	**+10.97**

Table 5. Individual performance of players for ball wins and ball losses. First listed are the starters of the home team, subsequently the starters of the away team.

Position	Ball wins	Ball losses	Danger Created	Danger Allowed	Danger +/-
ST	31	36	10.56	6.22	**4.34**
LCM	31	18	9.51	6.64	**2.86**
RCM	23	21	7.13	4.73	**2.39**
LM	14	21	6.35	4.09	**2.26**
LCB	11	8	3.09	0.94	**2.15**
RCB	13	8	3.80	2.45	**1.35**
CAM	14	16	2.32	2.67	**−0.35**
RB	19	14	4.94	7.34	**−2.40**
LB	21	31	4.44	9.60	**−5.16**
RM	17	35	4.18	9.77	**−5.59**
GK	28	16	0.12	10.72	**−10.6**
RCM	32	32	12.08	4.29	**7.79**
LB	31	22	9.84	5.43	**4.41**
LCM	21	22	8.47	4.42	**4.05**
ST	17	40	6.84	3.81	**3.04**
RM	18	26	6.78	4.15	**2.63**
CAM	18	19	7.80	6.62	**1.18**
LM	14	15	4.97	4.16	**0.81**
RB	34	26	8.59	8.11	**0.48**
LCB	22	17	4.18	6.99	**−2.82**
GK	25	10	0.59	4.43	**−3.85**
RCB	14	16	0.91	7.11	**−6.20**

7   Limitations and Conclusion

We have presented a feature-based analysis and model for the problem of xCounter, significantly refining our previous work [5]. Our results show that players in possession should attack as a compact unit to minimize the risk of conceding an opposing *counterattack*. On the other hand, players out of possession can already prepare for an own *counterattack* by positioning as potential pass options in case of a future ball win.

Our predictive model's results demonstrated the importance of hyperparameter configuration, where we experience that a low number of features already provided good results. Admittedly, the small gap to the location-based baseline results indicates that more experiments are required before a robust model can be obtained. Lastly, our approach is subject to a set of design choices that need to be carefully inspected. Overall, we see large potential in combining and evaluating xCounter in the light of existing sport-specific concepts.

A   Appendix

For the predictive XGBoost models, a range of different hyperparameters were examined. Therefore, training was done on the training set (70% of turnovers) and the performance of different hyperparameter configurations was compared on the test set (30% of turnovers). Due to the fact, that the focus of work does not lie on generating an automatic model, we avoid using a more sophisticated approach, e.g., using cross-validation or a separate validation set. A list of the evaluated hyperparameters is provided in Table 6. Admittedly, our search space is limited, yet we plan to expand it in future. An explanation of the different hyperparameter configurations of the best XGBoost models, encrypted as superscripts in Table 3, is given in Table 7.

Detailed lists of the best ranked features for both teams are presented in Tables 8 and 9.

Table 6. Hyperparameter search space used for optimizing the XGBoost models. The choice of search space was inspired by the optimal results documented by Bauer and Anzer [2] as experimentation with significantly different parameters did not offer promising results.

Hyperparameter	Description	Search Space
N_{top}	Number of features passed to the model	$[1, \ldots, 49]$
Loss	Function to compute the gradient in model optimization	{ squared error, absolute error, huber }
Learning Rate	Step size per update of model parameters	$\{.01, .05, 0.1, 0.5\}$
Max depth	Maximum depth of the decision tree	$\{5, 7, 10\}$

Table 7. Hyperparameter configurations of the superior XGBoost models (refer to Table 3 for evaluation results)

	N_{top}	Loss	Learning Rate	Max depth
A	1	squared error	0.01	5
B	1	huber	0.01	5
C	6	absolute error	0.05	5
D	9	squared error	0.01	5

Table 8. Most predictive features for the ball-winning team. The *Lastplayer* subgroup was added to the feature set after inspection of the initial results.

◄──── Direction of counterattack   ▮ xC Higher than Average   ▮ xC Lower than Average

Ball-winning Team				
Feature				
Team Subgroup	*Infront Ball*	*All Players*	*Around Ball*	*Around Ball*
Metric	*Compactness*	*Compactness*	*Compactness*	*Free Pl.-Count*[5]
Direction	*Horizontal*	*Horizontal*	*Horizontal*	
Feature Value Above	16.35m	14.75m	13.74m	2 Players
Pitch Zones w/ increased xCounter				
Aggregate	**3.82**	**3.66**	**3.59**	**2.87**
Feature				
Team Subgroup	*Infront Ball*	*All Players*	*Behind Ball*	*Behind Ball*
Metric	*Centroid to Ball*	*Compactness*	*Compactness*	*Compactness*
Direction	*Vertical*	*Vertical*	*Horizontal*	*Vertical*
Feature Value Above	13.42m	13.42m	14.24m	5.28m
Pitch Zones w/ increased xCounter				
Aggregate	**2.77**	**2.59**	**2.41**	**2.34**
Feature				
Team Subgroup	*Infront Ball*	*Infront Ball*	*Around Ball*	*All Players*
Metric	*Free Pl.-Count*	*Compactness*	*Compactness*	*Centroid to Ball*
Direction	*5*	*Vertical*	*Vertical*	*Vertical*
Feature Value Above	2.0m	13.71m	9.36m	14.41m
Pitch Zones w/ increased xCounter				
Aggregate	**2.26**	**1.91**	**1.88**	**1.84**
Feature				
Team Subgroup	*Around Ball*	*Behind Ball*	*Behind Ball*	*All Players*
Metric	*Centroid to Ball*	*Free Pl.-Count*[1.5]	*Player-Count*	*Centroid to Ball*
Direction	*Vertical*			*Horizontal*
Feature Value Above	6.74m	5.0m	5.0m	5.49m
Pitch Zones w/ decreased xCounter				
Aggregate	**1.62**	**1.56**	**1.36**	**1.3**

Table 9. Most predictive features for the ball-losing team. The *Lastplayer* subgroup was added to the feature set after inspection of the initial results.

◀— Direction of counterattack	▮ xC Higher than Average	▮ xC Lower than Average

Ball-losing Team

Feature				
Team Subgroup	Around Ball	Infront Ball	All Players	Behind Ball
Metric	Compactness	Player-Count	Compactness	Centroid to Ball
Direction	Vertical		Vertical	Vertical
Feature Value				
Below	10.89m	3 Players	12.54m	19.95m
Pitch Zones w/ decreased xCounter				
Aggregate	**5.68**	**3.46**	**2.83**	**2.40**

Feature				
Team Subgroup	Behind Ball	Around Ball	Infront Ball	Infront Ball
Metric	Centroid to Ball	Compactness	Compactness	Compactness
Direction	Horizontal	Horizontal	Horizontal	Vertical
Feature Value				
Below	12.36m	9.44m	16.6m	4.43m
Pitch Zones w/ decreased xCounter				
Aggregate	**2.13**	**2.11**	**2.09**	**1.88**

Feature				
Team Subgroup	All Players	All Players	Around Ball	Lastplayer
Metric	Centroid to Ball	Centroid to Ball	Centroid to Ball	Centroid to Ball
Direction	Horizontal	Vertical	Vertical	Vertical
Feature Value				
Below	5.71m	21.29m	7.14m	41.57m
Pitch Zones w/ decreased xCounter				
Aggregate	**1.86**	**1.78**	**1.78**	**1.68**

Feature				
Team Subgroup	All Players	Around Ball	Behind Ball	Infront Ball
Metric	Compactness	Player-Count	Compactness	Centroid to Ball
Direction	Horizontal		Vertical	Horizontal
Feature Value				
Below	12.62m	4 Okayers	16.57m	8.75m
Pitch Zones w/ decreased xCounter				
Aggregate	**1.19**	**1.13**	**0.92**	**0.74**

References

1. Balague, N., Torrents, C., Hristovski, R., Davids, K., Araújo, D.: Overview of complex systems in sport. J. Syst. Sci. Complex. **26**(1), 4–13 (2013). https://doi.org/10.1007/s11424-013-2285-0
2. Bauer, P., Anzer, G.: Data-driven detection of counterpressing in professional football: a supervised machine learning task based on synchronized positional and event data with expert-based feature extraction. Data Min. Knowl. Disc. **35**(5), 2009–2049 (2021). https://doi.org/10.1007/s10618-021-00763-7
3. Bauer, P., Anzer, G.: A goal scoring probability model for shots based on synchronized positional and event data in football (soccer). Front. Sports Active Living **3**, 53 (2021). https://doi.org/10.3389/fspor.2021.624475
4. Biermann, H., Theiner, J., Bassek, M., Raabe, D., Memmert, D., Ewerth, R.: A unified taxonomy and multimodal dataset for events in invasion games. In: Proceedings of the 4th International Workshop on Multimedia Content Analysis in Sports, pp. 1–10. ACM, Virtual Event China (2021). https://doi.org/10.1145/3475722.3482792
5. Biermann, H., Wieland, F.G., Timmer, J., Memmert, D., Phatak, A.: Towards expected counter - using comprehensible features to predict counterattacks. In: Brefeld, U., Davis, J., Van Haaren, J., Zimmermann, A. (eds.) MLSA 2022. CCIS, vol. 1783, pp. 3–13. Springer, Cham (2023). https://doi.org/10.1007/978-3-031-27527-2_1
6. Delaunay, B., et al.: Sur la sphere vide. Izv. Akad. Nauk SSSR, Otdelenie Matematicheskii i Estestvennyka Nauk **7**(793–800), 1–2 (1934)
7. Fernández, J., Bornn, L., Cervone, D.: A framework for the fine-grained evaluation of the instantaneous expected value of soccer possessions. Mach. Learn. **110**(6), 1389–1427 (2021). https://doi.org/10.1007/s10994-021-05989-6
8. Frencken, W., Lemmink, K., Delleman, N., Visscher, C.: Oscillations of centroid position and surface area of soccer teams in small-sided games. Eur. J. Sport Sci. **11**(4), 215–223 (2011). https://doi.org/10.1080/17461391.2010.499967
9. Hockeyviz: Smoothing: How to (2023)
10. Lago-Ballesteros, J., Lago-Peñas, C., Rey, E.: The effect of playing tactics and situational variables on achieving score-box possessions in a professional soccer team. J. Sports Sci. **30**(14), 1455–1461 (2012)
11. Lepschy, H., Wäsche, H., Woll, A.: Success factors in football: an analysis of the German Bundesliga. Int. J. Perform. Anal. Sport **20**(2), 150–164 (2020). https://doi.org/10.1080/24748668.2020.1726157
12. Liu, G., Luo, Y., Schulte, O., Kharrat, T.: Deep soccer analytics: learning an action-value function for evaluating soccer players. Data Min. Knowl. Disc. **34**(5), 1531–1559 (2020)
13. LLC, S: Playing Styles Definition by StatsPerform (2023)
14. Merhej, C., Beal, R.J., Matthews, T., Ramchurn, S.: What happened next? Using deep learning to value defensive actions in football event-data. In: Proceedings of the 27th ACM SIGKDD Conference on Knowledge Discovery & Data Mining, pp. 3394–3403. ACM, Virtual Event Singapore (2021). https://doi.org/10.1145/3447548.3467090
15. Pedregosa, F., et al.: Scikit-learn: machine learning in Python. J. Mach. Learn. Res. **12**, 2825–2830 (2011)
16. Raudonius, L., Allmendinger, R.: Evaluating football player actions during counterattacks. In: Yin, H., et al. (eds.) IDEAL 2021. LNCS, vol. 13113, pp. 367–377. Springer, Cham (2021). https://doi.org/10.1007/978-3-030-91608-4_36

17. Robberechts, P., Davis, J.: How data availability affects the ability to learn good xG models. In: Brefeld, U., Davis, J., Van Haaren, J., Zimmermann, A. (eds.) MLSA 2020. CCIS, vol. 1324, pp. 17–27. Springer, Cham (2020). https://doi.org/10.1007/978-3-030-64912-8_2
18. Sahasrabudhe, A., Bekkers, J.: A graph neural network deep-dive into successful counterattacks. In: MIT Sloan Sports Analytics Conference, vol. 17 (2023)
19. Tenga, A., Kanstad, D., Ronglan, L.T., Bahr, R.: Developing a new method for team match performance analysis in professional soccer and testing its reliability. Int. J. Perform. Anal. Sport 9(1), 8–25 (2009). https://doi.org/10.1080/24748668.2009.11868461
20. Van Haaren, J.: "Why would I trust your numbers?" On the explainability of expected values in soccer. arXiv preprint arXiv:2105.13778 (2021)

Pass Receiver and Outcome Prediction in Soccer Using Temporal Graph Networks

Pegah Rahimian[1(✉)], Hyunsung Kim[2], Marc Schmid[3], and Laszlo Toka[1,4]

[1] Budapest University of Technology and Economics, Budapest, Hungary
pegah.rahimian@edu.bme.hu
[2] Seoul National University, Seoul, South Korea
[3] Technische Universität München, Munich, Germany
[4] ELKH-BME Cloud Applications Research Group, Budapest, Hungary

Abstract. This paper explores the application of the Temporal Graph Network (TGN) model to predict the receiver and outcome of a pass in soccer. We construct two TGN models that estimate receiver selection probabilities (RSP) and receiver prediction probabilities (RPP) to predict the intended and actual receivers of a given pass attempt, respectively. Then, based on these RSP and RPP, we compute the success probability (CPSP) of each passing option that the pass is successfully sent to the intended receiver as well as the overall pass success probability (OPSP) of a given situation. The proposed framework provides deeper insights into the context around passes in soccer by quantifying the tendency of passers' choice of passing options, difficulties of the options, and the overall difficulty of a given passing situation at once.

Keywords: Soccer Analytics · Multi-Agent Analysis · Temporal Graph Network · Pass Receiver Prediction · Pass Outcome Prediction

1 Introduction

Passes are the most frequent event in soccer, so analyzing them is essential to evaluate players' performance or match situations [1,11]. Particularly, focusing on individual passing options in a given passing situation enables domain participants to characterize the general tendency of players' decision-making or assess their decisions. There are two main aspects of analyzing passing options: either in terms of player (i.e., selecting a player to receive the pass) [1,11] or space (i.e., selecting a specific location on the pitch to send the ball to) [6,16,18].

In reality, it is difficult for players to pass the ball to a specific point on purpose, so we focus on players rather than the space to concretize the passer's intention more intuitively. We employ Temporal Graph Network (TGN) [17] to predict the intended and actual receivers in a given passing situation. By leveraging the TGN's ability to capture temporal dependencies, we estimate for a given moment the receiver selection probability (RSP) that the passer intends to send the ball to each of the teammates and the receiver prediction probability (RPP) that each player becomes the actual receiver of the pass.

U. Brefeld et al. (Eds.): MLSA 2023, CCIS 2035, pp. 52–63, 2024.
https://doi.org/10.1007/978-3-031-53833-9_5

Based on these RSP and RPP, we compute the success probability (named as CPSP in our paper) of each passing option that the pass is successfully sent to the intended receiver as well as the overall pass success probability (OPSP) of a given situation. Especially, we mathematically prove that dividing the RSP of a teammate by the corresponding RPP is equal to the CPSP of the passing option to the teammate. We analyze 358,790 passes from the 330 Belgian Pro League matches to estimate their average success probabilities in 18 zones of the pitch for both the start and end locations of the passes.

The proposed framework provides deeper insights into the context around passes in soccer by quantifying the tendency of passers' choice of passing options, the difficulties of the options, and the overall difficulty of a given passing situation at once. Another contribution is that this study suggests the potential of applying the TGN model to team sports data for handling the interaction between players. Also, we have made the source code available online for reproducibility[1].

2 Related Work

Several studies have tried to quantify the risk of a pass in a given passing situation. Spearman et al. [18] proposed a physics-based framework named Pitch Control to estimate the probability of a pass being successful given that the pass is sent to each location on the pitch. Power et al. [11] employed logistic regression to estimate the risk and reward of a pass based on handcrafted features. Fernández et al. [6] performed a similar task to that of Pitch Control, but by implementing a CNN-based deep learning architecture instead of physics-based modeling. Anzer and Bauer [1] predicted the intended receiver leveraging the approach of Pitch Control, and trained an XGBoost [5] model to estimate the success probability of each passing option. Most recently, Robberechts et al. [16] proposed a framework named un-xPass that measures a passer's creativity.

Meanwhile, analyzing players' movements in soccer is a cumbersome task due to its spatiotemporal and permutation-invariant nature, so several methods have been proposed to deal with this nature. Some studies [6, 14–16] treated each moment of the data as an image and apply a convolutional neural network (CNN) to encode it, and others [10, 12, 13] sorted players by a rule-based ordering scheme starting from the ball possessor. A better approach to model interaction between players and the ball is to employ graph-based [3] or Transformer-based [19] neural networks. To name a few, Anzer et al. [2] and Bauer et al. [4] constructed graph neural networks (GNN) to detect overlapping patterns and to divide a match into multiple phases of play, respectively. Kim et al. [8] deployed Set Transformers [9] to predict the ball locations from player trajectories.

3 Decomposing the Pass Success Probability

In this section, we formulate a relationship between the selection and success probabilities of each passing option in a given passing situation. Based on this

---

[1] https://github.com/hsnlab/sports_analitica.

relationship, we calculate the success probability of each passing option as well as the overall pass success probability in the situation.

Strictly speaking, a pass is said to be "successful" only if it is sent to the intended receiver. However, since there is no direct way of knowing the intention of each pass, many studies simply define that a pass is successful if one of the passer's teammates receives the pass. This definition involves an assumption that for each successful pass, the actual receiver (who is a teammate of the passer) is the expected receiver to whom the passer intended to send the ball. In other words, for the random variables E and R indicating the expected and actual receivers of the pass in a given state $S = s$, respectively, we assume

$$P(E = R|S = s, O = o^+) = 1. \tag{1}$$

where $O = o^+$ denotes the event that the pass is successful. Starting from this assumption, we can prove the following proposition.

Proposition 1. For each teammate i of the passer,

$$P(R = i|S = s) = P(E = i, R = i|S = s).$$

Proof. Since $P(E = i, R = i|S = s) = P(R = i|S = s) \cdot P(E = i|S = s, R = i)$, it is enough to show that $P(E = i|S = s, R = i) = 1$ for every $i \in T^+$ where T^+ is the set of the passer's teammates: Suppose $P(E = i|S = s, R = i) < 1$ for some $i \in T^+$, then

$$P(E = R|S = s, O = o^+)$$
$$= \sum_{i \in T^+} P(E = i, R = i|S = s, O = o^+)$$
$$= \sum_{i \in T^+} P(E = i|S = s, O = o^+, R = i) \cdot P(R = i|S = s, O = o^+)$$
$$= \sum_{i \in T^+} P(E = i|S = s, R = i) \cdot P(R = i|S = s, O = o^+)$$
$$< \sum_{i \in T^+} P(R = i|S = s, O = o^+)$$
$$= 1 \quad \text{(by the definition of a successful pass)}.$$

This contradicts Eq. 1 and thus completes the proof. $\qquad \square$

Based on Proposition 1, we can decompose the overall pass success probability as follows:

$$P(O = o^+|S = s) = \sum_{i \in T^+} P(R = i|S = s) \tag{2}$$

$$= \sum_{i \in T^+} P(E = i, R = i|S = s) \tag{3}$$

$$= \sum_{i \in T^+} P(E = i|S = s) \cdot P(R = i|S = s, E = i). \tag{4}$$

Four types of probabilities are related to the above equations:

- **Overall pass success probability** $P(O = o^+|S = s)$ (OPSP) that a pass in a given state s is successful.
- **Receiver selection probability** $P(E = i|S = s)$ (RSP) that the passer at s intends to send the ball to a teammate i.
- **Receiver prediction probability** $P(R = i|S = s)$ (RPP) that i is the actual receiver of the pass.
- **Conditional pass success probability** $P(R = i|S = s, E = i)$ (CPSP) given that i is the expected receiver of the pass being successfully sent to i.

In Sect. 4, we construct separate TGN architectures to estimate RSPs and RPPs, respectively. Then, we can obtain the OPSP for a given state from Eq. 2, i.e., by adding up the RPPs for all the teammates of the passer. Moreover, from Proposition 1, dividing the RPP of each teammate by the corresponding RSP results in the CPSP indicating the success probability of the hypothetical pass from the passer to the teammate, i.e.,

$$P(R = i|S = s, E = i) = \frac{P(E = i, R = i|S = s)}{P(E = i|S = s)} = \frac{P(R = i|S = s)}{P(E = i|S = s)}. \tag{5}$$

4   Constructing Temporal Graph Networks

In this section, we explain the tasks of estimating RSPs and RPPs introduced in Sect. 3 using separate TGN models. The common goal of our RSP and RPP models is to find the most likely receiver (either expected or actual) in a given passing situation. What differentiates them is that the candidate receivers of the former are the teammates (10 in general) of the passer and those of the latter are all the players (21 in general) other than the passer. In Sect. 4.1 and 4.2, we elaborate on the common fundamentals of our TGN models. In Sect. 4.3, we describe how to train the TGN for each type of probability.

4.1   Model Definition

The TGN model for each task takes a sequence of time-stamped events that occurred during each "possession" in soccer matches and produces the probability of the pass being received by each of the players (or the teammates) on the pitch in a given game state. Here a possession is defined as a time interval that a team continues to touch the ball except for fewer than three consecutive actions by the opponents. Namely, we assume that a possession ends when the next three actions are performed by the opposite team.

First, we make a graph with **nodes** corresponding to players, and **interactions** (i.e., temporal edges) indicating pass attempts between players. We label an interaction as a successful pass if it connects the two nodes of the same team, and an unsuccessful pass otherwise. Also, we extract temporal features for each of the nodes and edges on top of event and tracking data collected from the given match. More specifically, **node features** include a player's (x, y) location, velocity, distance, and angle from the ball carrier, and a flag indicating whether the player is the ball carrier for each time-step. Meanwhile, **edge features** include the distance and relationship (i.e., teammates or opponents) between the two interacting nodes.

Then, we model a TGN as a sequence of events $G = \{x(t_1), x(t_2), ...\}$ at times $0 \leq t_1 \leq t_2 \leq \cdots$, where $x(t)$ is either (1) a **node-wise event** $\mathbf{v}_i(t)$ of a player i such as the change of his location or (2) an **interaction event** $\mathbf{e}_{ij}(t)$ represented by a temporal edge between two nodes i and j such as a pass or a change in the distance between the two players.

4.2 TGN Architecture

In this section, we elaborate on the building blocks of the proposed TGN. It consists of an encoder-decoder pair, where an encoder is a function that maps players' interactions to node embeddings and a decoder takes the node embeddings as input and performs link prediction of the future time-steps. Figure 1 depicts the architecture of our network, which consists of the following modules:

– **Memory:** A memory of the model $\{\mathbf{s}_i(t)\}_{i \in P}$ at time t is a representation of the node's history that the model has seen until t. It consists of a state vector $\mathbf{s}_i(t)$ for each player $i \in P$ with the set P of all the players in the game at t, which is updated after an event $x(t)$. (Note that $x(t)$ can be either node-wise or interactive.) When a substitute is sent onto the pitch and a new node is created, the network initializes a zero vector for it, and then updates the memory after each event the player is involved in.
– **Message Function:** For each event $x(t)$ involving player i, the model computes a message $\mathbf{m}_i(t)$ to update i's memory. When a node-wise event $\mathbf{v}_i(t)$ happens, a single message for i is computed as:

$$\mathbf{m}_i(t) = \mathrm{msg}_n(\mathbf{s}_i(t^-), t, \mathbf{v}_i(t)).$$

Likewise, an interaction event $\mathbf{e}_{ij}(t)$ induces the computation of messages for the passer i and the receiver j as follows:

$$\mathbf{m}_i(t) = \mathrm{msg}_s(\mathbf{s}_i(t^-), \mathbf{s}_j(t^-), \Delta t, \mathbf{e}_{ij}(t))$$
$$\mathbf{m}_j(t) = \mathrm{msg}_d(\mathbf{s}_j(t^-), \mathbf{s}_i(t^-), \Delta t, \mathbf{e}_{ij}(t))$$

where $\mathbf{s}_i(t^-)$ is the memory of i at the time of the last event before t in which the player is involved and $\mathrm{msg}_n, \mathrm{msg}_s, \mathrm{msg}_d$ are learnable message functions.
– **Message Aggregator:** Since each player i can be involved in multiple events until time t, we aggregate all the memories $\mathbf{m}_i(t_1), \ldots, \mathbf{m}_i(t_b)$ of i generated before t by averaging them, i.e.,

$$\bar{\mathbf{m}}_i(t) = \mathrm{mean}(\mathbf{m}_i(t_1), \ldots, \mathbf{m}_i(t_b)).$$

– **Memory Updater:** For each event $x(t)$, a learnable memory update function updates the memory $\mathbf{s}_i$ of each player i involved in the event:

$$\mathbf{s}_i(t) = \text{mem}(\bar{\mathbf{m}}_i(t), \mathbf{s}_i(t^-)).$$

In this work, we employ the structure of Long Short-Term Memory (LSTM) [7] for this memory update function.

– **Embedding:** Even if $\mathbf{s}_i$ is not updated at time t because the player i is not involved in the event $x(t)$, the context around i can change by interactions of other players. To reflect this, we also deploy the embedding module to generate the temporal embedding $\mathbf{z}_i(t)$ of i at any time t by

$$\mathbf{z}_i(t) = \text{emb}(i, t) = \sum_{j \in P_{-i}} h(\mathbf{s}_i(t), \mathbf{s}_j(t), \mathbf{e}_{ij}, \mathbf{v}_i(t), \mathbf{v}_j(t))$$

where P_{-i} is the set of all 21 players other than i and h is Temporal Graph Attention (TGA) proposed in Rossi et al. [17].

– **Link Prediction:** To predict the most likely receiver (either expected or actual) of a pass attempt, we put the temporal embeddings $\mathbf{z}_i(t)$ into a fully connected layer that outputs link values between nodes. After applying soft-max to these values, we obtain a set of probabilities that add up to 1 and mean which candidate would be the receiver of the pass. Note that any passer does not intend to send the ball to an opponent, so we restrain the candidates to the passer's teammates for the RSP model. Meanwhile, all the players including opponents are the candidates for the RPP model. See Fig. 2 depicting the resulting probabilities in a passing moment as an example.

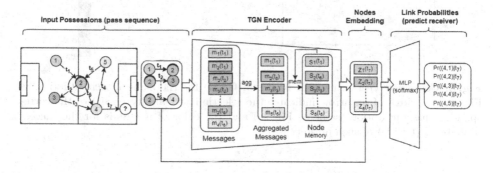

Fig. 1. TGN architecture for outcome prediction.

4.3 Training RSP and RPP Models

We train separate TGN models for estimating RSPs and RPPs, respectively. Both models take features for all the players in the state s. On the other hand, we impose different restrictions on model outputs as described in Sect. 4.2: While

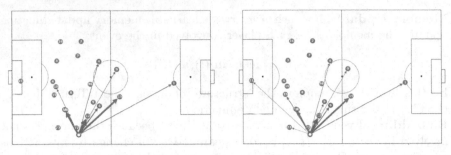

(a) Receiver selection probabilities   (b) Receiver prediction probabilities

Fig. 2. Visualizations of RSP and RPP for an example match situation. Every passing option from the ball carrier to a player with a probability larger than 0.01 is expressed as an arrow whose width indicates the probability value.

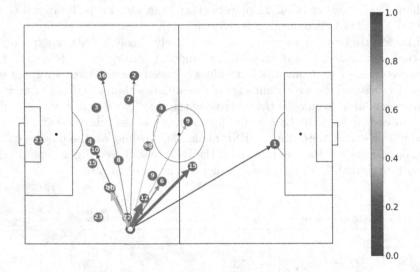

Fig. 3. Combined visualization of RSP and CPSP for the same match situation as Fig. 2. The width of an arrow indicates the selection probability (RSP) of the corresponding passing option (same as Fig. 2a) and the color of it stands for the success probability (CPSP) of such option.

only a teammate can be a candidate receiver for the RSP model, all the players including teammates and opponents are candidates for the RPP model.

For the RSP model, we aim to estimate $\hat{y}_{s,i}^{E} = P(E = i | S = s)$ for each of the passer's teammates i, the probability that the passer intends to send the ball to i in a given state s. While we cannot know the expected receiver of an unsuccessful pass, we have assumed that for a successful pass, the actual receiver is the expected receiver in Sect. 3. Hence, we take successful passes $\mathcal{D}^{+}$ in the training dataset and use the actual receivers of them as the true labels indicating the expected receivers for training. Namely, the model is trained by minimizing the cross-entropy loss

$$\mathcal{L}^E = \frac{1}{|\mathcal{D}^+|} \sum_{s \in \mathcal{D}^+} \sum_{i \in T^+} y_{s,i}^E \log \hat{y}_{s,i}^E$$

between the output $\hat{y}_{s,i}^E$ and the true label $y_{s,i}^E$. Here $y_{s,i}^E = 1$ if i receives the pass, and $y_{s,i}^E = 0$ otherwise.

For the RPP model, we want to estimate $\hat{y}_{s,i}^R = P(R = i|S = s)$ for each of the players i (either a teammate or an opponent), the probability that i actually receives the pass. Other than the RSP model, we do know the true receiver for every pass (either successful or failure) in the dataset. Thus, we train the model with the entire training dataset $\mathcal{D}$ by minimizing the cross-entropy loss

$$\mathcal{L}^R = \frac{1}{|\mathcal{D}|} \sum_{s \in \mathcal{D}} \sum_{i \in T^+ \cup T^-} y_{s,i}^R \log \hat{y}_{s,i}^R$$

where $y_{s,i}^R = 1$ if i receives the pass, and $y_{s,i}^R = 0$ otherwise.

While the two models are trained on different datasets, they can be applied to any passing situation regardless of its outcome. They produce $\hat{y}_{s,i}^E$ for each teammate i and $\hat{y}_{s,j}^R$ for each player j (either a teammate or an opponent) for the situation. Then, as mentioned in Sect. 3, we can compute the OPSP from Eq. 2 and the CPSP per teammate from Eq. 5, i.e.,

$$P(O = o^+|S = s) = \sum_{i \in T^+} P(R = i|S = s) = \sum_{i \in T^+} \hat{y}_{s,i}^R \tag{6}$$

$$P(R = i|S = s, E = i) = \frac{P(R = i|S = s)}{P(E = i|S = s)} = \frac{\hat{y}_{s,i}^R}{\hat{y}_{s,i}^E}. \tag{7}$$

For example, the OPSP of Fig. 2 can be obtained by summing the widths of red arrows in Fig. 2b. Also, the CPSP per the passer's teammate is calculated by dividing the width of the corresponding arrow in Fig. 2b by that of its counterpart in Fig. 2a. The results are illustrated as the arrows' colors in Fig. 3.

5   Experiments

5.1   Dataset

The dataset consists of high-resolution spatiotemporal tracking and event data covering all 330 games of the 2020–21 season of Belgian Pro League collected by Stats Perform. The tracking data include the (x, y) coordinates of all 22 players and the ball on the pitch for 25 observations per second. The event data includes on-ball action types such as passes, shots, dribbles, etc. annotated with additional features such as period ID, the ball carrier's ID, start and end locations of the ball. We then merged tracking data with event data. Each record of our merged dataset includes all players and the ball coordinates with their corresponding features for each snapshot, i.e., every 0.04 s.

Table 1. Feature sets of different models.

Model	Selected features
XGBoost trained with event data	Normalized start and end locations of the passes, pass length, pass angle, pass direction, a flag indicating whether the pass goes inside the penalty box, angle and distance to goal, pass type
XGBoost trained with event and tracking data	Velocity of the passer, velocities of the nearest defenders toward the passer and the receiver, Distances from the passer and receiver to their respective nearest defenders, the nearest defenders' angles to the passing line, time from regaining possession
TGN (trained with event and tracking data)	(1) Node features: player's location, velocity, distance and angle from the ball carrier, and a flag indicating whether the player is the ball carrier for each time-step. (2) Edge Features: distance and relationship (i.e., teammates or opponents) between the two interacting nodes

Table 2. Model performance on the test dataset.

Model	F_1 score	AUC	Log loss
Naive	–	0.50	0.45
XGBoost (event only)	0.81	0.79	0.38
XGBoost (event + tracking)	0.86	0.82	0.29
TGN	**0.95**	**0.92**	**0.18**

5.2 Evaluating Model Performance

We aim to evaluate the performance of our framework for estimating CPSPs. To this end, we trained our TGN models with 358,790 passes from the 330 Belgian Pro League matches. The data was split by using 80% of games for model training, 10% for validation, and 10% for test according to the chronological order of the matches in the league. Also, we implemented three other baseline models to estimate the success probability of a hypothetical pass for comparison. First, we implemented a naive model that assigns a fixed success probability of 84.5% (the average success rate in our dataset) to every pass. Second, we trained a binary classifier with XGBoost [5] using only the features that can be derived from event data (i.e., the first row in Table 1). Lastly, we trained XGBoost with hand-crafted features derived from event and tracking data [11] to showcase the necessity of positional data in prediction (i.e., the second row in Table 1). As a consequence, Table 2 demonstrate that our TGN model outperforms the other baselines, achieving 0.95 in F_1 score and 0.92 in Area Under the Curve (AUC).

5.3   Pass Difficulty in Different Areas of the Pitch

To show that the resulting success probabilities agree with our intuition, we compared the CPSPs in different areas of the pitch. Specifically, we split the pitch into 18 zones as in Fig. 4 and calculated the average CPSP for the passes starting from each zone. Also, we performed the same aggregation using the end locations of passes. The resulting average probabilities of each zone signify how it is challenging that a player in the area makes a successful pass (aggregation by starting zone) or that a player successfully sends to the ball to that area (aggregation by ending zone). Namely, the lower the average values of the zone, the more difficult to make a successful pass from or to the area.

Figures 4a and 4b depict the average CPSP for all passes in different areas of the pitch. The cooler colors of a pitch zone show lower average values indicating more difficulty. Both figures demonstrate that it is more difficult to make a pass in or towards the attacking area (i.e., zones in the central channel and the final third). Particularly, partitioning by the destination of a pass exhibits more deviation of probabilities than that by the origin. These observations accord with our general intuition that it is generally more challenging to succeed in passing in the scoring zone, and even harder to successfully send the ball to the zone.

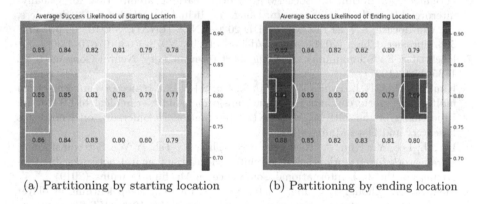

(a) Partitioning by starting location   (b) Partitioning by ending location

Fig. 4. Average CPSPs in different areas of the pitch.

6   Conclusion

In this study, we propose the application of a Temporal Graph Network (TGN) to pass receiver and outcome prediction in soccer. By leveraging the TGN's predictive capabilities, our framework can analyze a given passing situation with segmentalized components. Specifically, it quantifies the tendency of passers' choice of passing options, the difficulties of the options, and the overall difficulty of a given passing situation at once. A direction for future work is to assess the offensive and defensive performance of players leveraging our metrics.

Acknowledgment. Project no. 2021-1.2.4-TÉT-2021-00053 has been implemented with the support provided by the Ministry of Culture and Innovation of Hungary from the National Research, Development and Innovation Fund, financed under the 2021-1.2.4-TÉT funding scheme.

References

1. Anzer, G., Bauer, P.: Expected passes: determining the difficulty of a pass in football (soccer) using spatio-temporal data. Data Min. Knowl. Disc. **36**, 295–317 (2022)
2. Anzer, G., Bauer, P., Brefeld, U., Fassmeyer, D.: Detection of tactical patterns using semi-supervised graph neural networks. In: 16th MIT Sloan Sports Analytics Conference (2022)
3. Battaglia, P.W., et al.: Relational inductive biases, deep learning, and graph networks. CoRR abs/1806.01261 (2018). https://arxiv.org/abs/1806.01261
4. Bauer, P., Anzer, G., Shaw, L.: Putting team formations in association football into context. J. Sports Anal. **9**(6), 39–59 (2023)
5. Chen, T., Guestrin, C.: XGBoost: a scalable tree boosting system. In: Proceedings of the 22nd ACM SIGKDD International Conference on Knowledge Discovery and Data Mining (2016)
6. Fernández, J., Bornn, L.: SoccerMap: a deep learning architecture for visually-interpretable analysis in soccer. In: Dong, Y., Ifrim, G., Mladenić, D., Saunders, C., Van Hoecke, S. (eds.) ECML PKDD 2020. LNCS (LNAI), vol. 12461, pp. 491–506. Springer, Cham (2021). https://doi.org/10.1007/978-3-030-67670-4_30
7. Hochreiter, S., Schmidhuber, J.: Long short-term memory. Neural Comput. **9**(8), 1735–1780 (1997)
8. Kim, H., Choi, H.J., Kim, C.J., Yoon, J., Ko, S.K.: Ball trajectory inference from multi-agent sports contexts using set transformer and hierarchical bi-LSTM. In: Proceedings of the 29th ACM SIGKDD International Conference on Knowledge Discovery and Data Mining (2023)
9. Lee, J., Lee, Y., Kim, J., Kosiorek, A.R., Choi, S., Teh, Y.W.: Set transformer: a framework for attention-based permutation-invariant neural networks. In: Proceedings of the 36th International Conference on Machine Learning (2019)
10. Mehrasa, N., Zhong, Y., Tung, F., Bornn, L., Mori, G.: Deep learning of player trajectory representations for team activity analysis. In: 12th MIT Sloan Sports Analytics Conference (2018)
11. Power, P., Ruiz, H., Wei, X., Lucey, P.: Not all passes are created equal: objectively measuring the risk and reward of passes in soccer from tracking data. In: Proceedings of the 23rd ACM SIGKDD International Conference on Knowledge Discovery and Data Mining (2017)
12. Rahimian, P., Oroojlooy, A., Toka, L.: Towards optimized actions in critical situations of soccer games with deep reinforcement learning. In: Proceedings of the 8th IEEE International Conference on Data Science and Advanced Analytics (2021)
13. Rahimian, P., da Silva Guerra Gomes, D.G., Berkovics, F., Toka, L.: Let's penetrate the defense: a machine learning model for prediction and valuation of penetrative passes. In: Brefeld, U., Davis, J., Van Haaren, J., Zimmermann, A. (eds.) MLSA 2022. CCIS, vol. 1783, pp. 41–52. Springer, Cham (2022). https://doi.org/10.1007/978-3-031-27527-2_4

14. Rahimian, P., Van Haaren, J., Abzhanova, T., Toka, L.: Beyond action valuation: a deep reinforcement learning framework for optimizing player decisions in soccer. In: 16th MIT Sloan Sports Analytics Conference (2022)
15. Rahimian, P., Van Haaren, J., Toka, L.: Towards maximizing expected possession outcome in soccer. Int. J. Sports Sci. Coach. (2023)
16. Robberechts, P., Roy, M.V., Davis, J.: un-xPass: measuring soccer player's creativity. In: Proceedings of the 29th ACM SIGKDD International Conference on Knowledge Discovery and Data Mining (2023)
17. Rossi, E., Chamberlain, B., Frasca, F., Eynard, D., Monti, F., Bronstein, M.M.: Temporal graph networks for deep learning on dynamic graphs. CoRR abs/2006.10637 (2020). https://arxiv.org/abs/2006.10637
18. Spearman, W., Basye, A., Dick, G., Hotovy, R., Pop, P.: Physics-based modeling of pass probabilities in soccer. In: 11th MIT Sloan Sports Analytics Conference (2017)
19. Vaswani, A., et al.: Attention is all you need. In: Advances in Neural Information Processing Systems (2017)

Field Depth Matters: Comparing the Valuation of Passes in Football

Leo Martins de Sá-Freire$^{(\boxtimes)}$ and Pedro O. S. Vaz-de-Melo

Universidade Federal de Minas Gerais, Belo Horizonte, MG, Brazil
leomartins@dcc.ufmg.br, olmo@dcc.ufmg.br

Abstract. This study delves into the influence of missing spatial context information on the valuation of football actions through event data based metrics. Using actions from an entire Premier League season, we analyze successful passes originating from different field depths, considering the subsequent occurrence of goals. By comparing the value assignments by Valuing Actions by Estimating Probabilities (VAEP), we provide insights into the metric's ability to recognize the quality of passes in the early stages of attacks.

Keywords: Sports analytics · Event data · Machine Learning

1 Introduction

Valuation metrics have emerged in the field of football analytics as a way to quantify the impact of each action in a match [1]. With high performance and a wide range of useful employments, they have generated academic developments and industrial applications over the past years [3,7–12]. Among the state-of-the-art metrics, VAEP (Valuing Actions by Estimating Probabilities) [1] and xT (Expected Threat) [4]) stand out, and they have already been compared in previous research [2].

VAEP is particularly notable for its sensitivity to the specificities of each action [2]. By analyzing event data, it assigns values to actions by estimating goal probabilities at each moment of the game. This approach allows for valuing every move in the game based on the probability variation it generates.

However, event data does not contain the location of all players on the field for every stored event. Only the protagonist player of each action has their coordinates recorded. Consequently, this representation suffers from a significant loss of spatial context information, which inevitably limits the effectiveness of metrics utilizing it. One notable limitation is the neglect of positional advantage, which refers to the advantage resulting from the relation between players' positions from both teams.

This study was financed in part by the Coordenação de Aperfeiçoamento de Pessoal de Nível Superior - Brasil (CAPES) - Finance Code 001.

U. Brefeld et al. (Eds.): MLSA 2023, CCIS 2035, pp. 64–73, 2024.
https://doi.org/10.1007/978-3-031-53833-9_6

Positional advantage is among the key aspects of modern football [5,6]. In a game where the offensive process is increasingly integrated, it is possible to observe that many goals and dangerous plays are a consequence of coordinated movements that put the attacking team in equal or numerical superiority situations on the field. Many of these movements start far from the opponent's penalty area, with passes resulting from good readings by defenders, full-backs, and midfielders initiating an attack.

The advantage generated by this kind of pass seems to be mainly positional. Therefore, we raise the following question: Considering that VAEP is based on event data, can it recognize contributive passes in the early stages of an attack? Throughout this work, we will gather evidence to answer this question.

The proposed analysis consists of implementing a framework of VAEP applied to an entire season of the Premier League. From this, we will group successful passes that occurred throughout the championship according to the depth of the field from which they originated and the occurrence or non-occurrence of goals in the near future. Subsequently, we will compare the value assignment by VAEP in the different groups.

2   Methodology

This section presents an overview of the methodology utilized in the study, highlighting the fundamental approaches. Initially, the description of football event data will be provided. Following that, we will introduce the VAEP framework, which utilizes a machine learning algorithm to establish the probabilities of scoring or conceding a goal in each gamestate. Next, the process of assigning a value to each action will be explained. Finally, we will elucidate the grouping of examined passes and list the conducted analyses and tests.

2.1   Event Data

In football, event data refers to a data representation that captures the sequence of on-ball actions throughout a match. In this work we used the SPADL [1] format and the stored attributes of each event are described in Table 1. Although this data type includes a complete overview on each action on the ball, event stream data lacks spatial context information once it ignores the other players' positions during each action.[1]

2.2   VAEP

Event data allows us to represent a football match as a finite sequence of actions $(a_1, a_2, ..., a_n)$, where $n \in \mathbb{N}$. The VAEP framework is based on gamestates consisted of three consecutive actions. A gamestate S_i is defined as (a_{i-2}, a_{i-1}, a_i).

---

[1] An alternative data representation is tracking data, which constantly captures all players and ball coordinates. Although it details players positioning, it is more expansive, more challenging to acquire, and requires a significantly larger volume of instances to represent full matches.

Table 1. SPADL Attribute Descriptions

Attribute	Description
StartTime	The action's start time
EndTime	The action's end time
StartLoc	The (x, y) location where the action started
EndLoc	The (x, y) location where the action ended
Player	The player who performed the action
Team	The player's team
ActionType	The type of the action
BodyPart	The player's body part used for the action
Result	The result of the action

Then, each gamestate S_i is associated with the probabilities of the team t in possession of the ball scoring ($P_{scores}(S_i, t)$) or conceding ($P_{concedes}(S_i, t)$) a goal within the subsequent ten actions. These probabilities are separately estimated through a learning algorithm that utilizes features derived from the SPADL attributes of the 3 gamestate actions, as detailed in [1]. A binary label is used to indicate whether a goal occurs or not shortly after the action sequence. Finally, a value is assigned to each action a_i, denoted as $V(a_i)$. The calculation is performed as follows:

$$\Delta P_{scores}(S_i, t) = P_{scores}(S_i, t) - P_{scores}(S_{i-1}, t)$$

$$\Delta P_{concedes}(S_i, t) = P_{concedes}(S_i, t) - P_{concedes}(S_{i-1}, t)$$

$$V(a_i) = \Delta P_{scores}(S_i, t) - \Delta P_{concedes}(S_i, t)$$

From now on, we will refer to $\Delta P_{scores}(S_i, t)$ as the offensive value of action a_i.

For our implementation, we utilized a free event data sample provided by Wyscout, containing the five main European leagues in the 2017/18 season. We used the matches from La Liga, Ligue 1, Serie A, and Bundesliga for training the models and defined the matches from Premier League as the test dataset. Considering the results reported in [13], XGBoost was the chosen learning algorithm, with default hyperparameters except for those indicated in Table 2. The models performances were measured using the Normalized Brier Score (NBS) and the obtained values are displayed in Table 3. The Brier Score is defined as the mean squared error between the predicted probabilities and the corresponding binary outcomes. The normalization step involves dividing the Brier Score by the baseline Brier Score, where the predicted probabilities are equal to the observed frequency of the event in the dataset. A lower NBS indicates better calibration and higher reliability, signifying that the probabilities align well with the actual outcomes.

Table 2. Models Hyperparameters

Model	Algorithm	Objective	Learning Rate	Max Depth	Number of Estimators
Scores	XGBoost	Binary: Logistic	0.1	9	100
Concedes	XGBoost	Binary: Logistic	0.1	9	100

Table 3. Models Performance

Dataset	Size	Model	NBS
Train	1454120	Scores	0.814
Train	1454120	Concedes	0.876
Test	482901	Scores	0.847
Test	482901	Concedes	0.969

2.3 Groups and Tests

With the set of actions from the entire Premier League 17/18 season properly valuated by the metric, it is possible to conduct the desired investigation. Initially, we separated a dataset including all successful passes throughout the championship. From this dataset, we extracted four groups, 1-G, 1-NG, 3-G, and 3-NG, according to pass origin and the occurrence of goals by the team in possession in the subsequent ten actions. The criteria and the size of each group are presented in Table 4. We used the traditional division of the pitch into thirds, consisting of the defensive third (1st), the midfield third, and the attacking third (3rd), selecting only passes from the initial and the final thirds. The occurrence of goals is represented by the binary label of the scores model.

Table 4. Groups of successful passes.

Group	Pass origin	Label	Size
1-G	1st third	True	572 passes
1-NG	1st third	False	76036 passes
3-G	3rd third	True	1606 passes
3-NG	3rd third	False	56395 passes

We proceeded by first examining the Cumulative Distribution Functions (CDFs) of the offensive values in the groups of passes, comparing groups 1-G × 1-NG and 3-G × 3-NG. Additionally, we conducted Kolmogorov-Smirnov tests to analyze the differences between the groups. Next, we compared the CDFs of groups 1-G and 3-NG to gain insights into their offensive value distributions. Lastly, we closely examined a selection of high-valued passes through plots.

3   Results

With only event data attributes, it is not easy to accurately determine which passes in the first third of the field actually significantly increased the real probability of a subsequent goal. Still, it is reasonable to assume that there is a higher concentration of such passes among those that actually resulted in a goal.

This justifies why Group 1-G, which contains initial passes that resulted in a goal in the near future, will be the focus of our analysis. It is not possible to affirm that all the passes in this group actually made a significant contribution to the subsequent goal, but certainly, some of them were decisive.

To understand if the VAEP valuation based on event data can identify them, we will divide this section into three subsections. The first subsection will compare the offensive valuation differences of passes within the same third of the field. In the subsequent subsection, we will compare groups 1-G and 3-NG. Lastly, the final subsection will showcase specific pass examples and highlight notable cases.

3.1   Comparing Same Third Groups

We conducted the mentioned comparisons by analyzing the groups' Cumulative Distribution Functions (CDFs) of the offensive value distribution, as shown in Fig. 1. Additionally, we performed two Kolmogorov-Smirnov tests. The KS Statistic for groups 1-G and 1-NG is 0.10582 while the same calculation between 3-G and 3-NG is 0.23937.

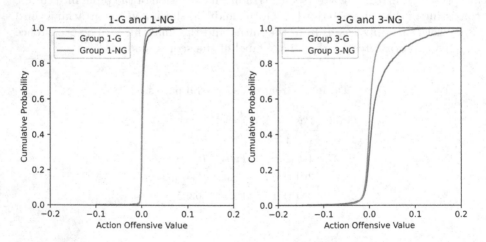

Fig. 1. Comparison of Cumulative Distribution Functions (CDFs) for groups 1-G and 1-NG (left), 3-G and 3-NG (right). The larger discrepancy between 3-G and 3-NG CDFs compared to 1-G and 1-NG CDFs indicates that the metric better differentiates passes that result in goals in the final third than in the first third.

These results show that there is a significant difference between the two comparisons. The performed test and the visualizations indicate that, although both comparisons point out differences between the groups, the discrepancy of values between 3-G and 3-NG is significantly larger than between 1-G and 1-NG. This indicates that the metric can better differentiate passes that result in goals in the final third than in the first third.

This result can be interpreted in different ways. One possible interpretation is that the factors that led to the subsequent goals in group 1-G occurred after the passes themselves. Thus, the variation in the label between groups 1-G and 1-NG is more associated with chance than with the differences between the passes in each group, which results in a similar valuation by VAEP in both groups. On the other hand, it is in the final third where the goal condition is really generated. Therefore, the metric appropriately differentiates good passes in the final third, which are abundant in group 3-G and receive better overall ratings than group 3-NG.

However, this interpretation does not align with what we can observe in contemporary football. In recent years, defenders have been increasingly involved in the offensive phase of the game, starting from their own field, breaking lines, finding long balls, and structuring counter-attacks. This is a cornerstone of various prominent tactical approaches today. Therefore, we believe in an alternative interpretation of the results.

The advantage generated by good passes in the early stages of the field is predominantly positional. Whether it is a pressure release, a first-line break, or a good long pass, the gain for the executing team lies in the relation between players' positions and the ball rather than in the attributes stored in event data. Conversely, in the final third of the field, the features involved in the model can more easily capture dangerous passes. Although positional relations are still relevant, there is also substantial importance on elements such as proximity to the goal and the speed of the sequence of plays. Because of this, VAEP can make a better distinction in the final third.

This second perspective on the results seems more plausible, but analyzing just one season is not sufficient to claim that the metric indeed underestimates good passes in the first third of the field. There is a significant difference in the number of passes in each group, which makes it challenging to employ certain approaches in this comparison. Nonetheless, even though they are not conclusive, the presented results serve as evidence to believe that underestimation does occur.

3.2   Comparing 1-G and 3-NG

Another comparison we conducted was between the CDFs of the offensive value distribution of passes from groups 1-G and 3-NG. The graph with both functions is displayed in Fig. 2. Clearly, the two groups contain actions that occurred in very different contexts. Still, this comparison provides us with some interesting insights. Examining the curves, we can observe a higher frequency of low values, particularly negative values, in group 3-NG. This aligns with expectations since,

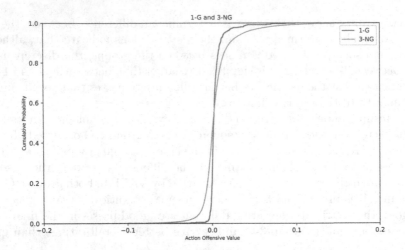

Fig. 2. Comparing CDFs of groups 1-G and 3-NG. Group 3-NG shows more frequent high values than group 1-G. This observation is intriguing since all passes in group 1-G resulted in goals, while none of the passes in group 3-NG did.

in the final third of the field, the probabilities of scoring are higher and, therefore, can be decreased by some passes. Though, when we look at the other end of the graph, we can see that the frequency of higher values is also greater in group 3-NG. This observation is intriguing since all passes in group 1-G resulted in goals, while none of the passes in group 3-NG did.

Once again, this analysis cannot be taken as conclusive. In addition to the inherent contextual difference between these two groups, there is a significant disparity in the number of passes in each. Even so, it is a surprising fact that corroborates the proposed investigation.

3.3   Notable Cases

To analyze some examples more closely, we selected the top 10 passes from group 1-G with the highest offensive values assigned by VAEP. These passes are represented in Fig. 3, where the bottom part of each plot represents the defending goal, and the top part represents the attacking goal.

The most prominent characteristic in this set is the depth of the passes. Except for the first one, all of them are long balls that cover a significant portion of the field. This observation aligns with expectations because ball advance is a feature that event data can represent and is intuitively correlated with the occurrence of a subsequent goal. At first glance, it is plausible that these passes were influential in creating the resulting goal.

Still, when we look at group 3-NG, we observe that 434 passes are better valuated than the one occupying the first position in group 1-G. In Fig. 4, we can see a random sample of 10 of these 434 passes.

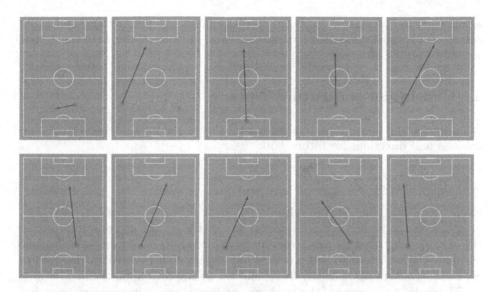

Fig. 3. Top 10 valued passes in group 1-G. There is a prominent characteristic of depth, with all but the first pass being long balls covering a substantial portion of the field.

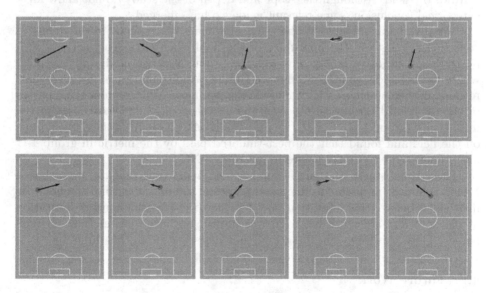

Fig. 4. Random sample of the top 434 valued passes in group 3-NG. In general the passes are short and there is a slight trend of progressiveness.

We can observe a notable trend in these passes: they are generally progressive, aiming for areas of the field closer to the opponent's goal, despite being shorter than the selected passes from group 1-G. While none resulted in a goal, they give the initial impression of increasing the likelihood of scoring. However, it is astonishing to find such a significant absolute number of passes that supposedly enhanced the goal probability more than any pass from the first third that actually resulted in a goal.

4   Conclusion and Future Work

After presenting the results, this section concludes the work by presenting conclusions and directions for future work.

4.1   Conclusion

Event data has considerable advantages, such as more accessible collection, greater availability, and lower memory demand. Despite its inherent limitations, efficient models based on this structure have already been shown to be feasible and are of great scientific and practical importance. This reinforces the need to explore characteristics, identify flaws, and try to improve upon them.

Throughout the scope of this work, we conducted an analysis aiming to understand if VAEP, with its original features, can distinguish good passes in the initial third of the field. Although the scope and depth of the study do not allow for a categorical conclusion, some relevant evidence has emerged.

Initially, it was possible to observe a significant discrepancy in the offensive valuation of passes in the final third of the field when comparing actions with positive and negative labels. The same was not observed in the initial third, where the value distributions are more similar. Additionally, we observed that, in general, there are more well-valuated passes among the negative-labeled passes in the final third (group 3-NG) than among the positive-labeled passes in the initial third (group 1-G). Finally, we presented some passes from these two groups on the field and found that the best-valuated pass by the metric in group 1-G has a lower score than 434 passes from group 3-NG.

These three stages of analysis support the hypothesis that the event-based VAEP is limited in distinguishing good passes in the initial third of the field. As mentioned before, this limitation may be due to the spatial context limitation of the data format, which has a greater impact on initial passes than on final passes. Thus, this study encourages further investigation in this direction.

4.2   Future Work

The evidence raised points to directions for future work. One possibility is to repeat the analysis on different datasets to ensure that what was observed in this Premier League season is not an exception. Additionally, making slight variations in the VAEP model, such as changing the outcome window of an action to determine labels, could be interesting. This would increase the likelihood that the grouped passes are more directly related to goal occurrence.

A longer-term and ongoing approach as a continuation of this work involves developing a second framework for VAEP that includes features extracted from tracking data. By re-valuating the actions using this second form of the metric, it would be possible to identify which passes had a significant change in value. This approach could guide a search for patterns within the original features to enhance and balance the functioning of the metric using event data.

References

1. Decroos, T., Bransen, L., Van Haaren, J., Davis, J.: Actions speak louder than goals: valuing player actions in soccer. In: Proceedings of the 25th ACM SIGKDD International Conference on Knowledge Discovery & Data Mining, pp. 1851–1861. Association for Computing Machinery, New York (2019). https://doi.org/10.1145/3292500.3330758
2. Van Roy, M., Robberechts, P., Decroos, T., Davis, J.: Valuing on-the-ball actions in soccer: a critical comparison of XT and VAEP. In: Proceedings of the AAAI-20 Workshop on Artificial Intelligence in Team Sports. AI in Team Sports Organizing Committee (2020)
3. Robberechts, P., Van Roy, M., Davis, J.: un-xPass: measuring soccer player's creativity. In: StatsBomb Conference (2022). https://statsbomb.com/wp-content/uploads/2022/09/Pieter
4. Singh, K.: Introducing Expected Threat (xT) (2023). https://karun.in/blog/expected-threat.html
5. Crow, B.: How the creation of different superiorities generates opportunities to progress the ball (2023). https://soccerdetail.com/2020/10/26/how-the-creation-of-different-superiorities-generates-opportunities-to-progress-the-ball/
6. Hodson, T.: Positional play: football tactics explained (2023). https://www.coachesvoice.com/cv/positional-play-football-tactics-explained-guardiola-cruyff-manchester-city/
7. Fernández, J., Bornn, L., Cervone, D.: Decomposing the immeasurable sport: A deep learning expected possession value framework for soccer. In: 13th MIT Sloan Sports Analytics Conference (2019)
8. Decroos, T., Bransen, L., Van Haaren, J., Davis, J.: VAEP: an objective approach to valuing on-the-ball actions in soccer. In: IJCAI, pp. 4696–4700 (2020)
9. Davis, J., et al.: Evaluating sports analytics models: challenges, approaches, and lessons learned. In: AI Evaluation Beyond Metrics Workshop at IJCAI 2022, vol. 3169, pp. 1–11. CEUR Workshop Proceedings (2022)
10. Pappalardo, L., Cintia, P., Ferragina, P., Massucco, E., Pedreschi, D., Giannotti, F.: PlayeRank: data-driven performance evaluation and player ranking in soccer via a machine learning approach. ACM Trans. Intell. Syst. Technol. (TIST) 10(5), 1–27 (2019). https://doi.org/10.1007/1234567890
11. Fernández, J., Bornn, L., Cervone, D.: A framework for the fine-grained evaluation of the instantaneous expected value of soccer possessions. Mach. Learn. 110(6), 1389–1427 (2021). https://doi.org/10.1007/1234567890
12. Nascimento, R.F.M., Rios-Neto, H.: Generalized action-based ball recovery model using 360 data. In: StatsBomb Conference (2022). https://statsbomb.com/wp-content/uploads/2022/09/Ricardo. Accessed 6 June 2023
13. Decroos, T., Davis, J.: Interpretable prediction of goals in soccer. In: Proceedings of the AAAI-20 Workshop on Artificial Intelligence in Team Sports (2019)

Basketball

Momentum Matters: Investigating High-Pressure Situations in the NBA Through Scoring Probability

Balazs Mihalyi[1]($\boxtimes$), Gergely Biczók[1,3], and Laszlo Toka[1,2]

[1] Budapest University of Technology and Economics, Budapest, Hungary
balazsmark.mihalyi@edu.bme.hu, biczok@crysys.hu, toka.laszlo@vik.bme.hu
[2] ELKH-BME Cloud Applications Research Group, Budapest, Hungary
[3] ELKH-BME Information Systems Research Group, Budapest, Hungary

Abstract. One of the defining characteristics of real basketball stars, and even great role players, is how well they perform under immense mental pressure. In this paper, we present a method to identify high-pressure situations during a basketball game through shooting success. In order to calculate the amount of pressure a team is facing going into a game, we use a prediction model to determine the importance of the given game for that team to reach their end-of-season goal. The model relies on features referring to game context, recent form, and pre-season aspirations. We then investigate the impact of our pre-game pressure metric, along with other factors, on the shooting performance of NBA players on six seasons' worth of data. We find that shotmaking in the NBA is mainly impacted by the so-called *momentum*, i.e., when a team outscores their opponent significantly over a short period of time.

Keywords: basketball · scoring · mental pressure · momentum · performance

1 Introduction

In the world of sports, there is an adjective for athletes who perform well in big moments: *clutch*. This expression is very well known in the NBA. NBA.com even has a tab, where they list traditional, advanced, and other statistics for players *in the clutch*. By their definition, the clutch is the final five minutes of a game, where the point differential is five or less.

Although earlier studies on the subject show that points scored near the end of a game, when the score is close, have a significant impact on the final outcome ([6]), games can be decided earlier than that. Giving up a big run can break a team even if it happens in the third quarter or early on in the fourth. The authors of [3] were the first ones to introduce pre-game elements to their definition of high-pressure scenarios. They used features describing game importance, team ambition, recent form, and game context to train a model on rankings acquired from a set of football experts.

U. Brefeld et al. (Eds.): MLSA 2023, CCIS 2035, pp. 77–90, 2024.
https://doi.org/10.1007/978-3-031-53833-9_7

The authors of [12] chose to identify high-pressure factors by examining scoring probability in the Italian "Serie A2". They have also found that pressure mounts late into a closely contested game.

To the best of our knowledge, there has been no work published on the subject of mental pressure in sports addressing momentum, although it is a commonly used term by analysts, play-callers, and fans when a team seemingly grows over their opposition. When momentum shifts, the athlete who gets on top could feel a certain superiority over their opponent. This is what the authors of [7] call *psychological momentum*, and it could be an important aspect of a basketball player's mental state during a game.

To carry out our analysis we used shooting [8] and play-by-play [10] data, along with standings and advanced box-score statistics [9]. The resulting dataset consisted of six full seasons, from the 2012–13 regular season to that of 2017–18, totaling 7, 379 games, and 1, 459, 374 shots (818, 720 2-pointers, 324, 183 3-pointers, and 316, 471 free throws).

The paper is organized as follows. In Sect. 2, we look at pre-game pressure, where we use a prediction model to infer game importance and thus, pre-game pressure. Then, in Sect. 3, we discuss the high-pressure scenarios we identified through scoring probability. In Sect. 4, we evaluate the shooting and playmaking performance of players under pressure. Finally, we conclude our work in Sect. 5.

2   Pre-game Pressure

When constructing our pre-game pressure metric, we use a feature set similar to the one in [3]; however, our final pressure score is game importance itself.

To determine team ambition, we assigned all 30 NBA teams in the 6 seasons under consideration to four clusters. During the clustering we used the following features: average experience and age of the roster, average salary of the 5 highest earning players on the team, average experience of the 5 highest earning players, number of all-stars on the team roster the year before, expected wins and championship odds before the season began, number of wins the team had 1, 2, 3 and 4 seasons ago, and playoff appearances and championships by the franchise. All this data was gathered from basketball-reference.com [1]. In the case of pre-season expected wins and championship odds, we used the way-back machine [2] to get sufficient data.

The results of the clustering can be seen in Table 1. There are two superior clusters, 0 and 2. Both of these have more experience on their roster than the other two, as well as more all-stars. The difference between the two clusters is their success in recent seasons. Members of cluster 0 have been winning teams for years, while teams in cluster 2 have been losing teams some years ago, but are winning presently. Members of cluster 3 are the opposite of teams in cluster 2. They have been getting worse and worse over the last few seasons, but their highest-paid players are quite experienced. These teams are likely just entering a rebuild, but have not yet gotten rid of their aging veterans. Teams in cluster 1 are in complete demise. They are young and bad, and seemingly not going anywhere. For some examples of teams in certain clusters look for Fig. 7 in the Appendix.

Table 1. Means of the most interesting features in the 4 clusters

Cluster	avg exp	avg age	all-stars last year	expected wins	wins 1 yr ago	wins 2 yrs ago	wins 3 yrs ago	wins 4 yrs ago
0	6.82	28.90	1.39	46.33	50.20	52.24	52.30	51.04
1	4.90	27.41	0.21	31.96	29.51	31.41	34.76	38.30
2	5.94	27.13	1.32	47.03	45.21	39.82	34.24	30.89
3	4.56	24.34	0.17	29.11	34.00	38.44	43.33	43.72

As mentioned above, to define the amount of mental pressure a team faced prior to a game, we used a game outcome prediction model. The features used to train this model were the ones acquired from [9], along with team ambition features assessed during clustering. To predict game outcomes we used a Multilayer Perceptron (MLP) model. After feature selection, we were left with 27 features, mostly consisting of factors that experts usually look at when assessing a team's strength entering a game, such as special records for the teams (home and away wins and losses), recent performance, margins of victory, and a simple rating system (a team rating that takes into account average point differential and strength of schedule).

After training the model, we calculated the pre-game pressure scores. A calculation for team t can be seen in Eq. (1), where PreGamePres_t is the pre-game pressure value of team t, ExpectedWins_t is the mean of the number of wins expected for teams in the same cluster with team t before the season, Wins_t is the number of games the team has won so far in the current season, PredWins_t is the number of wins the team will add to Wins_t according to the MLP model's predictions, and MeanProb_t is the mean of the prediction confidence values of the MLP model. When a team is about to play their final game of the season, their pre-game pressure is simply $1 - \text{WinProb}_t$, where WinProb_t is the probability that they are going to win their last game.

$$\text{PreGamePres}_t = \frac{\text{ExpectedWins}_t - (\text{Wins}_t + \text{PredWins}_t)}{\text{MeanProb}_t} \tag{1}$$

An example of pre-game pressure scores throughout an entire season can be seen in Fig. 1. The team is the Los Angeles Clippers, who were put in cluster 2 that year, meaning they were slowly entering contender status at the time, but were still relatively young. They started off the season with very low pre-game pressure scores, but at one point in early February they lost 7 games out of 9, and pressure started to mount.

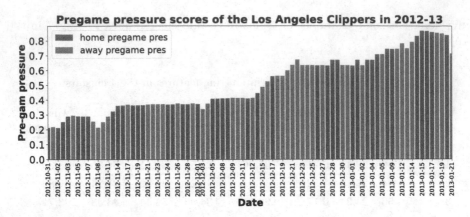

Fig. 1. Pre-game pressure scores of the LA Clippers in the 2012–13 season

3 Identifying High-Pressure Scenarios

Our approach to identifying high-pressure situations is inspired by the one presented in [12], but with a different feature set. Indeed, the main difference is including features that could describe momentum and pre-game pressure. These were:

- *SHOTMAKING_L2M*, the shot-making streak of the shooter in the last 2 min. The value is $+m$ if the shooter made the last m shots they attempted and $-m$ if they missed their last m shots;
- *PERF_DELTA*, the difference in the shooting percentages of the shooter in previous games and the current game;
- *SCOREMARGIN_L5M*, the score margin in the last 5 min before the shot was taken from the shooter's team's point of view; and
- *pregame_pressure_cluster*, the pre-game pressure the shooter's team was under entering the game.

The other features were *PERIOD*, the quarter in which the shot was taken; *SECLEFT*, the number of seconds left in the quarter when the shot was taken; *LAST_SHOT*, 1 if the shooter made their previous shot of the same type, 0 otherwise; *SCOREMARGIN*, the score difference between the two teams from the shooter's team's perspective; and *SHOTTYPE*, 1 if the shot taken was a 2-pointer, 2 if it was a 3-pointer, and 3 if it was a free throw.

In our earlier attempts we used features created from tracking data acquired from [11]. These features were shot-clock (the number of seconds remaining on the shot-clock), closest defender (the distance between the shooter and the closest defender to him), and average defender distance (the average distance between the shooter and the defenders). Although these features added extra context to each individual shot, our previous analysis proved them indifferent to shooting success.

For easier interpretability, we first transformed all numerical features into categorical ones, by training a CART [5], and a Random Forest [4] classifier on the original data, and calculated the mean of the decreases in heterogeneity for every threshold used for every feature, at every node. Equation (2) shows the calculation of the drop at a single node:

$$HT_i = impurity_i - \frac{impurity_j - impurity_k}{2} \tag{2}$$

where HT_i is the decrease in heterogeneity allowed by node i, $impurity_i$ is the Gini impurity of node i, and $impurity_j$ and $impurity_k$ are the impurities of the left- and right child-node of node i. Table 2 shows the results of the categorization.

After finalizing our dataset we trained a CART model on our target feature, *SHOT_MADE_FLAG*, to attain scoring probabilities depending on the above-mentioned factors. Figure 5 shows the resulting decision tree (see Appendix). Upon first glance, *SCOREMARGIN_L5M* and *SECLEFT* dominate the tree. These two features alone were enough to define high-pressure situations: "There are more than 8 min and 20 s left, and the shooter's team has not outscored

Table 2. Categories created from numerical variables, with thresholds.

Variable	Category	Thresholds
SECLEFT	quarter-end	SECLEFT < 60.5
	quarter-middle	60.5 ≤ SECLEFT < 500.5
	quarter-start	500.5 ≤ SECLEFT
pregame_pressure_cluster	low pre-game pr	pregame_pressure_cluster < 0.4
	normal pre-game pr	0.4 ≤ pregame_pressure_cluster < 0.7
	high pre-game pr	0.7 ≤ pregame_pressure_cluster
SHOTMAKING_L2M	cold hand	SHOTMAKING_L5M < 0.5
	hot hand	0.5 ≤ SHOTMAKING_L5M
PERF_DELTA	below −0.4	PERF_DELTA < −0.4
	between −0.4 and −0.2	−0.4 ≤ PERF_DELTA < −0.2
	between −0.2 and 0.4	−0.2 ≤ PERF_DELTA < 0.4
	more than 0.4	0.4 ≤ PERF_DELTA
SCOREMARGIN	less than −22.5	SCOREMARGIN < −22.5
	bw −22.5 and -10.5	−22.5 ≤ SCOREMARGIN < −10.5
	bw −10.5 and -6.5	−10.5 ≤ SCOREMARGIN < −6.5
	bw −6.5 and 12.5	−6.5 ≤ SCOREMARGIN < 12.5
	bw 12.5 and 18.5	12.5 ≤ SCOREMARGIN < 18.5
	more than 18.5	18.5 ≤ SCOREMARGIN
SCOREMARGIN_L5M	less than −11.5	SCOREMARGIN_L5M < −11.5
	bw −11.5 and 0.5	−11.5 ≤ SCOREMARGIN_L5M < 0.5
	bw 0.5 and 12.5	0.5 ≤ SCOREMARGIN_L5M < 12.5
	more than 12.5	12.5 ≤ SCOREMARGIN_L5M

the opposing team so far in the quarter". In other words, NBA players shot the basketball much better when they gained momentum over their opponent in the first few minutes of a quarter. Players shot both 2- and 3-pointers much worse when these conditions were not true. Players made their 2-pointers 49.2% of the time, but when under high pressure, they only made 31.5%. For 3-pointers, these numbers are 35.6% and 15.2%, respectively. A potential way to stabilize things when a team allows their opponent to go on a run early into a quarter could be to get to the free throw line. Although free throw shooting also gets worse when a team did not win the last 5 min, the 78.3% to 71.9% drop is more favorable compared to the other two shot types.

It would make sense that momentum in the first few minutes of the first quarter stems from pre-game pressure. To test this hypothesis we built a decision tree without the feature $SCOREMARGIN\_L5M$, exclusively on shots in the first quarter. Figure 6 shows that in the first 11 min of first quarters, players shoot 2-pointers better (52% vs. 49.5%) when the pre-game pressure is low (see Appendix). Although there are much fewer shots in such situations (32, 482 vs. 112, 453), the tree is still robust in these leaves.

4   Evaluation of Players' Performance in High-Pressure Situations

To evaluate players' shooting performance under pressure we calculated the shooting performance of players that took at least 1500 of each shot type in the investigated time period. To calculate a player's shooting performance, we subtracted the likelihood of every shot they took from the shots' $SHOT\_MADE\_FLAG$ values (1 if made, 0 if missed). Thus, every missed shot was assigned a negative value, and every made shot was given a positive one. The absolute value of the scores for missed shots was greater if the player missed a shot with a high probability of going in. On the other hand, if a player made a shot with a lower scoring probability, they got a higher score for actually making it. Note that the performance value for a single shot is in the range of $[-1; 1]$.

The overall shooting performance of player x, for shot type T (2-pointer, 3-pointer, or free throw) was calculated according to Eq. (3). This metric is a slightly modified version of the one presented in [12].

$$SP_x(T) = \frac{\sum\limits_{s_x \in S_x} (\text{SHOT\_MADE\_FLAG}_{s_x} - \pi_{s_x})}{\sum\limits_{s_x \in S_x(T)} s_x} \tag{3}$$

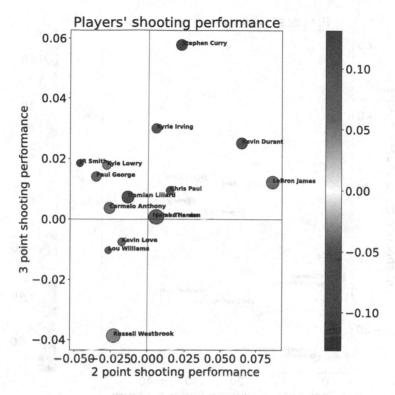

Fig. 2. Players' 2-pointer (x-axis), 3-pointer (y-axis), and free throw (color) shooting performance between the 2012–13 and 2017–18 NBA seasons (Color figure online)

where $S_x(T)$ denotes the set of type T shots player x took, and s_x is one of these shots. SHOT_MADE_FLAG$_{s_x}$ is the value of the *SHOT_MADE_FLAG* variable for shot s_x, and π_{s_x} is the scoring probability of s_x according to our decision tree.

The results can be seen in Fig. 2. This figure, as well as Figs. 3, and 4, are simplified since some of the players seen on them changed teams during the investigated time period. Stephen Curry's 3-point dominance is very apparent, but the whole upper right section of the figure is interesting. Apart from Stephen Curry, we see Kevin Durant, LeBron James, and James Harden (barely) there as well. These players won the Most Valuable Player award 5 times out of the possible 6 during the investigated time period. The only other MVP not there in the best quarter of the plot is Russell Westbrook, who was better than average only at free throw shooting while under pressure.

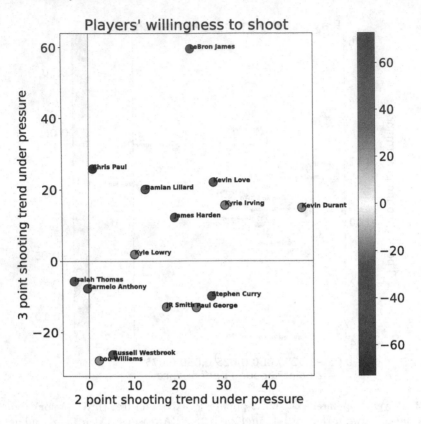

Fig. 3. 2-point (x-axis), 3-point (y-axis), and free throw (colors) shooting trends between the 2012–13 and 2017–18 NBA seasons (Color figure online)

Apart from shooting performance, we also investigated players' willingness to shoot. As players can get intimidated under high pressure, and, therefore, lose their confidence to shoot the basketball, this is worth investigating. Equation (4) shows the formula for calculating the shooting trend of player x.

$$ST_x = \left[\frac{\frac{\sum\limits_{s_x \in S_{x,p}} s_x}{\sum\limits_{s_t \in S_{t,p}} s_t}}{\frac{\sum\limits_{s_x \in S_x} s_x}{\sum\limits_{s_t \in S_t} s_t}} - 1 \right] \cdot 100 \tag{4}$$

Essentially, we take the ratio between the fraction of team shots player x has taken under pressure and the same ratio overall. $S_{s,p}$ denotes the set of shots

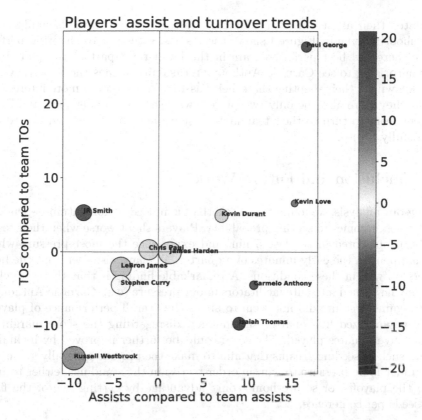

Fig. 4. Assist (x-axis), turnover (y-axis), and assist to turnover ratio (colors) trends between the 2012–13 and 2017–18 NBA seasons (Color figure online)

player x has taken under pressure, and $S_{t,p}$ is the same for his team. S_x and S_t are the set of shots player x and his team took, in that order. This is a slightly modified version of the formula presented in [12].

Players' shooting trends under pressure can be seen in Fig. 3. Almost every player seems to take more 2-pointers and get to the free-throw line less under pressure. The latter trend usually means that a player is less aggressive than usual; however, in this case, it could also be explained by the fact that our high-pressure criterion can only be true in the first few minutes of a quarter, where there are usually fewer free throw attempts than in the later stages.

Apart from shooting, a player can also impact a basketball game with his passing ability, by setting up his teammates to score. On the other hand, they can also hurt their team by turning the ball over. To see how the players who met the 1500-shot criterion did in this aspect of the game under pressure, we calculated their assist, turnover, and assist-to-turnover ratio trends similarly to their shooting trends. Figure 4 shows the results. Contrary to shooting performance, here the best performers are in the lower-right part of the plot. It is quite surprising to see Carmelo Anthony and Isaiah Thomas there, as they are more known for their shooting than their passing. What is even more interesting is that they were also the only two players who shot less under pressure. Both of them seem to turn to their teammates when under pressure, and they do it successfully.

5   Conclusion and Future Work

During our analysis, we found that basketball is indeed a momentum-dependent sport when it comes to scoring probability. Players shoot worse when their team has been outscored in the last 5 min, and experience the most pressure when that happens in the early minutes of a quarter. We have also seen that the best players do well in these conditions. A remarkable finding is that there are elite scorers who turned into elite facilitators under pressure (e.g., Carmelo Anthony).

Pre-game pressure did not seem to affect the overall performance of players when we analyzed first-quarter shotmaking, disregarding the score margin in the last five minutes played. The score could be further improved by including factors such as seeding. Teams that aim to make the playoffs generally go out to play under more pressure to win, in order to rise in the standings, either to just make the playoffs, or secure home-court advantage by getting one of the first four seeds per conference.

Acknowledgement. Project no. 2021-1.2.4-TÉT-2021-00053 has been implemented with the support provided by the Ministry of Culture and Innovation of Hungary from the National Research, Development and Innovation Fund, financed under the 2021-1.2.4-TÉT funding scheme.

Appendix

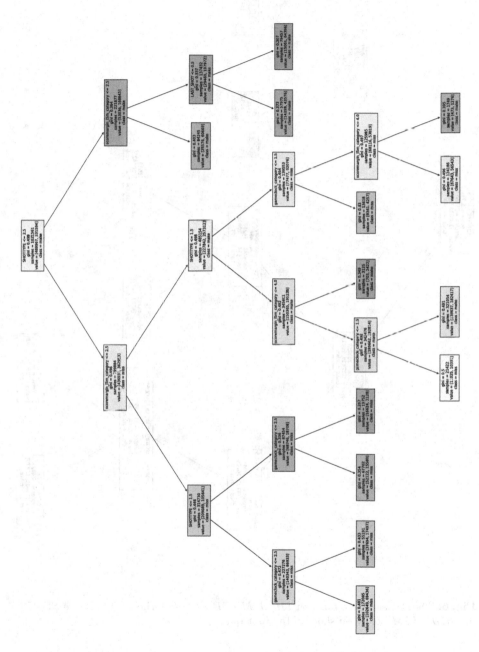

Fig. 5. The decision tree built on *SHOT_MADE_FLAG*

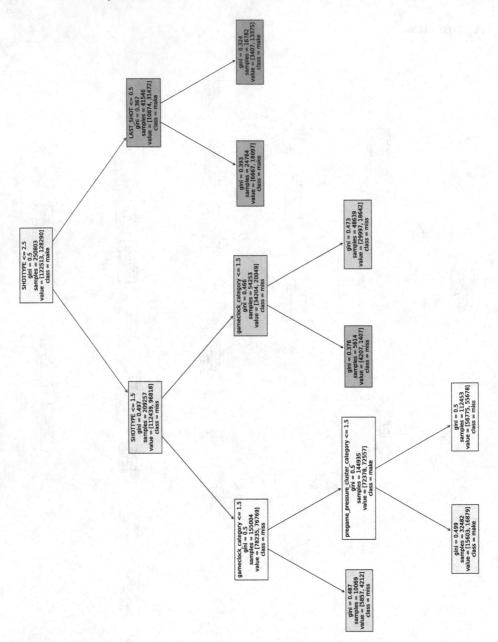

Fig. 6. The decision tree built on *SHOT_MADE_FLAG*, without the feature *SCORE-MARGIN_L5M*, solely on shots in the first quarter

full_name	abbreviation	season	cluster
Boston Celtics	BOS	2012-13	0
Chicago Bulls	CHI	2012-13	0
Los Angeles Lakers	LAL	2012-13	0
San Antonio Spurs	SAS	2012-13	0
Golden State Warriors	GSW	2017-18	0
Cleveland Cavaliers	CLE	2012-13	1
Minnesota Timberwolves	MIN	2012-13	1
New Orleans Pelicans	NOP	2013-14	1
Detroit Pistons	DET	2013-14	1
Los Angeles Lakers	LAL	2016-17	1
Utah Jazz	UTA	2017-18	2
Boston Celtics	BOS	2016-17	2
Atlanta Hawks	ATL	2015-16	2
Oklahoma City Thunder	OKC	2012-13	2
Los Angeles Clippers	LAC	2012-13	2
Philadelphia 76ers	PHI	2014-15	3
Dallas Mavericks	DAL	2016-17	3
Chicago Bulls	CHI	2017-18	3
Brooklyn Nets	BRK	2017-18	3
Memphis Grizzlies	MEM	2017-18	3

Fig. 7. Some examples to the clustering of teams' pre-season aspirations detailed in Sect. 2

References

1. Basketball Statistics & History of every Team & NBA and WNBA players. https://www.basketball-reference.com/
2. Internet archive: Wayback machine. https://archive.org/web/
3. Bransen, L., Robberechts, P., Van Haaren, J., Davis, J.: Choke or shine? Quantifying soccer players' abilities to perform under mental pressure. In: MIT Sloan Sports Analytics Conference (2019)
4. Breiman, L.: Random forests. Mach. Learn. **45**(1), 5–32 (2001)
5. Breiman, L., Friedman, J.H., Olshen, R.A., Stone, C.J.: Classification and Regression Trees. Routledge, Abingdon-on-Thames (2017)
6. Goldman, M., Rao, J.M.: Effort vs. concentration: the asymmetric impact of pressure on NBA performance. In: MIT Sloan Sports Analytics Conference (2012)
7. Iso-Ahola, S.E., Dotson, C.O.: Psychological momentum: why success breeds success. Rev. Gen. Psychol. **18**(1), 19–33 (2014)
8. Patel, S.: nba_api, September 2018. https://github.com/swar/nba_api
9. Rossotti, P.: NBA Enhanced Box Score and Standings (2012–2018), March 2018. https://www.kaggle.com/datasets/pablote/nba-enhanced-stats
10. schadam26: Br_scrape, January 2021. https://github.com/schadam26/BR_Scrape/

11. Seward, N.: Sportvu movement tracking data, February 2018. https://github.com/sealneaward/nba-movement-data
12. Zuccolotto, P., Manisera, M., Sandri, M.: Big data analytics for modeling scoring probability in basketball: the effect of shooting under high-pressure conditions. Int. J. Sports Sci. Coach. **13**(4), 569–589 (2018)

Are Sports Awards About Sports? Using AI to Find the Answer

Anshumaan Shankar[1], Gowtham Veerabadran Rajasekaran[1],
Jacob Hendricks[1], Jared Andrew Schlak[1], Parichit Sharma[1], Madhavan K. R.[1],
Hasan Kurban[1,2,3(✉)], and Mehmet M. Dalkilic[1,2]

[1] Computer Science Department, Indiana University, Bloomington, IN 47405, USA
{shankaa,goveera,jbhendri,jschlak,parishar,madhkr,dalkilic}@iu.edu
[2] Data Science Program, Indiana University, Bloomington, IN 47405, USA
[3] Department of Electrical and Computer Engineering, Texas A&M University at
Qatar, Doha, Qatar
hasan.kurban@qatar.tamu.edu

Abstract. Sports awards have become almost as popular as the sports
themselves bringing not only recognition, but also increases in salary,
more control over decisions usually in the hands of coaches and general
managers, and other benefits. Awards are so popular that even at the
start of a season pundits and amateurs alike predict or argue for athletes. It is odd that something so apparently data-driven does not work
in determining whether it is, indeed, data-driven. The simple question
arises, "Are sports awards about sports?" Using ML (over a hundred
potential models) this work aims to answer this question for professional
basketball: Most Valuable Player, Most Improved Player, Rookie of the
Year, and Defensive Player of the Year. Pertinent data is gathered including voting percentages. Our results are very interesting. MVP can be
predicted well from the data, while the other three are more difficult.
The findings suggest that either the data is insufficient (although no
more sports data can be found) or more likely non-tangible factors are
playing critical roles. This outcome is worth reflecting on for fans of all
stripes: should sports awards be about sports? The source code along
with instructions on running it to can be found in our github repository.

Keywords: NBA · Award Prediction · Regression · Sports Analytics

1 Introduction

At the conclusion of each National Basketball Association (NBA) season, individual awards are presented to players who have demonstrated exceptional performance in specific categories. Judges cast votes and a simple majority wins.
These awards, in particular, the Most Valuable Player (MVP), Defensive Player
of the Year (DPY), Most Improved Player (MIP), and Rookie of the Year (RoY),
hold great prestige and often foster intense debates throughout the off-season.

U. Brefeld et al. (Eds.): MLSA 2023, CCIS 2035, pp. 91–102, 2024.
https://doi.org/10.1007/978-3-031-53833-9_8

The general belief is that superior performance dictates the outcome. For instance, an MVP typically achieves the highest averages in points, rebounds, and assists; however, history shows many outcomes being driven by what are apparently other factors.

Interestingly, for an event that brings debate, salary increases, trades *etc.*, awards have received limited formal research. In this work, AI is leveraged to predict the four major NBA awards. Using a novel machine learning (ML) approach, where over ninety models are examined, we demonstrate a compelling approach to predicting awards that also gives insight into, perhaps, what might be intangibles. In fact, the question of whether statistics are sufficient to predict awards is directly answered.

2   Background

Sports Analytics [5,6,10,17–21,24,25,28] has become critical to discovering winning patterns hidden in sports data, that is collected during each game and prediction of award winners through the same. While some award decisions are explained by superior "stats" (statistics) or player performance, there may be other extraneous factors involved influencing the final outcome. Some of these may include salary [22], voter fatigue, luck [2] and social elements [8]. Due to such factors, there is some ambiguity around the meaning of these awards (what does "most valuable" actually mean?) and the basis on which they are given. Building on previous works on this topic [1,4] that use individual statistics for MVP prediction, This paper seeks to achieve accurate predictions for four NBA awards based on player statistics as well as explore whether there are any factors impacting the awards in addition to player performance.

The data (years 1950–2023) are drawn from several sources: older archived player data [11], recent player data [9], team data for every year [12], and individual award voting by year [3]. Four data sets (denoted MVP, MIP, RoY, DPY) were created differing on size dictated by eligibility. For size, $|MVP| = |DPY| \approx 18\,K$, $|MIP| \approx 13K$, $|RoY| \approx 3K$. For features, $MVP, DPY, RoY \in \mathbb{R}^{27}$ and $MIP \in \mathbb{R}^{52}$ because it also includes most of the data from the player's previous year to learn how much a player has improved over time. The class label of each dataset is a value $[0,1]$ reflecting the percentage of votes.

See Fig. 1 for the pipeline. MVP and DPY data consist of player data for each year including typical stats *e.g.*, shots taken, shots made, and location of shot. RoY data is constrained to rookies. The MIP dataset has all players who have played at least a year in the NBA. A majority of missing values >75% in the years 1950–1981 resulted in only using 1982 onward. Missing values were replaced with zero.

Because of space limitations, only MVP is presented in detail. As part of our work, the sufficiency of the data (*wrt* prediction) for MVP is investigated using a modified version of the offensive rating [23]. Figure 2 plots the offensive rating of all players across all years, showing that the MVP consistently ranks above the 95th percentile, often reaching the top.

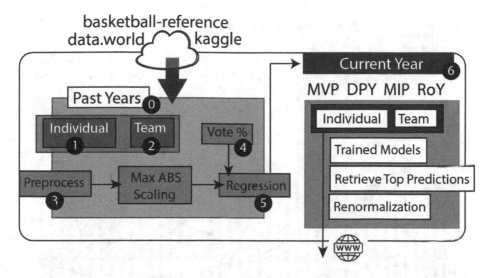

Fig. 1. The green boxes illustrate model training and the blue box shows how the trained model is used. 0: previous years are used as the training data. 1, 2: Individual player statistics and team win statistics are used as the dataset, 3: preprocess the data to remove unneeded features and entries. 4: award vote percentage is used as the class label. 5: regression architectures are used to build models. 6: Player data from the current year is fed into the model to get results. (Color figure online)

Notably, in the year 2022, the top three performers align with the top three candidates for the MVP award, suggesting that the offensive rating metric can serve as a fair indicator of performance. Figure 3 (top) plots points + assists per game scored by each player. The MVP consistently outperforms the majority of players typically ranking within the top 5th percentile. Figure 3 (bottom) shows that many players remain candidates in subsequent years. The rationale behind this analysis was to ascertain the presence of players with prior NBA experience, which could potentially impact their likelihood of receiving MVP votes and being considered contenders for the award. Notably, it is observed that a significant overlap ranges from approximately 75% to 85% across all years, indicating a substantial number of players who carry on from one season to the next can win. Our analysis revealed the existence of more than 20 players who received votes for the MVP award in at least five different years but have never won. These results do not encompass the current 2022–23 season, which explains why Joel Embiid appears in the visualization despite winning the award this season.

3 Experimental Overview

Four experiments were done to predict the chances of a player winning an award in a specific category (greatest percentage vote) that included over 90 AI models currently available in R [14]. Selected models vary greatly *e.g.*, tree-based regressor, support vector machine-based regressor, ordinary linear regression models

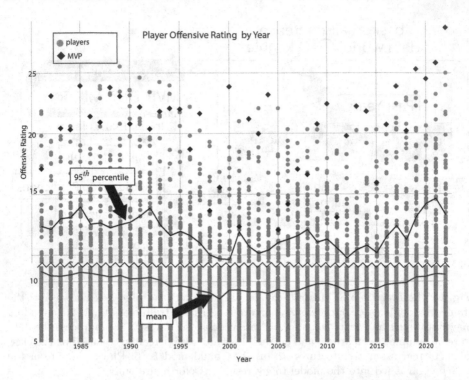

Fig. 2. MVP winners (red) consistently outperform other players (light blue) in Offensive ratings. They consistently achieve scores above the 95th percentile (black arrow & line) and the mean performance (green arrow & line) in each year. (Color figure online)

with regularization, random forest, and deep learning models. Models competed to be the best predictors must (1) complete computation within 15 min; (2) have no error. After meeting both conditions, 30 models remained for MVP, MIP, and DPY (all the same). For RoY the number of models was 76. Model training is done on each data set individually and we report the top models and their summary statistics. Performance is evaluated *via* two different metrics: Root Mean Squared Error (RMSE) and Mean Absolute Error (MAE).

3.1 Data Processing

Irrelevant Features were removed and all values are converted to the same scale by normalizing using maximum absolute scaling. The data is split in the ratio 85:15 for training and test sets, and the training data is further split into validation sets as described below. The target column is the number of votes and the remaining columns are used as the predictor variables.

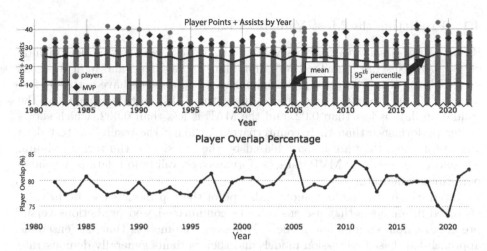

Fig. 3. (top) MVP winners consistently outperform other players in points + assists consistently achieving scores above both the 95th percentile (black arrow & line) and the mean performance (green arrow & line) in each year. (bottom) Overlaps of 75% to 85% of players in successive years in the NBA indicate many of the same players remain candidates. (Color figure online)

3.2   Implementation Details

To improve model generalization, we employ k-fold cross-validation ($k = 5$) by partitioning the data into k subsets, where the model is trained on k-1 subsets while the kth fold is used as a validation set for measuring performance. Each round of k-fold cross-validation is repeated five times to further increase the model's robustness. The model training is performed on a 64-bit Ubuntu system with 512 GB of RAM consisting of 24 AMD cores, and the version of R programming language is 4.2.2.

4   Results and Analysis

Performance of top 20 models are presented in Fig. 4. Box plots in sub-figure A and B demonstrate the spread of RMSE and MAE on the validation data, and the bar plots in subfigure B, D indicate the RMSE and MAE values on test data. We note that models won't perform equally well across both validation and test data, because of the inherent nature of MVP data *i.e.*, only a few tuples have non-zero values, and of those, only one win. Since validation data spans a major portion of the training set, the best models should be chosen by giving more weight to the performance of validation data. This phenomenon is common to all data sets used in this work due to the sparsity in the target column and is a general problem in AI [13].

4.1   Predicting the Most Valuable Player

Results (Fig. 4) show that across validation and test sets, top models include cubist, pcaNNet, qrnn xgbTree, M5, knn, kknn and avNNet, and indicates that averaged neural network, tree and neighbor based approaches have better performance than their counterparts. Interestingly, the RMSE of these models on the validation data is less than 0.02, and the MAE is less than 0.002, which shows better performance than their counterparts. Although the results on test data seem promising, they are in part biased by the sparsity in the target column. Therefore, as noted, for MVP data, performance on validation data is a reliable performance indicator.

Interestingly, the performance landscape of the top models can be broadly classified into models that use ensemble or committee-based predictions versus predictions from stand-alone models. Moreover, the models that use ensemble approach-tree-based regression models and their variants generally demonstrate the best performance across the evaluation metrics. We think the reason behind this specific performance landscape is motivated by the accurate selection of features either in the form of 1) rules identified by tree-based models that associate different weights with specific features for regression, and use a committee of models to smooth final predictions (opposed to conventional linear regression), or 2) using PCA to identify the features with high variance-removing noisy or outlier features thus resulting into better training and predictions.

Out of the 7 models that have the lowest average i.e. (RMSE < 0.02), 3 models-cubist, xgbTree and M5 are tree-based, avNNet is a bagging model that averages the predictions from various single hidden layer neural networks, and knn is the nearest neighbor method that predicts based on the closest neighbors. Although, all the top 7 models have RMSE < 0.02, yet cubist attained the best performance by using a relatively sophisticated approach i.e. correcting the predictions made by a committee of tree-based regressors by using a weighted nearest neighbor approach [15]. xgbTree which implements gradient tree boosting [7], and M5 which uses linear regressors in the terminal leaves of the tree (without nearest neighbor smoothing) have slightly higher RMSE than cubist. An illustrative example of the rule extracted by M5 (a tree-based model) is shown below:

```
IF
PTS <= 0.492
AST <= 0.369
THEN
```

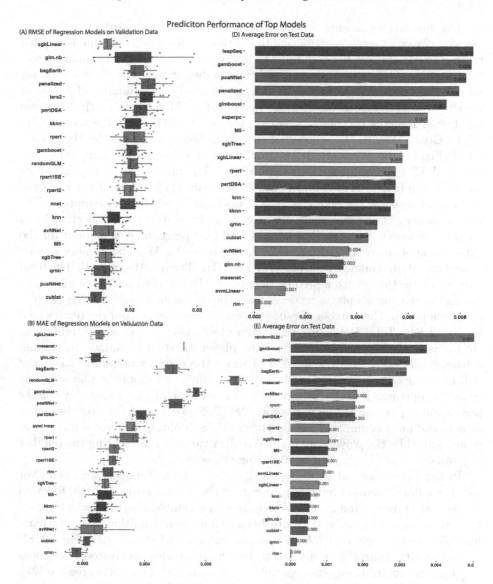

Fig. 4. Comparative performance of top models while predicting the Most Valuable Player (MVP) of the year.

$$target = 0.0001 * G - 0.0001 * GS - 0.0003 * MP - 0.0009 * FG \quad (1)$$
$$-0.0018 * FGA - 0.001 * FG + 0.0008 * X3P + 0.0025 * X2P$$
$$-0.0006 * X2PA - 0.0005 * X2P - 0.0006 * eFG$$
$$-0.0003 * FT + 0.0003 * FTA + 0.0011 * ORB$$
$$+0.0021 * DRB - 0.0027 * TRB + 0.0004 * AST + 0.0003 * STL$$
$$+0.0002 * BLK - 0.0001 * TOV - 0.0002 * PF + 0.0016 * PTS$$
$$+0.0003 * Win + 0.0006$$

The formula represents a weighted sum of different statistical metrics to assess a player's overall contribution to the team. This particular rule is applied when PTS(points) ≤ 0.492 and AST (assists) is ≤ 0.369. Here is an explanation of each variable: G (Games Played): The total number of games in which the player participated during the season; GS (Games Started): The number of games in which the player was in the starting lineup; MP (Minutes Played): The total number of minutes the player spent on the court throughout the season; FG (Field Goals Made): The number of successful field goals made by the player; FGA (Field Goals Attempted): The total number of field goals attempted by the player; $X3P$ (Three-Point Field Goals Made): The number of three-point shots made by the player; $X2P$ (Two-Point Field Goals Made): The number of two-point shots made by the player; $X2PA$ (Two-Point Field Goals Attempted): The total number of two-point shots attempted by the player; eFG (Effective Field Goal Percentage): A metric that adjusts field goal percentage to account for the extra value of three-point shots; FT (Free Throws Made): The number of successful free throws made by the player; FTA (Free Throws Attempted): The total number of free throws attempted by the player; ORB (Offensive Rebounds): The number of rebounds a player retrieves from the opponent's basket; DRB (Defensive Rebounds): The number of rebounds a player retrieves from the team's own basket; TRB (Total Rebounds): The sum of offensive and defensive rebounds; AST (Assists): The number of times the player assists a teammate in making a basket; STL (Steals): The number of times the player successfully steals the ball from the opponent; BLK (Blocks): The number of shots the player blocks from the opponent; TOV (Turnovers): The number of times the player loses possession of the ball to the opponent; PF (Personal Fouls): The total number of personal fouls committed by the player; PTS (Points): The total number of points scored by the player; in (Team Wins): A variable representing the number of games won by the player's team during the season.

In the case of neural network-based models, the top models are: pcaNNet which applies dimension reduction to reduce the feature space of data, followed by network training, and avNNet which uses an ensemble of networks to improve the predictions. Evidently, both are better than their traditional counterpart-nnet that neither applies PCA nor uses an ensemble of models [26]. For RMSE > 0.02, rpart2, rpart1SE, rpart are all tree-based models motivated from ideas in [16], randomGLM combines ensemble approach with forward regression [27]. Although, from a practical standing, models with RMSE < 0.02 are virtually indistinguishable from models with RMSE between 0.02–0.03, the observed performance landscape gives ample evidence to associate better performance with superior modeling mechanics and methodology.

Table 1 shows the predictions for the top three players predicted to win each award, as well as the actual award winners for the 2020 season including two measures to help assess the outcome. First, the Jaccard Similarity:

$$J(A, B) = \frac{A \cap B}{A \cup B} \tag{2}$$

This was used to evaluate the predictions by comparing the top 10 predicted players and the top 10 actual players. The similarity algorithm was run on each dataset for every year from 2000 to 2023 to assess performance over multiple years. The average Jaccard Similarity score was then calculated. The MVP dataset achieved a score of 0.74 ± 0.12, which outperforms the other models. The RoY dataset had a score of 0.62 ± 0.13, DPY had a score of 0.47 ± 0.15, and MIP had a score of 0.5 ± 0.14. These scores suggest that, while the MVP is mostly data-driven, the other awards apparently include other criteria (perhaps including human bias). Making this analysis available might provide voters with incentives to become more transparent.

Table 1. Comparison of actual and predicted awards winner for the 2020 season. The average rank assessment and Jaccard similarity score respectively are shown $n = 24$. Observe that MVP is clearly the most data-driven.

Best Model	MVP	MIP	DPY	RoY
Predicted	1. Antetokounmpo	1. Graham	1. Gobert	1. Morant
	2. James	2. Young	2. Davis	2. Ayton
	3. Harden	3. Adebayo	3. Covington	3. Williamson
Actual	1. Antetokounmpo	1. Ingram	1. Antetokounmpo	1. Morant
	2. James	2. Adebayo	2. Davis	2. Nunn
	3. Harden	3. Tatum	3. Gobert	3. Williamson
Mean S	0.00	0.62	0.37	0.33
Mean J	0.60	0.70	0.40	0.60

Table 2. Predictions of 2023 Awards.

MVP	MIP	DPY	RoY
1. Jokic	1. Markkanen	1. Claxton	1. Banchero
2. Tatum	2. Murphy III	2. Jackson Jr	2. Gray
3. Antetekounmpo	3. Jones	3. Robinson	3. Ivey

Second, The rank assessment score:

$$S((p_1, p_2, \ldots, p_k)) = \frac{1}{2k} \sqrt{(k - p_1)^2 + ((k - 1) - p_2)^2 + \cdots + (1 - p_k)^2} \quad (3)$$

Each p_k value is set based on the player's actual ranking for the award that year. If a predicted value finished first overall, set the p_k to 3. Similarly, if the predicted player finished second or third, set the value to 2 or 1 respectively. If a predicted player did not finish in the top three, the value is set to $k+1$. Similar to the Jaccard calculations, this score function was run on all years from 2000 to 2022 and the average was calculated. The MVP model achieves a score of 0.40 ± 0.18, MIP gets a score of 0.54 ± 0.09, DPY has a score of 0.51 ±, 0.15, and RoY got a score of 0.35 ± 0.18.

For the defensive player, and most improved player, the model does not perform quite as well. For these two awards, it was found that the metrics which make a player a good choice do not necessarily show up in the stats. Many variables, such as guarding match-ups, positioning, and general work ethic, are all critical parts of what makes a good defensive or improving player, but what variables are used is not evident. Since the models failed, perhaps the data was not sufficient. The answer is that we accessed all available data that is ostensibly used to determine the award.

In Table 2, the top three predictions made by the model for this year's awards are presented. The model accurately forecasted the winners of the MIP and RoY awards. While the model anticipated Claxton to receive the DPY award, it was ultimately awarded to Jackson Jr., who the model had predicted as the runner-up. Additionally, the model correctly placed Jokic and Antetekounmpo in the top three predictions. However, the award was ultimately bestowed upon Joel Embiid, who was predicted by the model to secure the fourth position in the voting.

Judging from the results of the awards, the models are performing fairly successfully. They predicted two awards correctly. For the two other awards, the mistakes made are understandable considering the tight competition of those awards this year. From a data science perspective, this means other factors, likely intangible, are playing roles.

5   Conclusion and Future Work

In the future, there are plans to expand the prediction model to include the WNBA and explore automatic award predictions for other sports such as Ice Hockey, Football, and Baseball. This expansion aims to broaden the scope of the model and apply it to different sports domains, enabling predictions for various awards.

It is noteworthy that the Defensive Player of the Year (DPY) and Most Improved Player (MIP) awards seems to rely on factors beyond the measured statistics in the dataset. Despite the limitations in predicting these awards, considering it as a learning experience and understanding the boundaries of automatic award predictions is valuable. Recognizing the limitations of the model allows for future improvements and refinements in the prediction process.

Overall, the model's performance is considered to be successful. It can generate reasonable predictions for most cases and often produces accurate results, particularly for the MVP and Rookie of the Year (RoY) awards. This work serves as a foundation for future endeavors and models in the field of data-driven award predictions. By expanding the model's capabilities, it opens up possibilities for further research and advancements in the realm of data-based award predictions across various sports.

References

1. Albert, A., de Mingo López, L., Allbright, K., Gómez Blas, N.: A hybrid machine learning model for predicting USA NBA all-stars. Electronics **11**(1), 97 (2022). https://doi.org/10.3390/electronics11010097
2. Aoki, R.Y., Assuncao, R.M., Vaz de Melo, P.O.: Luck is hard to beat: the difficulty of sports prediction. In: Proceedings of the 23rd ACM SIGKDD International Conference on Knowledge Discovery and Data Mining (KDD '17), pp. 1367–1376. Association for Computing Machinery, New York, NY, USA (2017). https://doi. org/10.1145/3097983.3098045
3. Basketball-Reference.com: Awards - 2023 (2023). https://www.basketball-reference.com/awards/awards2023.html
4. Chapman, A.: The Application of Machine Learning to Predict the NBA Regular Season MVP. Phd thesis, Utica University (2023)
5. Chen, M.: Predict NBA regular season MVP winner. In: International Conference on Industrial Engineering and Operations Management. Bogota, Colombia, October 2017
6. Chen, M., Chen, C.: Data mining computing of predicting NBA 2019–2020 regular season MVP winner. In: 2020 International Conference on Advances in Computing and Communication Engineering (ICACCE), pp. 1–5. Las Vegas, NV, USA (2020). https://doi.org/10.1109/ICACCE49060.2020.9155038
7. Chen, T., Guestrin, C.: XGBoost: a scalable tree boosting system. In: Proceedings of the 22nd ACM SIGKDD International Conference on Knowledge Discovery and Data Mining, pp. 785–794 (2016)
8. Coleman, B.J., DuMond, J.M., Lynch, A.K.: An examination of NBA MVP voting behavior: does race matter? J. Sports Econ. **9**(6), 606–627 (2008). https://doi.org/10.1177/1527002508320653
9. Etocco, E.: NBA Player Stats (2023). https://data.world/etocco/nba-player-stats
10. Forese, J., Gelman, J., Reed, D., Lorenc, M., Shields, B.: Modern NBA coaching: balancing team and talent. In: 2016 MIT Sloan Sports Analytics Conference (2016)
11. Gilermo, D.R.: NBA Players Stats (2023). https://www.kaggle.com/datasets/drgilermo/nba-players-stats?resource=download&select=player+data.csv
12. Gmoney: NBA Team Records by Year (2023). https://data.world/gmoney/nba-team-records-by-year
13. Johnson, J., Khoshgoftaar, T.: Survey on deep learning with class imbalance. J. Big Data **6**(27) (2019). https://doi.org/10.1186/s40537-019-0192-5
14. Kuhn, Max: Building predictive models in r using the caret package. J. Stat. Softw.**28**(5), 1–26 (2008). https://doi.org/10.18637/jss.v028.i05, https://www.jstatsoft.org/index.php/jss/article/view/v028i05
15. Kuhn, M., Weston, S., Keefer, C., Coulter, N.: Cubist models for regression. R Package Vignette R Package Version 0.0 **18**, 480 (2012)
16. Lewis, R.J.: An introduction to classification and regression tree (CART) analysis. In: Annual Meeting of the Society for Academic Emergency Medicine in San Francisco, California, vol. 14. Citeseer (2000)
17. Maszczyk, A., Golás, A., Pietraszewski, P., Roczniok, R., Zajac, A., Stanula, A.: Application of neural and regression models in sports results prediction. Procedia. Soc. Behav. Sci. **117**, 482–487 (2014). https://doi.org/10.1016/j.sbspro.2014.02.249
18. Maymin, A., Maymin, P., Shen, E.: NBA chemistry: positive and negative synergies in basketball. In: 2012 MIT Sloan Sports Analytics Conference (2012)

19. McCabe, A., Trevathan, J.: Artificial intelligence in sports prediction. In: Fifth International Conference on Information Technology: New Generations (ITNG 2008), pp. 1194–1197. Las Vegas, NV, USA (2008). https://doi.org/10.1109/ITNG.2008.203

20. McIntyre, A., Brooks, J., Guttag, J., Wiens, J.: Recognizing and analyzing ball screen defense in NBA. In: 2016 MIT Sloan Sports Analytics Conference (2016)

21. Miljković, D., Gajić, L., Kovačević, A., Konjović, Z.: The use of data mining for basketball matches outcomes prediction. In: IEEE 8th International Symposium on Intelligent Systems and Informatics, pp. 309–312. Subotica, Serbia (2010). https://doi.org/10.1109/SISY.2010.5647440

22. Nagarajan, R., Zhao, Y., Li, L.: Effective NBA player signing strategies based on salary cap and statistics analysis. In: 2018 IEEE 3rd International Conference on Big Data Analysis (ICBDA), pp. 138–143. Shanghai, China (2018). https://doi.org/10.1109/ICBDA.2018.8367665

23. nbn23.com: Basketball Statistics (Year). https://www.nbn23.com/improve-efficiency-basketball-statistics/

24. Oh, M., Keshri, S., Iyengar, G.: Graphical model for basketball match simulation. In: 2015 MIT Sloan Sports Analytics Conference (2015)

25. Papageorgiou, G.: Data mining in sports: daily NBA player performance prediction (2020). https://hdl.handle.net/11544/29991. Accessed 30 May 2023

26. Ripley, B., Venables, W., Ripley, M.B.: Package 'nnet'. R Package Version 7(3–12), 700 (2016)

27. Song, L., Langfelder, P., Horvath, S.: Random generalized linear model: a highly accurate and interpretable ensemble predictor. BMC Bioinform. 14(1), 1–22 (2013)

28. Wang, N., Chen, M.: Simple poker game design, simulation, and probability. In: IEOM Bogota Proceedings, pp. 1297–1301 (2017)

The Big Three: A Practical Framework for Designing Decision Support Systems in Sports and an Application for Basketball

Francisco Javier Sanguino Bautiste[(✉)], Dustin Brunner, Jonathan Koch, Timothé Laborie, Liule Yang, and Mennatallah El-Assady

ETH AI Center, Zürich, Switzerland
jsanguino@ethz.ch

Abstract. In a world full of data, Decision Support Systems (DSS) based on ML models have significantly emerged. A paradigmatic case is the use of DSS in sports organisations, where a lot of decisions are based on intuition. If the DSS is not well designed, feelings of unusefulness or untrustworthiness can arise from the human decision-makers towards the DSS. We propose a design framework for DSS based on three components (ML model, explainability and interactivity) that overcomes these problems. To validate it, we also present the preliminary results for a DSS for rival team scouting in basketball. The model reaches state of the art performance in game outcome prediction. Explainability and interactivity of our solution also got excellent results in our survey. Finally, we propose some lines of research for DSS design using our framework and for team scouting in basketball.

Keywords: Machine Learning · Explanability · Interactivity · Basketball · Game outcome prediction

1 Introduction

In sports, the strategic decisions made by coaches and analysts play a crucial role in the success of a team. With the advent of modern data science technologies, there is a growing opportunity to leverage these advancements to aid in the design and optimization of team strategies.

Nevertheless, the adoption of new Decision Support Systems (DSS) in high-performance sports organizations can be challenging. In fact, it is hard to incorporate data-based decision-making in the daily operations of the team. A considerable number of decision-making processes in sports are intuitive and the

F. J. S. Bautiste, D. Brunner, J. Koch, T. Laborie and L. Yang—Equal contribution.

Supplementary Information The online version contains supplementary material available at https://doi.org/10.1007/978-3-031-53833-9_9.

U. Brefeld et al. (Eds.): MLSA 2023, CCIS 2035, pp. 103–116, 2024.
https://doi.org/10.1007/978-3-031-53833-9_9

cognitive processes to understand recommendations by DSS are mainly analytical. This makes cognitive biases appear [6]. This is especially relevant for DSS that use Machine Learning (ML) algorithms. In most cases, ML algorithms are *black-boxes* and it is difficult for humans to understand the system's output based on the inputs. Therefore, human decision-makers are left with a sensation of untrustworthiness, uselessness and even falsehood towards those systems [48].

As a matter of fact, in this world full of data, DSS are vastly common and these kinds of challenges exist in other fields as well. Frameworks consisting of an ML model, an explanation for that model and some kind of interactivity between the user and the data have proven useful to improve trust in them.

Contributions

Past work in sports has explored model explanation and interactivity with data separately. There is a lack of work that uses both tools together in DSS. In this paper, we present a preliminary framework that closes that gap and improves the understanding of DSS. The framework consists of three components: model, explanation and interactivity. It has the potential to be used for any task in any statistical sport. As an application, we focus on team scouting in basketball to propose a novel methodology to understand why teams win.

2   Literature Overview

Past literature in sports analytics builds upon the fact that transitioning from observational analysis to automatic statistical analysis based on data provides huge opportunities [10,39]. The integration of data-driven approaches in physical conditioning has been a long-standing reality [24,27]. Nevertheless, the advent of modern data collection techniques has enabled comprehensive game analysis. From tactical investigations [4,13] to the exploration of mental aspects [12], nearly all facets of the game can now be studied with data-driven methodologies.

The growing prevalence of data-driven decision-making in diverse fields, including sports, underscores the need for research addressing the successful implementation and optimization of ML-based DSS for non-technical decision-makers. Particularly relevant is the work of Kayande et al. [22], which proposes a framework to understand potential problems of DSS when used by humans decision-makers. In the context of sports, there has been past work highlighting the challenges of adding these kinds of systems in professional organisations [41,48]. There have also been some attempts of proposing frameworks to facilitate the incorporation of such systems into sports organisations [2,44]. However, these frameworks mainly focus on organisations and not on how DSS should be designed in order to overcome those challenges. Other papers focus on the development of DSS for specific tasks [35,43]. Our work closes this gap by proposing a general framework to design DSS based on ML in sports by adding two components (model explanation and interactivity) to the traditional ML pipeline (only composed by a model). With these three components (ML model, explanation, interactivity), we aim to close the 3 gaps pointed out by Kayanda et al. [22].

Next, we explore ML Explainability and Human-Computer Interaction in sports, showcasing their distinct roles. We also review basketball analytics and game outcome prediction in basketball to set the context for our application.

ML Explainability in Sports. ML Explainability has proven essential when a ML system needs to meet certain requirements such as scientific understanding, safety or ethics [7]. Within the context of sports, previous literature has focused in scientific understanding. ML models with an explanability component have been recognized as valuable tools for generating hypotheses, particularly for tactical analysis, by identifying correlations between input and output variables.

Song et al. [46] tried to explain American football defence using visual explanations (saliency maps). In the work done by Fernandes et al. [21], Decision Trees were used to aid American football coaches in making decisions for the next play (pass or rush) due to their transparency. In volleyball, Lalwani et al. [26] trained a Neural Network (NN) to predict the result of matches and used SHAP to identify the most relevant factors for winning. Silver et al. [45] also use SHAP values to pinpoint the critical factors when predicting the outcome of a batter versus a pitcher matchup in baseball with a NN. Finally, Wang et al. [50] apply LIME (Local Interpretable Model-agnostic Explanation) on NN and Random Forests to analyze the game style based on the boxscore in the NBA.

As seen in the literature, the current state-of-the-art predominantly involves using ML models followed by the utilization of standard explainability methods.

Human-Computer Interaction in Sports. Interactivity has been a more prolific field than explainable ML in sports. Past work has focused mainly on data visualization [8,16,38]. Notably, both the contributions of practitioners and academic research play a vital role in this field.

In basketball, journalists' works such as Goldsberry's *shotmaps* [14] or Whitehead's *bubbles map* [52] have incorporated compelling narratives into data visualisation. Additionally, Fu et al. [11], Chen et al. [5] and Losada et al. [29] have proposed interactive dashboards for exploring basketball data.

Apart from basketball, [51] showcases a notable example of combining Machine Learning with data visualization by employing infographics to present Neural Network outputs to rubgy coaches, offering valuable tactical decision support. However, it is worth noting that there is a scarcity of research on interactivity with ML models beyond mere visualization in sports. Allowing human decision-makers to directly interact with the models could potentially unlock even more profound insights and facilitate more informed decision-making processes.

Sports Analytics in Basketball. The proliferation of data science techniques within the field of sports has also permeated basketball analytics. The field began studying the concept of possessions and how to optimize them, with the works by Oliver [36] and Kubatko et al. [25]. With the appearance of new data collection systems, new data sources have emerged, enabling more comprehensive quantitative game analysis. Page et al. [37] and Mandic et al. [34], uses box-score data, summarizing basic game statistics. Play-by-play data, that describes the time series of events in a game, is used by Grassetti et al. [15], and Vracar et al. [49]. Lastly, tracking data, that provides player localtions at every moment, has been used by Sampaio et al. [42], Reina et al. [40], and Abdelkrim et al. [1].

Studying Winning in Basketball. Predicting winning has been one of the most traditional perspectives to studying the game of basketball using data [3,18]. In fact, the seminal work [36] proposed 4 factors to predict winning. We focus on pre-game prediction rather than in-game prediction [33]. There has been past work focusing in predicting with season statistics [19,53] or individual player performance [20]. Based on boxscore statistics, Loeffelholz et al. [28] trained Neural Networks over the boxscore statistics (70.67% accuracy) and compared it to the accuracy of human experts (68.67%). Thabtah et al. [47] trained several models over different sets of features obtained directly from the boxscore, the best model was a reported accuracy was Decision Tree with 83% accuracy.

3   The Big Three: Model, Explanation and Interactivity

As proposed in Kayanda et al. [22], there are three potential gaps when using a DSS (Fig. 1). We present a framework for sports analytics DSS, consisting of 3 components: ML model, model explanation, and interactivity, each closing a specific gap. The framework is versatile enough to potentially apply it in any statistically quantifiable sport. To effectively implement the framework, designing each component separately is essential. Interviews with domain experts can be a valuable tool. To facilitate this process, it is advisable to identify the most relevant person within the organization. Moreover, co-creating the solution with experts can enhance engagement and foster better utilization of the DSS.

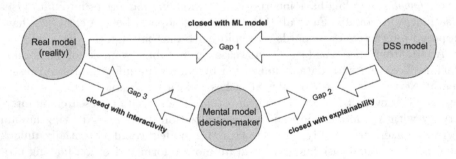

Fig. 1. Gaps proposed by [22] and solutions from our framework.

- Gap 1: closed with **ML model** component. In ML, it is commonly observed that models with higher performance tend to be more opaque, such as Neural Networks. However, with the addition of interaction and explainability components, the necessity for transparent models diminishes. Consequently, any superior performing model can be employed to enhance performance.

- Gap 2: closed with **explainability** component. Accordingly, to past literature, model transparency is key when adopting machine learning-based DSS
  within the sports domain [17]. We contend that incorporating an explainability method into the process will lead to increased user trust in the DSS. The
  type of explanation needed will depend on the task [9].
- Gap 3: closed with **interactivity** component. Running what-if analyses is
  crucial for coaches to gain insights into various scenarios and understand the
  reality of their team or game. By incorporating an interactive component,
  such as a dashboard, the coach's mental model can closely align with the
  actual circumstances. This enables them to make informed decisions based
  on a more accurate representation of the situation at hand.

4   BasketXplainer: A DSS for Basketball

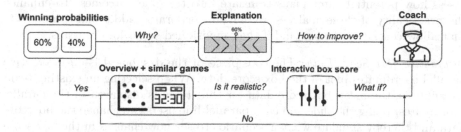

Fig. 2. Workflow from a user of our solution

A key aspect of designing a game plan is trying to modify some aspects of the it
to maximize the probabilities of winning. Traditionally, coaches have relied on
intuition. We have developed a Data-Driven DSS[1] to help coaches in scouting
teams and formulating game plans, showcasing our three-component framework.

The workflow, depicted in Fig. 2, illustrates how coaches can utilize Bas-
ketXplainer to create game plans based on data. The system's reception among
domain experts has been promising, validating its potential in enhancing
decision-making processes in basketball analytics.

Model. A crucial requirement is a predictive model capable of estimating the
chances of winning a game. For this purpose, we selected boxscore data as inputs,
motivated by their well-balanced combination of actionability (controlability
through a corresponding game plan) and widespread availability.

We used LightGBM [23], a gradient-boosting framework utilizing tree-based
algorithms. Training the model on NBA boxscores from the regular season from
2012–2013 to 2021–2022[2], we focused on: assists (AST), blocks (BLK), defensive

---

[1] Publicly accessible in http://b5-winning-in-basketball.course-xai-iml23.isginf.ch/.
[2] We omit season 2019–2020. Accessible at https://www.kaggle.com/datasets/nathan
lauga/nba-games.

rebounds (DREB), 3-point attempts (FG3A), field goal attempts (FGA), free throw attempts (FTA), offensive rebounds (OREB), steals (STL), and turnovers (TO). Statistics directly impacting the score, such as field goals made (FGM), 3-pointers made (FG3M), and free throws made (FTM), are deliberately excluded.

Explainability. Understanding what factors are the most important to win a game can help coaches designing a game plan. As professional teams do not have a lot of time between games, preparing just the most important aspects of the next game is crucial. From an ML perspective, this can be done using SHAP (SHapley Additive exPlanations) [31]. It assigns to each input feature an importance value for a particular prediction based on how much it contributes to the model output. For its implementation, we used TreeExplainer [30] for the LightGBM model and a force plot [32] for visualisation.

Interactivity: Dashboard. Our primary focus has been conducting what-if analyses. Coaches can greatly benefit from exploring multiple scenarios to assess how potential game plans translate into tangible outcomes. To enhance the practicality of these analyses, we have incorporated additional components that allow coaches to understand if their envisioned scenarios are realistic.

Interactive Box Score Data. The core piece of the dashboard is an interactive parallel coordinates plot of the box score data. When selecting an existing team for analysis, the mean box score data for that team is displayed in the parallel coordinates. Using the sliders in each parallel line users can change the boxscore data and thereby simulate what-if scenarios to see how changes in the box score will impact the predicted outcome of the matchup. Additionally, the mean boxscore data of the 5 most similar teams is shown in the background along with the number of possessions of each team. This allows direct comparison to check if the simulation is run with realistic data.

Winning Probability. The trained ML model is used to infer the winning chances of the two teams based on the provided box score data. Every change to the box scores displays new winning probabilities. Users can use this to understand how changes in the box score will influence the predicted outcome.

Similar Matchups. Though we are providing predictions for the outcome of future games, it is also helpful for users to be able to look back at past games of teams to see how they previously performed. When users manually adapt the box score from an existing team, we calculate the distance of this new, custom box score to all the existing teams and provide the user with the closest matching one. That way, even with a custom box score, users can look at the closest matching historic matchups and what the outcomes of those games were.

Feature Importance. We use SHAP as an explainability tool for users to understand the ML model's outcomes. The contribution of each input feature to the output is displayed graphically and intuitively, even without any technical knowledge of the underlying theory. Like all the other elements, it dynamically adapts whenever users make any changes to the input box score data.

League Overview. The offensive performance and defensive performance of a team are calculated and visualized to show how the team performs in the league compared to all other teams. To represent offensive performance, an Offensive Performance (OP) statistic is calculated. The calculation of OP is similar to the calculation of offensive rating. For each team,

$$OP = 100 * \frac{\text{PTS}}{(\text{Poss}_{\text{team}} + mean(\text{poss}_{\text{opponents}}))}$$

The Defensive Performance (DP) statistic is calculated as

$$DP = 100 * \frac{\text{BLK} + \text{DREB} + \text{STL}}{(\text{poss}_{\text{team}} + mean(\text{poss}_{\text{opponents}}))}$$

which represents how well the team is guarding other teams on average.

5   Results and Analysis

5.1   Model

The ML model (Gap 1) has been evaluated with accuracy, a standard machine learning metric. We have used $10,948$ games, from which $6,329$ were won by the home team (label 1). Therefore, the dataset is balanced.

For the input, *Boxscore* uses the boxscore data specified in Sect. 4 for both teams, containing 18 features. On the other hand, *Difference* calculates the difference between the boxscore metrics between home and away as an input, utilizing 9 features as input.

Before training the model, the data is normalized following equation

$$x'_{i,j} = \frac{x_{i,j} - \mu_j}{\sigma_j} \tag{1}$$

where $x_{i,j}$ is the original i-th sample of the j-th feature, $\mu_j = \frac{1}{n}\sum_{i=1}^{n} x_{i,j}$ is the mean of the j-th feature over all samples and $\sigma_j = \sqrt{\frac{1}{n}\sum_{i=1}^{n}(x_{i,j} - \mu_j)^2}$ its standard deviation. $x'_{i,j}$ is the final value used for training.

To find the best hyperparameters for the LightGBM classifier, we have conducted a grid search over a predefined set of hyperparameter values. For each combination of hyperparameters, we have performed 5-fold cross-validation, dividing the data into five subsets and iterating through training and testing on different splits. From this process, the mean accuracy over those splits was obtained. We report the result for the best combination hyperparameters. For prediction, we use the best model within that 5 splits.

The results of our models can be seen in Table 1[3]. For ease of comparison, we included the accuracies reported in the most relevant papers with similar features. The abbreviations used can be found in the supplementary material.

---

[3] The code to reproduce the results can be found in https://github.com/fjsanguino/nba-game-outcome-prediction.

Although Oliver's Four Factors are engineered features intended to enhance game outcome prediction, we conducted an additional experiment by training a Logistic Regression model on them without any regularization or bias term for comparison. The input for this model consists of the four factors for each team (8 features), as described in [25]. This comparison allows us to evaluate the effectiveness of our actionable metrics in relation to traditional engineered features that are prepared for the task.

Table 1. Model Comparison

Model	Features used	Accuracy(%)
Boxscore	FGA, FG3A, FTA, DREB, OREB, AST, STL, TO, BLK	85.40%
Difference	FGA, FG3A, FTA, DREB, OREB, AST, STL, TO, BLK	**86.77%**
Neural Network in [28]	FG%, 3P%, FT%, DREB, OREB, AST, STL, TO, BLK, PF, PTS	71.67%
Decision Tree in [47]	FGA, FG%, 3P%, FTM, DREB, REB, TOV, PF	83.00%
Oliver's Factors	eFG%, TOV%, OREB%, FT%	**94.72%**

As seen in Table 1, our model improves the accuracy of methods using simple boxscore data. However, it falls short when compared to methods with engineered features specifically tailored for game outcome prediction, such as Oliver's factors. Despite this, it is crucial to consider that such engineered features are not suitable for our application due to their lack of actionability.

5.2   Explainability and Interactivity

The other two components of the framework, explainability and interactivity, were evaluated through interviews with domain experts, recognizing the significance of the user's mental model in closing the gaps (See Fig. 1). The interview had a quantitative part with closed questions and a qualitative part with open-ended questions. After a brief introduction to the interface, domain experts were presented a use case were they had to predict the winner using boxscore data, give explanations of their reasoning and come up with a game plan for the home team. The quantitative part consisted some general enough questions to be used in any sport DSS using our Big Three framework. A detailed description of the structure of interviews can be consulted in the suplementary material.

The domain experts are five people from the coaching staff from teams in Spanish men's and women's leagues. Among them, four belong to the top-ranked league, while the fifth individual is associated with the third league. Three fulfill the role of data analysts, and two are assistant coaches.

Table 2. Survey Results

Gap2: Explainability	
Q1: How coherent is the explanation of the model compared to your explanation?	1.2 / 2
Q2: How satisfied with this kind of explanation?	1.2 / 2
Gap3: Interactivity	
Q3: How useful has been the interactivity (what-if analysis) for the use case proposed?	1.8 / 2
General Questions	
Q4: Is the information obtained from the DSS transferable to court decisions?	1.6 / 2
Q5: Would it be easy to include this DSS in your daily routine?	1.8 / 2
Q6: Does it add new perspectives? Is it innovative?	1.4 / 2
Q7: How effective ($\frac{information}{time}$) is the solution compared to what you use now?	1.6 / 2

Table 2 displays the survey results. Although we asked them for the predicted outcome of the game without showing them the actual model output, we don't include such a question because the model's performance has been evaluated in the previous section. Q1 evaluates the similarity of their reasoning for why the game was won before and after presenting the SHAP values with the actual SHAP explanation. Q2 measures the comprehensibility of the SHAP explanation after it was shown to them. Notably, all interviewees admit a lack of confidence in their answers for both Q1 and Q2 (and, previously, for guessing the game outcome), as it is difficult to predict outcomes based only on the metrics used. However, they demonstrated relative confidence in the rest of the questions.

Another conclusions of the open ended questions were:

They were Expecting a Tool with Information that Could be Quickly Transferred to the Court. During the expectation check, before the interface was shown to them, a recurring theme was the desire for a tool with information that could be readily applied on the court. The interviewees emphasized the importance of actionable metrics in facilitating data-driven decision-making for devising effective game plans. Specifically, the two assistant coaches mentioned using data systems as warnings, while the two data analysts looked for key headlines that could be communicated to the coaching staff. After the use case, they highlighted that our solution fulfilled this. Our system allowed rapid identification of key factors to win a game, which, was one of the most important factors to decide whether to use a DSS or not.

Explainability was Key to Improving Trust in the Model. During the interviews' use case, this component was used as a guideline to discover what factors were key to the model's decision. Domain experts checked the Feature Importance plot after seeing the outcome of the model. It seemed that this guided two-step discovery improved the trust in the system a lot (Gap 2), especially when the domain expert's initial guess differed from the model's output. There was one individual that did not quite get what the plot of Feature Importance meant due to confusing colouring. This made him more reluctant to believe the model's output. Additionally, one data analysts, used to working with other types of metrics, was expecting more detailed explanations, including ratios.

Their Mental Model was Coherent with the Interactivity Designing. The interactive box score component proved to be the most engaging during the interviews. The interviewees spent a significant time on it performing simulations in order to come up with a game plan. Two of them adopted a systematic approach by categorizing the metric into rebound, shooting and turnovers. Then, they modified all the statistics of one category imagining different scenarios and assessing their impact on winning probabilities. For instance, one of them thought that increasing three-point attempts would increase the winning probability, so he increased the FG3A and FGA and decreased FTA because if you shoot three-pointers a basketball team receives fewer fouls in general. All these modifications were qualitative (i.e. increase or decrease), and none of them focused on how much exactly. Some highlighted that the interactivity helped them explore more scenarios than they normally consider. And, therefore, decreasing the gap 3 of the framework between the user's mental model and the reality.

6   Conclusion and Future Work

In this paper, we have defined a general framework for designing Decision Support Systems (DSS) based on Machine Learning models in the domain of sports. The framework consists of 3 components that close all the potential gaps that produce user mistrust when using a DSS. To illustrate our approach, we have developed a tailored DSS for basketball game planning. Our solution allows coaches to scout the rival team using an ML model for predicting the outcome, SHAP values to explain the model's prediction and an interactive dashboard to perform what-if analysis while checking if the potential game plan is realistic. The model has a comparable accuracy to past literature and the preliminary feedback from domain experts regarding explainability and interactivity was excellent.

6.1   Research Opportunities

Regarding the Big Three: Our Framework. To further explore the benefit of our framework, a good research opportunity would be what kind of models (i.e. predictive, clustering, generative, anomaly detection...) would be useful for what kind of task and under what kind of circumstances (pre-game, in-game). The same applies to the kind of explanation (deductive, inductive, comparative) and interaction.

Regarding BasketXplainer and Scouting Rival Teams in Basketball

Improving the Model to Make it Specific. One domain expert expressed a major concern regarding the relevance of data used to train the predictive model, particularly regarding distribution shifts. For instance, using *LEB ORO* (Spanish second men's league) data to predict outcomes in the NBA would not be logical due to differences in leagues. However, there might be insufficient data to train an ML model for a specific league or team, prompting the exploration of ideas like fine-tuning, weighted training, or ensemble training to address this challenge and leverage useful representations from basketball games in other leagues.

Adding Other Metrics. A recurring desire expressed in all interviews was the possibility of incorporating personalized metrics into the dashboard, allowing for a deductive workflow that integrates their domain knowledge. However, gathering this specific data poses a significant challenge, as it often requires manual collection through game video analysis. Despite this obstacle, coaches recognized the potential benefits of including personalized data in our application. This could open up new avenues of research to explore the effectiveness of personalized metrics in basketball's winning dynamics. Some coaches even requested the inclusion of additional metrics relevant to their teams, such as differentiating assists for three-pointers and two-pointers, further enhancing their ability to leverage their mental models within the system.

Adding Other Player's Statistics. In a similar line, our interviewees praised our solution for providing valuable insights into the team's overall performance, aiding in game plan preparation. However, they emphasized the need to consider individual player contributions, leading to a new research direction on effectively integrating individual performance in team sports while preserving quality interactions.

Acknowledgements. We sincerely thank Francisco Camba Rodriguez for the insightful conversations and the feedback given. We also thank all the coaches for their time and willingness to participate in the interviews. This project was supported by the ETH AI Center. It was also partly supported by a fellowship from "la Caixa" Foundation (ID 100010434). The fellowship code is LCF/BQ/EU21/11890127.

References

1. Abdelkrim, N.B., El Fazaa, S., El Ati, J.: Time-motion analysis and physiological data of elite under-19-year-old basketball players during competition. Br. J. Sports Med. **41**(2), 69–75 (2007)

2. Browne, P., Sweeting, A.J., Woods, C.T., Robertson, S.: Methodological considerations for furthering the understanding of constraints in applied sports. Sports Med.-Open **7**(1), 1–12 (2021)
3. Bunker, R., Susnjak, T.: The application of machine learning techniques for predicting match results in team sport: a review. J. Artif. Intell. Res. **73**, 1285–1322 (2022)
4. Bunker, R.P., Thabtah, F.: A machine learning framework for sport result prediction. Appl. Comput. Inform. **15**(1), 27–33 (2019)
5. Chen, W., et al.: Gameflow: narrative visualization of NBA basketball games. IEEE Trans. Multimed. **18**(11), 2247–2256 (2016)
6. Daniel, K.: Thinking, fast and slow (2017)
7. Doshi-Velez, F., Kim, B.: Considerations for evaluation and generalization in interpretable machine learning. In: Escalante, H., et al. (eds.) Explainable and Interpretable Models in Computer Vision and Machine Learning. SSCML, pp. 3–17. Springer, Cham (2018). https://doi.org/10.1007/978-3-319-98131-4_1
8. Du, M., Yuan, X.: A survey of competitive sports data visualization and visual analysis. J. Vis. **24**, 47–67 (2021)
9. El-Assady, M., et al.: Towards XAI: structuring the processes of explanations. In: Proceedings of the ACM Workshop on Human-Centered Machine Learning, Glasgow, UK, vol. 4 (2019)
10. Fister, I., Jr., Ljubič, K., Suganthan, P.N., Perc, M., Fister, I.: Computational intelligence in sports: challenges and opportunities within a new research domain. Appl. Math. Comput. **262**, 178–186 (2015)
11. Fu, Y., Stasko, J.: Supporting data-driven basketball journalism through interactive visualization. In: Proceedings of the 2022 CHI Conference on Human Factors in Computing Systems, pp. 1–17 (2022)
12. Gao, X., Uehara, M., Aoki, K., Kato, C.: Prototyping sports mental cloud. In: 2017 5th International Conference on Applied Computing and Information Technology/4th International Conference on Computational Science/Intelligence and Applied Informatics/2nd International Conference on Big Data, Cloud Computing, Data Science (ACIT-CSII-BCD), pp. 141–146. IEEE (2017)
13. Goes, F., et al.: Unlocking the potential of big data to support tactical performance analysis in professional soccer: a systematic review. Eur. J. Sport Sci. **21**(4), 481–496 (2021)
14. Goldsberry, K.: How mapping shots in the NBA changed it forever. FiveThirtyEight. FiveThirtyEight, 2 May 2019
15. Grassetti, L., Bellio, R., Di Gaspero, L., Fonseca, G., Vidoni, P.: An extended regularized adjusted plus-minus analysis for lineup management in basketball using play-by-play data. IMA J. Manag. Math. **32**(4), 385–409 (2021)
16. Gudmundsson, J., Horton, M.: Spatio-temporal analysis of team sports. ACM Comput. Surv. (CSUR) **50**(2), 1–34 (2017)
17. Herold, M., Goes, F., Nopp, S., Bauer, P., Thompson, C., Meyer, T.: Machine learning in men's professional football: current applications and future directions for improving attacking play. Int. J. Sports Sci. Coach. **14**(6), 798–817 (2019)
18. Horvat, T., Job, J.: The use of machine learning in sport outcome prediction: a review. Wiley Interdiscip. Rev. Data Min. Knowl. Discov. **10**(5), e1380 (2020)
19. Horvat, T., Job, J., Logozar, R., Livada, Č: A data-driven machine learning algorithm for predicting the outcomes of NBA games. Symmetry **15**(4), 798 (2023)
20. Hubáček, O., Šourek, G., Železný, F.: Exploiting sports-betting market using machine learning. Int. J. Forecast. **35**(2), 783–796 (2019)

21. Joash Fernandes, C., Yakubov, R., Li, Y., Prasad, A.K., Chan, T.C.: Predicting plays in the national football league. J. Sports Anal. **6**(1), 35–43 (2020)
22. Kayande, U., De Bruyn, A., Lilien, G.L., Rangaswamy, A., Van Bruggen, G.H.: How incorporating feedback mechanisms in a DSS affects DSS evaluations. Inf. Syst. Res. **20**(4), 527–546 (2009)
23. Ke, G., et al.: LightGBM: a highly efficient gradient boosting decision tree. Adv. Neural Inf. Process. Syst. **30** (2017)
24. Kellmann, M.: Preventing overtraining in athletes in high-intensity sports and stress/recovery monitoring. Scand. J. Med. Sci. sports **20**, 95–102 (2010)
25. Kubatko, J., Oliver, D., Pelton, K., Rosenbaum, D.T.: A starting point for analyzing basketball statistics. J. Quant. Anal. Sports **3**(3) (2007)
26. Lalwani, A., Saraiya, A., Singh, A., Jain, A., Dash, T.: Machine learning in sports: a case study on using explainable models for predicting outcomes of volleyball matches. arXiv preprint arXiv:2206.09258 (2022)
27. Lapham, A., Bartlett, R.: The use of artificial intelligence in the analysis of sports performance: a review of applications in human gait analysis and future directions for sports biomechanics. J. Sports Sci. **13**(3), 229–237 (1995)
28. Loeffelholz, B., Bednar, E., Bauer, K.W.: Predicting NBA games using neural networks. J. Quant. Anal. Sports **5**(1) (2009)
29. Losada, A.G., Therón, R., Benito, A.: BKViz: a basketball visual analysis tool. IEEE Comput. Graph. Appl. **36**(6), 58–68 (2016)
30. Lundberg, S.M., et al.: From local explanations to global understanding with explainable AI for trees. Nat. Mach. Intell. **2**(1), 56–67 (2020)
31. Lundberg, S.M., Lee, S.I.: A unified approach to interpreting model predictions. Adv. Neural Inf. Process. Syst. **30** (2017)
32. Lundberg, S.M., et al.: Explainable machine-learning predictions for the prevention of hypoxaemia during surgery. Nat. Biomed. Eng. **2**(10), 749–760 (2018)
33. Maddox, J.T., Sides, R., Harvill, J.L.: Bayesian estimation of in-game home team win probability for national basketball association games. arXiv preprint arXiv:2207.05114 (2022)
34. Mandić, R., Jakovljević, S., Erčulj, F., Štrumbelj, E.: Trends in NBA and Euroleague basketball: analysis and comparison of statistical data from 2000 to 2017. PLoS ONE **14**(10), e0223524 (2019)
35. Märtins, J., Westmattelmann, D., Schewe, G.: Affected but not involved: two-scenario based investigation of individuals' attitude towards decision support systems based on the example of the video assistant referee. J. Decis. Syst. 1–25 (2022)
36. Oliver, D.: Basketball on Paper: Rules and Tools for Performance Analysis. Potomac Books, Inc., Dulles (2004)
37. Page, G.L., Fellingham, G.W., Reese, C.S.: Using box-scores to determine a position's contribution to winning basketball games. J. Quant. Anal. Sports **3**(4) (2007)
38. Perin, C., Vuillemot, R., Stolper, C.D., Stasko, J.T., Wood, J., Carpendale, S.: State of the art of sports data visualization. In: Computer Graphics Forum, vol. 37, pp. 663–686. Wiley Online Library (2018)
39. Rein, R., Memmert, D.: Big data and tactical analysis in elite soccer: future challenges and opportunities for sports science. Springerplus **5**(1), 1–13 (2016)
40. Reina Román, M., García-Rubio, J., Feu, S., Ibáñez, S.J.: Training and competition load monitoring and analysis of women's amateur basketball by playing position: approach study. Front. Psychol. **9**, 2689 (2019)

41. Robertson, S., Bartlett, J.D., Gastin, P.B.: Red, amber, or green? Athlete monitoring in team sport: the need for decision-support systems. Int. J. Sports Physiol. Perform. **12**(s2), S2-73 (2017)
42. Sampaio, J., McGarry, T., Calleja-González, J., Jiménez Sáiz, S., Schelling i del Alcázar, X., Balciunas, M.: Exploring game performance in the national basketball association using player tracking data. PloS one **10**(7), e0132894 (2015)
43. Schelling, X., Fernández, J., Ward, P., Fernández, J., Robertson, S.: Decision support system applications for scheduling in professional team sport. the team's perspective. Front. Sports Active Living **3**, 678489 (2021)
44. Schelling, X., Robertson, S.: A development framework for decision support systems in high-performance sport. Int. J. Comput. Sci. Sport **19**(1), 1–23 (2020)
45. Silver, J., Huffman, T.: Baseball predictions and strategies using explainable AI. In: The 15th Annual MIT Sloan Sports Analytics Conference (2021)
46. Song, H., et al.: Explainable defense coverage classification in NFL games using deep neural networks (2023)
47. Thabtah, F., Zhang, L., Abdelhamid, N.: NBA game result prediction using feature analysis and machine learning. Ann. Data Sci. **6**(1), 103–116 (2019)
48. Torres-Ronda, L., Schelling, X.: Critical process for the implementation of technology in sport organizations. Strength Cond. J. **39**(6), 54–59 (2017)
49. Vračar, P., Štrumbelj, E., Kononenko, I.: Modeling basketball play-by-play data. Expert Syst. Appl. **44**, 58–66 (2016)
50. Wang, Y., Liu, W., Liu, X.: Explainable AI techniques with application to NBA gameplay prediction. Neurocomputing **483**, 59–71 (2022)
51. Watson, N., Hendricks, S., Stewart, T., Durbach, I.: Integrating machine learning and decision support in tactical decision-making in rugby union. J. Oper. Res. Soc. **72**(10), 2274–2285 (2021)
52. Whitehead, T.: Explaining synergy's offensive roles (2023). https://synergysports.com/synergy-offensive-roles/. Accessed 3 June 2023
53. Zdravevski, E., Kulakov, A.: System for Prediction of the Winner in a Sports Game. In: Davcev, D., Gomez, J.M. (eds.) ICT Innovations 2009. ICT Innovations 2009, pp. 55–63. Springer, Berlin, Heidelberg (2010). https://doi.org/10.1007/978-3-642-10781-8_7

Other Team Sports

What Data Should Be Collected for a Good Handball *Expected Goal* model?

Alexis Mortelier[1(✉)], François Rioult[1], and John Komar[2]

[1] Normandie Univ, UNICAEN, ENSICAEN, CNRS, GREYC, 14000 Caen, France
`alexis.mortelier@unicaen.fr`
[2] National Institute of Education, Nanyang Technological University, Singapore, Singapore

Abstract. Expected goal models (xG) are of great importance as they are the most accurate predictor of future performance of teams and players in the world of soccer. This metric can be modeled by machine learning, and the models developed consider an increasing number of attributes, which increases the cost of learning it. The use of xG is not widespread in handball, so the question of learning it for this sport arose, in particular which attributes are relevant for learning. Here, we used a *wrapper* approach to determine these relevant attributes and guide teams through the data collection stage.

Keywords: Handball · Expected goal · Machine learning

1 Introduction

Expected goal (xG)[1] models are important as accurate predictors of future team and player performance. At team level, these models are better at predicting performance than current goal difference or number of shots, such as the Total Shot Ratio (TSR)[2].

Models of xG are commonly used for soccer and hockey [34]. Here we considered their use for handball, which is absent from the literature. Our study also attempted to clarify what types of data are required for the design of a robust xG model for handball. For example, can we be satisfied with analyzing player positions alone, or do we need to take account of match events (passing, fouls, shooting)? Taking each type of information into account represents a cost that needs to be considered: budgets and resources vary from one sport to another, and even from one team to another within the same sport. Depending on the available budget, data acquisition technologies will provide rich, comprehensive data, or poor, summary data.

We are therefore interested here in whether a dataset must necessarily be rich to obtain relevant xG values, and how this impacts its learning cost. Indeed, data

---

[1] https://www.statsperform.com/opta-analytics/.
[2] https://www.scisports.com/total-shots-ratio/.

© The Author(s), under exclusive license to Springer Nature Switzerland AG 2024
U. Brefeld et al. (Eds.): MLSA 2023, CCIS 2035, pp. 119–130, 2024.
https://doi.org/10.1007/978-3-031-53833-9_10

availability affects the ability to learn good models of xG [29]. In the search for young talent, a minor league team has very little data, so it's interesting to define an approach that allows us to judge the quality of the xG with summary data, so as not to miss out on the next recruit.

To answer the question of the relevance of the attributes needed to calculate xG, we used *machine learning* techniques in this article. These techniques make it possible to establish a model of the xG and the conditions for calculating this model. Calculation performance (accuracy, convergence speed) indicates the relevance of the attributes used: if the attribute improves learning quality, then it is relevant to consider it. This approach is called *wrapper* [20].

2   State of the Art

2.1   The xG Metric

In collective ball sports, goals are the most important events. Depending on the sport, these goal events may occur rarely, as in soccer, where goal events have a low probability of occurrence during a match [37]. Analysts therefore prefer to focus their attention on shots, which are more numerous than goals. This has led to the creation of measures such as the *Total Shot Ratio* or TSR [21], which evaluates the dominance of teams based on their share of shots in matches. The limitation of TSR, however, is that it does not take into account the quality of a shot. For example, a shot on goal without a goalkeeper has the same value as a shot from midfield defended by an entire team.

With the democratization of data analysis, several derivatives of this measure were created. Shot differential, Fenwick[3] differential (shot differential between teams) and Corsi[4] differential (which considers shots on target and blocked shots differently) have become popular for analyzing the performance of hockey teams and players [23]. These statistics were chosen because each has proven to be a very good indicator of performance at team level.

As not all shots are equal, a method is needed to measure the quality of a given shot or series of shots, and this is how the xG models were developed. xG is a statistical metric based on the shooter's position to calculate a probability of turning a shot into a goal. However, in sports where goal events occur most frequently, such as handball, which has around 40 goals per match for two and a half times as many shots, xG models are not used.

Historically, xG models were introduced to soccer in 2012 by Sam Green for statistics site Opta[5]. In soccer, the company StatsBomb[6] provides one of the most recognized xG[7] calculation services. StatsBomb uses this metric[8] in a

---

[3] https://en.wikipedia.org/wiki/Fenwick_(statistic).
[4] https://en.wikipedia.org/wiki/Corsi_(statistic).
[5] https://www.statsperform.com/opta/.
[6] https://statsbomb.com/.
[7] https://statsbomb.com/soccer-metrics/expected-goals-xg-explained/.
[8] https://statsbomb.com/what-we-do/soccer-data/.

variety of ways. In soccer circles, it is a benchmark calculation method on a par with that provided by Opta.

Models for predicting the probability of a shot turning into a goal are based on a history of similar shots. For example, for ten shots at a position, if seven are turned into goals, then the xG value for the position will be 0.7. These models can consider a wide variety of attributes, giving varied information, in order to predict the xG value of a particular shot. StatsBomb and Opta use up to 35 attributes, each advancing an xG value closer to reality. These models share a base of attributes that include the angle or distance of the shot in relation to the goal, the position of the goalkeeper, the number of defenders exerting pressure on the shooter [6,9,15,16,25,39]. In general, the addition of new attributes does not seem to improve the quality of xG models, but may be relevant for certain isolated cases.

While the xG metric indicates the most favorable positions for scoring a goal, it does not provide information on the quality of a shot: a shot with a high xG value may be stopped by the goalkeeper, the mechanics of the shot may be poor, or it may go out of frame. xG gives an indication of the position in which a player should place himself to take the shot, in order to increase his chances of turning it into a goal.

2.2   Use of xG

In the literature, xG can be used in several ways. Comparing the value of xG to the number of goals scored can indicate a player's scoring ability or luck. A player who regularly scores more goals than his total xG probably has above-average shooting/finishing ability [1].

xG models are used for a variety of reasons: predicting match scores [38,40], measuring scoring efficiency by estimating goal expectancy [30], judging the efficiency of soccer shots [28] or assessing the quality of positioning without the ball, preceding shots that may lead to goals [34]. The uses of the xG value are numerous and can be adapted to measure other qualities, such as passing, possession, etc. [24,26,41].

xG is also a collective performance attribute, as the model calculates the shooting situations that a team could have converted into a goal ($xG_{inflicted}$) as well as the chances that could have led to a goal being conceded ($xG_{conceded}$). A team's goal differential ($xG_{inflicted} - xG_{conceded}$) can indicate how a team should behave: a negative goal differential but a positive one could indicate that a team has had little luck or has a below-average finishing ability [1].

xG can be refined to differentiate between a team's abilities in different situations: open play, free kick, corner, etc. For example, a team that has conceded more goals from free-kicks than its xG on free-kicks is probably below average at defending these set-pieces. A team's $xG_{conceded}$ is an indicator of its ability to prevent goal-scoring opportunities. A team will have a lower than predicted $xG_{conceded}$ if it protects itself from shots with a high probability of being scored.

3   Handball Data

3.1   Data Acquisition

There are two types of dataset for team sports: spatio-temporal data and event data.

The *spatio-temporal* data are the trajectories of the players or the ball ; they provide location, direction and speed information for each of the entities [12].

Event data provides logs of player-related events (pass, shot, catch, goalkeeper stop, etc.) or technical events (red card, start of time, stop of time, foul, etc.) for a match. Each of these events can be associated with a distance, duration or direction, and is time-stamped.

These two ways of looking at data require different technologies and technical or financial resources. For example, Indoor Position System (IPS) sensors [33] are inexpensive but not very accurate, while video [27,31,32] is accurate but requires expensive processing.

3.2   Qatar 2015 Data

The data analyzed here comes from 88 matches of the 2015 Handball World Championship held in Qatar. These data were obtained by video analysis and manual annotation of the events, the integrity of this trajectory capture system have been measured in [4]. This dataset has been little studied [5,13,14].

These data combine spatio-temporal and event-based information: each player's trajectory at 10 Hz and details of match events such as passes, receptions, shots and goals. For each match, a statistical summary table is available for each player. This table communicates individual information, such as walking distance, running distance, shooting distance at 7 m and 9 m, as well as the player's role for each match.

3.3   Dataset Enrichment

From this dataset, it is possible to pre-calculate various attributes providing additional information on the state of play, such as the distance of the shot from the goal, the angle of opening, etc. More complex attributes provide information on the pressure exerted on the shooter. For example, Voronoï [2] regions are used to determine the area a player can reach before all others (assuming all players have the same speed). If individual speeds are taken into account, the dominant region [36] or zone of influence [35] can be calculated. These tools are widely used to analyze team sports such as football [18].

Each player has a dominant zone. The boundaries of these zones are delimited by the bisectors between the players: the closer the neighbors, the smaller the player's zone. The area of the zone is ultimately indicative of the pressure exerted on a player.

The Delaunay triangulation [8] of a discrete set P of points is the dual graph of the Voronoï diagram associated with P. Each cell of the Voronoï diagram is associated with a vertex in the Delaunay triangulation. These vertices are connected by an edge if the cells are adjacent. The number of edges connecting a player to defenders is a relevant indicator of the pressure exerted on that player.

4   Method for Calculating xG

4.1   Sample Calculation

The first method for calculating the xG metric involves sampling the data to determine the ratio between the number of goals scored and the number of shots taken for each shooting position. Since shots are always taken from different positions, the field is divided into a grid with cells of varying size, depending on the precision required. The ratio between the number of goals scored and the number of shots taken is then calculated for each grid cell. The ratio obtained reflects *the ground truth* provided by the data. These values can be visualized using a heat map. The advantage of this method is that only the shooter's position is required to determine this ground truth.

4.2   Model Calculation

The second method for obtaining the xG metric is to design a model. A model is a function that takes as input various arguments such as the angle of the goal opening, the distance of the shot, etc., and gives as output the value of the xG.

For example, if we denote $xG(d, \theta)$ the function of arguments d the shooting distance from the goal and θ the opening angle of the goal, we could define this function as equal to $\frac{1}{d\theta}$. Indeed, this function has good properties because the goal probability is inversely proportional to distance and opening angle. However, the exact expression of this function is not known, not least because it depends on many other arguments, such as the size of the shooter.

What's more, each handball expert has his or her own unique personal experience and intuitions. It would be difficult to reach a consensus on the precise definition of the *expected goal.*

Determining the right model and therefore the exact expression of the function is a task taken on by machine learning, based on ground truth. For the remainder of this presentation, we have used seven of the most widely used learning algorithms: RANDOMFOREST [3], logistic regression [22], decision trees [19] and gradient boosting [7,17]: XGBOOST, CATBOOST and ADABOOST. We don't need to go into the technical details of how these algorithms work, but the essential point is to understand that, from a series of matches between shooting situations and the outcome of the shot, the algorithm calculates the most accurate model that functionally relates a shot to its outcome.

The models under study operate in a *supervised classification* mode. Their role is namely to classify shooting opportunities according to their outcome, positive or negative. In practice, these models calculate the probability of shot success and use an activation threshold to make the classification decision. The performance of a model is evaluated by its recall, precision, F1-score and area under the ROC curve [10].

4.3 *Wrapper*: Attribute Selection Approach

In order to determine the handball attributes needed to learn a good handball model, a technique known as attribute selection is required. These techniques can be very costly if they have to exhaustively test all potential attribute combinations: for n attributes, there are in fact $2^n - 1$ possible combinations. In practice, we distinguish between the *filter* [11] and *wrapper* [20] approaches. The *filter* approach examines the statistical characteristics of attributes, such as correlation coefficients. The *wrapper* approach iteratively selects the attributes that induce good performance of the learning algorithm employed (see Fig. 1).

The *wrapper* approach thus performs a search in the space of attribute subsets, guided by the performance of the model learning algorithm. The evaluation criterion is simply the algorithm's performance measure, which depends on the calculated model. The *wrapper* approach enables finer selection than the *filter* approach, but at the cost of a longer computation time.

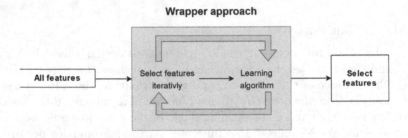

Fig. 1. *wrapper* approach.

In the experiments in Sect. 5, we're not looking for the optimal attribute configuration. We simply compare several emblematic families (see Table 1):

1. the first *pos* configuration considers only the shooter's position;
2. the second $(pos + \theta + d)$ adds the opening angle θ of the goal and the distance to the goal d;
3. *event data* contains position data plus information on match events (time elapsed since previous shot, goal differential, scores, etc.).
4. *spatial data* focus on the geometric characteristics of the game situation at the moment of shooting (goalkeeper position, shooter speed, number of defenders, etc.);
5. *combined data* consider all attributes.

The attributes chosen come from the literature on different xG models for football [6,9,15,16,25,39]. All these models use a base consisting of the shooter's position, the opening angle of the goal and the distance to the goal.

However, distance and angle are calculated from the shooter's x and y positions. They are therefore a priori redundant with the shooter's position. This is

Table 1. Attribute families for calculating xG.

data	pos	pos + θ + d	event	spatial	combined
shooter's (x, y) position	×	×	×	×	×
angle θ of goal opening		×	×	×	×
distance from goal		×	×	×	×
time elapsed since previous shot			×		×
goal difference			×		×
shooter's team score			×		×
opposing team's score			×		×
does the shooter's team lead?			×		×
ball possession time			×		×
goalkeeper's position(x, y)				×	×
distance from goalkeeper to goal				×	×
shooter's speed				×	×
game situation (counter-attack or placed attack)				×	×
dominant region area				×	×
number of connections in the Delaunay graph				×	×
number of defenders				×	×

why the model will be trained, on the one hand with the positions alone, and on the other with the addition of distance and angle. This distinction will enable us to decide whether the position is sufficient to calculate a good model.

For event data, the attributes are directly derived or calculated from the raw data. The characterization of the game situation (placed attack or transition game) is determined from the positions of the team's players: after a change in the team in possession of the ball, a transition situation is characterized by a surplus of players, indicating the delay of one or more defenders.

For spatial data, the area of the shooter's dominant Voronoï region and the number of neighbors in the Delaunay graph are considered. This information is thought to be indicative of the pressure exerted on the shooter.

5   Results

5.1   Sample Calculation

On the Qatar 2015 data, shot density, goal density and xG are represented by heat maps in Fig. 2. Although this article asks which attribute families should be considered for good xG learning, it seems relevant to visualize and analyze ground truth.

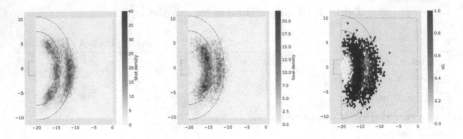

Fig. 2. Shot density (left), goal density (middle) and xG (right) in handball.

Most shots are taken from the 6 m and 9 m lines. On the other hand, their success seems to depend on the distance from the goal: the further away the shooter is, the more the angle of his shot seems likely to face the goal. The density suggests a shooting cone, with the wide base closest to the goal, and its apex closer to midfield. We can assume that there is a correlation between the chance of success on goal and the angle and distance of the shooter. Due to the atypical topography of a handball pitch, which prohibits players from entering the 6m zone, we observe a higher success rate for shots in this area. Indeed, an attacker can enter the zone for a brief moment while in the air, and thus be in a duel with the goalkeeper, with no defender to get in the way.

5.2 *Wrapper* Approach

Table 2 shows performance (accuracy, precision, recall, etc.) for each attribute family depending on model chosen. Learning times are in seconds for the reference attribute family (*pos* only), and in percentage relatively to the reference.

In our experiments, we found that the RANDOMFOREST algorithm performed best. For RANDOMFOREST, the F1-score is between 0.75 and 0.78 – recall and precision are almost identical – and the AUC varies between 0.71 and 0.75. This is the sign of a high-performance model that predicts rather correctly whether there is a goal in a given situation. The other models have an F1-score between 0.66 and 0.72, and an AUC between 0.63 and 0.67: RANDOMFOREST performs much better than the others.

As attribute richness increases, the improvement in learning quality is not very significant (F1-score of 0.75 for positions alone, 0.78 for all attributes). An increase in learning time is observed between the simplest configuration (*pos*) and the richest configuration (*combined data*).

We can also see that there is very little difference between event and spatial attribute configurations. The extra cost involved in calculating spatial attributes, such as those associated with the Delaunay graph, which requires the position of all players, is not always justified. This is characteristic of handball, whereas in soccer, the richness of attributes is important and the consideration of spatial attributes is necessary.

Table 2. Models performances on different attribute families.

input	model	accuracy	precision	recall	F1-score	AUC	learning time
pos	RANDOMFOREST	**0.72**	**0.77**	**0.74**	**0.75**	**0.71**	258 s
	LOGISTIC REGRESSION	0.64	0.64	0.69	0.66	0.63	16 s
	DECISION TREE	0.67	0.75	0.69	0.72	0.66	2 s
	XGBOOST	0.66	0.75	0.68	0.71	0.66	29 s
	CATBOOST	0.65	0.71	0.68	0.70	0.65	106 s
	ADABOOST	0.65	0.72	0.68	0.70	0.64	34 s
pos+θ+d	RANDOMFOREST	**0.73**	**0.78**	**0.74**	**0.76**	**0.72**	+62%
	LOGISTIC REGRESSION	0.63	0.64	0.69	0.66	0.63	+21%
	DECISION TREE	0.65	0.71	0.68	0.70	0.65	+28%
	XGBOOST	0.66	0.73	0.68	0.71	0.65	+33%
	CATBOOST	0.65	0.73	0.68	0.70	0.65	+60%
	ADABOOST	0.65	0.72	0.68	0.70	0.64	+70%
event data	RANDOMFOREST	**0.74**	**0.79**	**0.76**	**0.77**	**0.73**	+75%
	LOGISTIC REGRESSION	0.63	0.63	0.69	0.66	0.63	+1631%
	DECISION TREE	0.65	0.74	0.67	0.70	0.65	+700%
	XGBOOST	0.66	0.73	0.69	0.71	0.66	+177%
	CATBOOST	0.66	0.74	0.68	0.71	0.65	+54%
	ADABOOST	0.65	0.72	0.68	0.70	0.64	+70%
spatial data	RANDOMFOREST	**0.75**	**0.77**	**0.78**	**0.78**	**0.75**	+84%
	LOGISTIC REGRESSION	0.64	0.64	0.69	0.67	0.64	+768%
	DECISION TREE	0.65	0.73	0.67	0.70	0.65	+2000%
	XGBOOST	0.70	0.74	0.73	0.73	0.69	+134%
	CATBOOST	0.66	0.72	0.69	0.70	0.65	+148%
	ADABOOST	0.67	0.73	0.69	0.71	0.66	+114%
combined data	RANDOMFOREST	**0.75**	**0.77**	**0.78**	**0.78**	**0.75**	+49%
	LOGISTIC REGRESSION	0.64	0.64	0.69	0.67	0.64	+2406%
	DECISION TREE	0.65	0.67	0.69	0.68	0.64	+4450%
	XGBOOST	0.68	0.73	0.70	0.72	0.67	+144%
	CATBOOST	0.67	0.72	0.70	0.71	0.66	+102%
	ADABOOST	0.66	0.72	0.68	0.70	0.65	+238%

6   Conclusion

Adapting the calculation of the xG metric to handball is a crucial step in analyzing team performance in this sport. An *wrapper* approach was used to determine the relevant attributes for learning xG. In soccer, the position of the shooter, the distance to the goal and the position of the defenders are relevant. However, adapting the soccer models for handball, which include a large number of attributes, did not significantly improve model accuracy.

The way in which the calculation of the xG metric is adjusted is influenced by the availability of data, as well as by the cost that the team is willing to incur to collect this data. In handball, our experiments have shown that it is not mandatory to invest huge resources in data collection, and that only the shooting positions could be sufficient. This is a significant advance in the analysis of player and team handball performance, which could have practical applications in the field of training and strategy.

Acknowledgements. This work was partially funded by the ANR and the Normandy Region as part of the HAISCoDe project.

References

1. Anzer, G., Bauer, P.: A goal scoring probability model for shots based on synchronized positional and event data in football (soccer). Front. Sports Active Living **3**, 624475 (2021)
2. Aurenhammer, F.: Voronoi diagrams: a survey of a fundamental geometric data structure. ACM Comput. Surv. **23**(3), 345–405 (1991)
3. Breiman, L.: Random forests. Mach. Learn. **45**, 5–32 (2001)
4. Buchheit, M., Allen, A., Poon, T.K., Modonutti, M., Gregson, W., Di Salvo, V.: Integrating different tracking systems in football: multiple camera semi-automatic system, local position measurement and GPS technologies. J. Sports Sci. **32**(20), 1844–1857 (2014)
5. Cardinale, M., Whiteley, R., Hosny, A.A., Popovic, N.: Activity profiles and positional differences of handball players during the world championships in Qatar 2015. Int. J. Sports Physiol. Perform. **12**(7), 908–915 (2017)
6. Cavus, M., Biecek, P.: Explainable expected goal models for performance analysis in football analytics (2022). https://doi.org/10.48550/ARXIV.2206.07212, https://arxiv.org/abs/2206.07212
7. Chen, T., et al.: Xgboost: extreme gradient boosting. R Package Version 0.4-2 **1**(4), 1–4 (2015)
8. Delaunay, B.: Sur la sphére vide. Proceedings du Congrés international des mathématiciens de 1924, pp. 695–700 (1924)
9. Fairchild, A., Pelechrinis, K., Kokkodis, M.: Spatial analysis of shots in MLS: a model for expected goals and fractal dimensionality. J. Sports Anal. **4**(3), 165–174 (2018)
10. Fawcett, T.: Roc graphs: Notes and practical considerations for researchers. Technical report HPL-2003-4, HP Laboratories (2003)
11. Germano, M.: Turbulence: the filtering approach. J. Fluid Mech. **238**, 325–336 (1992)
12. Gudmundsson, J., Horton, M.: Spatio-temporal analysis of team sports. ACM Comput. Surv. (CSUR) **50**(2), 1–34 (2017)
13. Hansen, C., Sanz-Lopez, F., Whiteley, R., Popovic, N., Ahmed, H.A., Cardinale, M.: Performance analysis of male handball goalkeepers at the world handball championship 2015. Biol. Sport **34**(4), 393 (2017)
14. Hansen, C., Whiteley, R., Wilhelm, A., Popovic, N., Ahmed, H., Cardinale, M., et al.: A video-based analysis to classify shoulder injuries during the handball world championships 2015. Sportverletzung Sportschaden: Organ der Gesellschaft fur Orthopadisch-traumatologische Sportmedizin **33**(1), 30–35 (2019)
15. Herold, M., Goes, F., Nopp, S., Bauer, P., Thompson, C., Meyer, T.: Machine learning in men's professional football: current applications and future directions for improving attacking play. Int. J. Sports Sci. Coach. **14**(6), 798–817 (2019). https://doi.org/10.1177/1747954119879350

16. Hewitt, J.H., Karakuş, O.: A machine learning approach for player and position adjusted expected goals in football (soccer) (2023). https://doi.org/10.48550/ARXIV.2301.13052, https://arxiv.org/abs/2301.13052
17. Ke, G., et al.: Lightgbm: a highly efficient gradient boosting decision tree. Adv. Neural Inf. Process. Syst. **30** (2017)
18. Kim, S.: Voronoi analysis of a soccer game. Nonlinear Anal. Model. Control **9**(3), 233–240 (2004). https://doi.org/10.15388/NA.2004.9.3.15154, https://www.journals.vu.lt/nonlinear-analysis/article/view/15154
19. Kingsford, C., Salzberg, S.L.: What are decision trees? Nat. Biotechnol. **26**(9), 1011–1013 (2008)
20. Kohavi, R., John, G.H.: The wrapper approach. In: Liu, H., Motoda, H. (eds.) Feature Extraction, Construction and Selection. The Springer International Series in Engineering and Computer Science, vol. 453, pp. 33–50. Springer, Boston, MA (1998). https://doi.org/10.1007/978-1-4615-5725-8_3
21. Lago-Ballesteros, J., Lago-Peñas, C.: Performance in team sports: identifying the keys to success in soccer. J. Hum. Kinet. **25**(2010), 85–91 (2010)
22. LaValley, M.P.: Logistic regression. Circulation **117**(18), 2395–2399 (2008)
23. Macdonald, B.: Adjusted plus-minus for NHL players using ridge regression with goals, shots, fenwick, and corsi. J. Quant. Anal. Sports **8**(3) (2012). https://doi.org/10.1515/1559-0410.1447
24. Macdonald, B.: An expected goals model for evaluating NHL teams and players. In: Proceedings of the 2012 MIT Sloan Sports Analytics Conference (2012)
25. Madrero Pardo, P.: Creating a model for expected Goals in football using qualitative player information. Ph.D. thesis, UPC, Facultat d'Informàtica de Barcelona, Departament de Ciéncies de la Computació, June 2020. http://hdl.handle.net/2117/328922
26. Madrero Pardo, P.: Creating a model for expected goals in football using qualitative player information. Master's thesis, Universitat Politècnica de Catalunya (2020)
27. Pettersen, S.A., et al.: Soccer video and player position dataset. In: Proceedings of the 5th ACM Multimedia Systems Conference, pp. 18–23 (2014)
28. Rathke, A.: An examination of expected goals and shot efficiency in soccer. J. Hum. Sport Exerc. **12**(2), 514–529 (2017)
29. Robberechts, P., Davis, J.: How data availability affects the ability to learn good XG models. In: Brefeld, U., Davis, J., Van Haaren, J., Zimmermann, A. (eds.) Machine Learning and Data Mining for Sports Analytics. MLSA 2020. CCIS, vol. 1324, pp. 17–27. Springer, Cham (2020). https://doi.org/10.1007/978-3-030-64912-8_2
30. Ruiz, H., Lisboa, P., Neilson, P., Gregson, W.: Measuring scoring efficiency through goal expectancy estimation. In: ESANN 2015 proceedings of the European Symposium on Artificial Neural Networks, Computational Intelligence and Machine Learning, pp. 149–154 (2015)
31. Sanford, R., Gorji, S., Hafemann, L.G., Pourbabaee, B., Javan, M.: Group activity detection from trajectory and video data in soccer. In: Proceedings of the IEEE/CVF Conference on Computer Vision and Pattern Recognition Workshops, pp. 898–899 (2020)
32. Scott, A., Uchida, I., Onishi, M., Kameda, Y., Fukui, K., Fujii, K.: Soccertrack: A dataset and tracking algorithm for soccer with fish-eye and drone videos. In: Proceedings of the IEEE/CVF Conference on Computer Vision and Pattern Recognition, pp. 3569–3579 (2022)
33. Serpiello, F., et al.: Validity of an ultra-wideband local positioning system to measure locomotion in indoor sports. J. Sports Sci. **36**(15), 1727–1733 (2018)

34. Spearman, W.: Beyond expected goals. In: Proceedings of the 12th MIT Sloan Sports Analytics Conference, pp. 1–17 (2018)
35. Taki, T., Hasegawa, J.: Visualization of dominant region in team games and its application to teamwork analysis. In: Proceedings Computer Graphics International 2000, pp. 227–235 (2000). https://doi.org/10.1109/CGI.2000.852338
36. Taki, T., Hasegawa, J.I., Fukumura, T.: Development of motion analysis system for quantitative evaluation of teamwork in soccer games. In: Proceedings of 3rd IEEE International Conference on Image Processing, vol. 3, pp. 815–818. IEEE (1996)
37. Tenga, A., Ronglan, L.T., Bahr, R.: Measuring the effectiveness of offensive match-play in professional soccer. Eur. J. Sport Sci. **10**(4), 269–277 (2010)
38. Tiippana, T., et al.: How accurately does the expected goals model reflect goalscoring and success in football? (2020)
39. Umami, I., Gautama, D., Hatta, H.: Implementing the expected goal (xG) model to predict scores in soccer matches. Int. J. Inform. Inf. Syst. **4**(1), 38–54 (2021). https://doi.org/10.47738/ijiis.v4i1.76, http://ijiis.org/index.php/IJIIS/article/view/76
40. Umami, I., Gautama, D.H., Hatta, H.R.: Implementing the expected goal (xG) model to predict scores in soccer matches. Int. J. Inform. Inf. Syst. **4**(1), 38–54 (2021)
41. Van Haaren, J.: Why would i trust your numbers? On the explainability of expected values in soccer. arXiv preprint arXiv:2105.13778 (2021)

Identifying Player Roles in Ice Hockey

Rasmus Säfvenberg, Niklas Carlsson[ID], and Patrick Lambrix[(✉)][ID]

Linköping University, Linköping, Sweden
patrick.lambrix@liu.se

Abstract. Understanding the role of a particular player, or set of players, in a team is an important tool for players, scouts, and managers, as it can improve training, game adjustments and team construction. In this paper, we propose a probabilistic method for quantifying player roles in ice hockey that allows for a player to belong to different roles with some probability. Using data from the 2021–2022 NHL season, we analyze and group players into clusters. We show the use of the clusters by an examination of the relationship between player role and contract, as well as between role distribution in a team and team success in terms of reaching the playoffs.

Keywords: Sports analytics · Ice Hockey

1 Introduction

Ice hockey is a fast-paced team sport that emphasizes both physical prowess and technical ability [10]. However, the expectations and responsibilities of players vary, not only based on playing position, but also on the role of the player. The three traditional groups of positions in ice hockey are goaltenders, defenders, and forwards [21], where the latter two positions are referred to as skaters. However, the roles of the players are not always that clear cut. For instance, while defenders are typically given the highest responsibility for preventing the opposition from scoring, there are defenders who specialize in offensive contribution [21].

The benefits of categorizing players into roles are multi-fold. For team staff it will allow the choices and design of rosters and line-ups to be more effective in-game. Additionally, the construction of team rosters is also constrained from an economic standpoint. In the National Hockey League (NHL), the salary cap prevents a team from having salary expenditure above a fixed amount [6]. On an individual level, if there is a disagreement in expectations of the player's role between a player and a team, the development of the player may be hampered and the likelihood of attaining success is lowered for both parties [14].

Work on player roles has been performed in different sports (e.g. [1,19]). Prior work regarding player roles in ice hockey has typically utilized methods that assign each player into a distinct cluster, e.g., using k-means, and used a limited set of performance metrics, e.g., points, plus-minus, and penalty minutes, which may leave some roles or role nuances undiscovered [6,21]. In comparison,

U. Brefeld et al. (Eds.): MLSA 2023, CCIS 2035, pp. 131–143, 2024.
https://doi.org/10.1007/978-3-031-53833-9_11

the aim of this paper is to identify different player roles for skaters in ice hockey using performance metrics that span more aspects of the game than previous work, as well as a wider basis for discovering different player roles. Further, players can be assigned to different roles to different degrees.

The contributions of this paper are as follows. First, we identify player roles by using a larger set of performance metrics than previous work, allowing us to discover new roles and/or key components in understanding a role, and by using fuzzy clustering, allowing each player to belong to a role to some degree, rather than assigning each player to a distinct role. Further, we show applications to team constructions in terms of player contract comparison and team composition for successful and less successful teams. Our findings have value to players, scouts, and managers.

The remainder of the paper is organized as follows. Section 2 describes the data used for the analysis while Sect. 3 introduces the method including preprocessing, principal component analysis and fuzzy clustering. Section 4 presents and contextualizes the results. Further, we show two applications. In Sect. 5 we compare players to players with similar roles with respect to their salaries and in Sect. 6 we investigate the relationship between team composition based on roles and reaching the playoffs. Limitations of the study are addressed and concluding remarks are drawn in Sect. 7.

2   Data

We use data from 2021–2022 NHL regular season obtained from the official website of the NHL[1] and their public API, as well as salary data from CapFriendly[2]. The data combines play-by-play data with shift data. From this data, a set of variables was derived (Table 1). Variables regarding goals, assists, and expected goals are used to evaluate offensive quality and frequency among players. Plus-minus $(+/-)$, xGF, xGF%, and xGF% Relative serve as proxies for team performance while the player is on the ice. Giveaways gives some measure of puck control, while takeaways and blocks represent defensive contributions. Hits, net hits, penalties, net penalties, penalty minutes, and number of penalties per group all portray player aggression and physical play. The number of penalties per group variables are also split into the penalties the player is given as well as the penalties that are drawn, to distinguish between players who are the instigator and the receiver. Offensive zone starts can depict if a player is more offensively or defensively orientated. The time on ice variables capture how much ice time the player has, while the coordinate variable describes where the player typically is when performing each event. Finally, weight characterizes player physique, which is used to gauge the physical dimension of players and its impact on player role. Furthermore, the variables xGF%, and xGF% Relative serve as a proxy for puck possession, and, as [22] explains, can negate the weaknesses of the traditional plus-minus metric.

---

[1] https://www.NHL.com.
[2] https://www.capfriendly.com.

Table 1. Variables in the data.

Variable	Description
Goals	Number of goals scored by the player
Assists	Number of passes by the player leading to goals
xG	How many goals a player is expected to score
xG difference	Goals - xG
S%	Percentage of shots on goal that become goals
+/−	+/− while the player is on the ice
xGF%	xGF on ice/(xGF on ice + xGF off ice) during 5 on 5
xGF% Relative	xGF% on ice - xGF% off ice during 5 on 5
Giveaway	Unforced loss of control of puck by the player
Takeaway	Retrieval of the puck from opponent
Blocks	Number of blocked shots by the player
Hits	Number of hits by the player on opposing players
Net hits	Hits given - Hits received
Fights	Number of fights the player was involved in
Penalties	Number of penalties on the player
Net penalties	Penalties on - Penalties drawn
Penalty minutes	Total penalty minutes for the player
Penalties per group	Groups are physical, restraining, stick, (other not used)
Penalties drawn per group	Groups are physical, restraining, stick, (other not used)
OZS%	% of starts in the offensive zone for the player
PP%	% of time played in powerplay
SH%	% of time played while shorthanded
OT%	% of time played in overtime
Median X coordinate	Median X coordinate for each event
Median Y coordinate	Median absolute Y coordinate for each event
TOI*	Total time on ice for the player
5 on 5 TOI*	Total time on ice during full strength for the player
Height	Player's height in inches
Weight	Player's weight in pounds

* Not included as a variable for modeling.

3   Method

The analysis consisted of preprocessing, dimensionality reduction and clustering.

3.1   Preprocessing

In the Preprocessing step, a threshold was used of 200 min for minimum number of minutes played during the season to exclude players who had insufficient playing time. The number of defenders satisfying this requirement was 263 (out of 345), and the number of forwards 485 (out of 659). We then split the data into two subsets, one for defenders and one for forwards, to take positional variations into consideration. Further, all[3] performance-related variables with counts, i.e.,

---

[3] Except xGF, which used 5 on 5 TOI.

not variables with percentages, were then standardized by dividing by total time on the ice (TOI) and multiplied by 60 (number of minutes in a game in regulation time). The variables were also normalized by subtracting the variable's mean and dividing by its corresponding standard deviation.

3.2   Principal Component Analysis

Next, principal component analysis (PCA) was utilized to perform dimensionality reduction on the data, as clustering in high dimensions tends to become ineffective [2]. The selection of the number of principal components was primarily based on parallel analysis [12,13] to reduce the probability that too many components are kept. This selection method was shown to be among the best performing in [17]. Based on experiments regarding the robustness for the method [12] we ran 100,000 iterations using the 95th percentile as the basis for selecting the number of components.

3.3   Clustering

As we wanted to model that players can take on different roles to certain degrees and that roles tend to have overlapping elements, we opted to use a fuzzy clustering algorithm rather than the crisp clustering algorithms used in previous work. In fuzzy clustering, the objects are assigned a probability of belonging to a given cluster, where the probabilities of cluster membership of an object sum to one. In this paper, we used the fuzzy c-means algorithm [3,9]. The objective in fuzzy c-means algorithm is to create k fuzzy partitions among a set of n objects from a data vector $\mathbf{x}$ by solving (1) until convergence.

$$\min_{\mathbf{U},\mathbf{C}} J_m = \sum_{i=1}^{n} \sum_{j=1}^{k} u_{ij}^m d^2(\mathbf{x}_i, \mathbf{c}_j) \quad s.t. \quad u_{ij} \in [0,1], \sum_{j=1}^{k} u_{ij} = 1 \qquad (1)$$

In (1), d denotes the distance between object i and the j:th cluster centroid c_j. Moreover, u_{ij} is the degree of membership for object i to cluster j. The hyperparameter m controls the degree of fuzziness, where a higher m leads to a fuzzier solution [4]. It can also be shown that the fuzzy solution converges to the crisp solution as $m \to 1$ [15] and as $m \to \infty$ then $u_{ij} \to \frac{1}{k}$.

There is no optimal m that suits all cases [4]. However, $m \in [1.5, 3.0]$ tends to give satisfactory results in general [4] or are typical values [24], $m = 2$ results in compact and well separated clusters [9], but can also negatively affect the clustering [8,20]. The formula that we use for deciding m was proposed in [20].

$$f(n,p) = 1 + \left(\frac{1418}{n} + 22.05\right) d^{-2} \left(\frac{12.33}{n} + 0.243\right) d^{-0.0406 \log(n) - 0.1134}, \qquad (2)$$

which only depends on the number of objects n and the dimensions p.

Similar to its crisp clustering counterpart, k-means, the fuzzy c-means algorithm also requires that the number of clusters k are specified in advance. A popular method for deciding how many clusters should be formed is to compare a set of candidate k by considering one or more cluster validity indices [16]. In [23] a large set of different fuzzy cluster validity indices are compared. Although no singular validity index is optimal for all data, the modified partition coefficient (MPC) was one of the indices that partitioned many of the investigated data sets into the best number of clusters. The MPC is an extension of the partition coefficient (PC) [3]:

$$V_{PC} = \frac{1}{n} \sum_{i=1}^{n} \sum_{j=1}^{k} u_{ij}^2 \in \left[\frac{1}{k}, 1\right], \tag{3}$$

PC exhibits a monotonic evolution as k increases. As a result, [7] proposed the MPC, which is defined as:

$$V_{MPC} = 1 - \frac{k}{k-1}(1 - V_{PC}) \in [0, 1]. \tag{4}$$

Similarly to the PC, MPC quantifies the extent of sharing between fuzzy subsets. For both indices, the optimal number of clusters is given by the k that maximizes the index [23].

Although some cluster validity indices are typically only considered for fuzzy clustering, extensions of crisp clustering validity indices have also been proposed, an example being a fuzzy extension of the silhouette width criterion, which is frequently used in crisp clustering [5]. The silhouette of an object i is computed by

$$s_i = \frac{a_i - b_i}{\max\{a_i, b_i\}} \in [-1, 1], \tag{5}$$

where a_i describes the average dissimilarity for object i to all other objects belonging to the same crisp cluster, while b_i is the minimum average dissimilarity to the clusters where object i is not assigned [18]. Moreover, the crisp silhouette is defined as the average of the silhouette over all objects. However, in the context of fuzzy clustering, the crisp silhouette does not account for information regarding the degree of cluster overlap between two clusters. To generalize this criterion to fuzzy clustering, the fuzzy silhouette (FS) is defined by:

$$V_{FS} = \frac{\sum_{i=1}^{n}(u_{ig} - u_{ig'})^\alpha s_i}{\sum_{i=1}^{n}(u_{ig} - u_{ig'})^\alpha}, \tag{6}$$

where u_{ig} and $u_{ig'}$ represent the two largest elements from $\mathbf{U}_i$ [5] while $\alpha \geq 0$ is a weighting coefficient that is commonly set to 1 [11]. One distinction between the crisp and fuzzy silhouette is that the latter computes the weight for each term, based on the two fuzzy clusters that are found to be the best match. The optimal number of k is obtained by maximizing the index [5].

4 Results

4.1 Principal Component Analysis

Figure 1 shows the proportion of variance explained by each component generated by the PCA for defenders and forwards, respectively. The first six components are

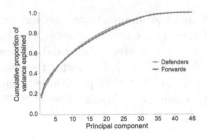

Fig. 1. Proportion of variance explained for defenders and forwards

responsible for the majority of the variance in the data, by providing an explanation of at least 50% of the variance. However, the proportion of explained variance decreases rapidly, and in order to explain, e.g., 90% of the variance, at least 26 and 27 components are required for defenders and forwards, respectively. We used parallel analysis to determine the set of components, which resulted in the selection of the first eight for defenders and nine components for forwards. These choices explain approximately 55–57% of the variance for each respective position group.

4.2 Fuzzy Clustering

For obtaining values for m in fuzzy c-means we used Eq. 2 which resulted in 2.407 for defenders and 2.179 for forwards. For k we used Eqs. 4 and 6 to evaluate cluster cohesion. $k = 2$ produced the most distinct clusters for defenders and forwards and less cohesive clusters were observed for values larger than $k = 3$ (defenders) and $k = 4$ (forwards). In addition to these metrics, the cluster assignment of players was also compared to domain knowledge to guide the final choice. More specifically, the players who belong to the same cluster should share the same style of play, regardless of if other possible roles, i.e., clusters, have some overlap. As a result, $k = 3$ and $k = 4$ were chosen for defenders and forwards, respectively, as they provide more cohesive clusters while also allowing the number of roles to be as descriptive as possible.

Figure 2 shows the distribution of the probabilities representing cluster membership. We note that the densities of probabilities for defenders are more similar than forwards, where cluster F4 has a high peak close to zero. Furthermore, clusters D1 and D3 among defenders have similar distributions while cluster D2 is more centered. For forwards, both clusters F1 and F3 appear to span the entire range of possible values between zero and one, while clusters F2 and F4 have a somewhat smaller range. Except for cluster D2 among defenders, the densities reach a peak between 0 and 0.25.

To explore the variables characterizing each cluster, we retrieve the cluster centroids, which are expressed in terms of principal components. We then obtain approximate centroids corresponding to the original variables by computing an inverse transform of the centroids and the selected principal components. Moreover, since the data was standardized to have unit variance prior to conducting

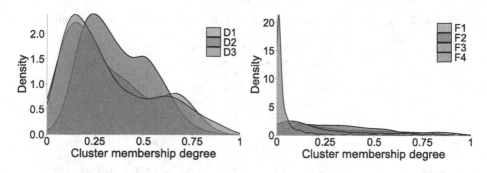

Fig. 2. Cluster membership degrees for defenders (left) and forwards (right).

PCA we also invert this procedure by multiplying by the standard deviation and adding the mean for each variable. Using this method, we then obtain approximate centroids on the original variable scales, expressed in per 60 min of ice time (Table 2).

Among defenders, a higher probability to belong to cluster D1 is connected to the most offensively skilled defenders, who assist their team's attacking presence by contributing more goals, assists, xG, and takeaways while also playing closer to the opposition's net. They also start in the offensive zone and in powerplay situations, more often than defenders in the other clusters. In cluster D3 we find the most physical defenders, as the number of fights, hits, and penalties are the highest, alongside the largest average weight. Their offensive contribution, with respect to xG, assist, and OZS% rank is lowest. They also garner the highest share of time played while shorthanded, but lowest in overtime and while shorthanded. Finally, the third cluster, D2, contains the defensive specialists, where goals, penalty minutes, and hits are at their lowest, in combination with playing closer to their own net. They are also the shortest and lightest.

Regarding forwards, the players in cluster F4 can be described as physical players, with the highest weight in combination with most fights, hits, and penalty minutes. The offensive production is second lowest, and they tend to be preferred in defensive situations. The offensive specialists can be found in cluster F3, where goals, assists, and xG are at their highest, which also can be seen in their play closer to the opposition's goal. Moreover, players in F3 also draw the most non-physical penalties. These players also block the most shots. A lower, but still second highest, offensive proficiency characterizes the players in F2, alongside positive xGF% values. Finally, the two-way forwards reside in F1, with skating that covers the entirety of the rink. Additionally, the lowest xG and goals are created by these players, alongside the lowest +/− and xGF On. However, they rank the highest for time played while shorthanded and percentage of starts in the defensive zone.

Table 2. Approximate cluster centroids of the original variables per 60 min.

Variable	F1[a]	F2[b]	F3[c]	F4[d]	D1[e]	D2[f]	D3[g]
Goals	0.536	0.784	1.189	0.596	0.304	0.172	0.165
Assists	0.782	1.057	1.535	0.663	1.032	0.701	0.592
xG	0.649	0.823	1.023	0.711	0.271	0.187	0.174
xG difference	−0.113	−0.039	0.166	−0.116	0.033	−0.015	−0.010
S%	0.090	0.108	0.143	0.093	0.059	0.041	0.040
+/−	−0.532	−0.221	0.274	−0.370	0.164	−0.180	−0.097
xGF%	0.469	0.497	0.525	0.471	0.510	0.487	0.486
xGF%Rel	−0.024	−0.001	0.024	−0.025	0.010	−0.008	−0.014
Giveaways	1.270	1.513	1.918	1.463	1.872	1.740	1.793
Takeaways	1.512	1.618	1.848	1.277	1.125	0.846	0.818
Blocks	2.137	1.747	1.441	2.220	3.737	4.214	4.672
Hits	6.122	4.668	3.023	12.749	3.427	4.229	6.279
Net hits	1.006	−0.202	−0.976	6.655	−0.874	−1.008	0.822
Fights	0.058	0.024	0.019	0.460	0.020	0.027	0.107
Penalties	0.691	0.661	0.642	2.007	0.629	0.573	0.929
Net penalties	−0.029	−0.080	−0.207	0.456	0.207	0.187	0.398
Penalty minutes	3.591	3.299	3.368	11.621	2.310	2.145	3.796
Physical penalties drawn	0.145	0.120	0.127	0.833	0.094	0.101	0.228
Physical penalties on	0.148	0.117	0.119	0.921	0.091	0.093	0.244
Restraining penalties drawn	0.395	0.425	0.488	0.459	0.208	0.176	0.170
Restraining penalties on	0.330	0.333	0.309	0.529	0.340	0.321	0.440
Stick penalties drawn	0.162	0.182	0.217	0.189	0.113	0.102	0.119
Stick penalties on	0.151	0.157	0.159	0.318	0.148	0.117	0.180
OZS%	0.502	0.501	0.500	0.499	0.500	0.500	0.498
PP%	0.161	0.303	0.522	0.087	0.340	0.149	0.060
SH%	0.205	0.144	0.140	0.124	0.287	0.281	0.359
OT%	0.121	0.225	0.464	0.035	0.423	0.192	0.120
Median X Blocker	−61.418	−61.600	−62.203	−60.421	−71.531	−71.816	−72.058
Median X Giveaway	−9.247	7.064	22.694	−12.545	−54.876	−62.295	−64.705
Median X Hit taken	46.848	52.974	56.480	42.968	−79.173	−82.887	−83.735
Median X Hitter	50.035	53.585	45.437	63.619	−74.427	−75.385	−72.842
Median X Penalty drawn	38.681	48.730	55.660	29.017	−44.261	−51.050	−52.665
Median X Penalty	−1.786	7.576	2.976	16.351	−66.892	−67.643	−68.462
Median X Shooter	69.933	70.348	69.813	70.270	51.044	49.973	48.561
Median X Takeaway	4.481	12.296	8.304	7.197	−43.224	−49.087	−48.726
Median Y Blocker	3.240	3.550	3.366	4.741	2.374	2.665	2.824
Median Y Giveaway	13.743	11.202	8.965	15.791	11.802	12.917	14.816
Median Y Hit taken	14.749	13.006	11.718	17.486	19.306	19.300	21.594
Median Y Hitter	12.296	12.299	12.062	11.374	19.586	20.391	23.384
Median Y Penalty drawn	10.509	8.171	4.680	6.694	11.419	12.341	10.447
Median Y Penalty	10.644	9.845	7.487	6.765	6.644	9.580	7.123
Median Y Shooter	1.855	1.680	1.872	1.931	8.742	11.059	13.364
Median Y Takeaway	8.543	7.226	5.514	11.394	14.730	16.196	16.270
Height (inches)	72.832	72.776	72.648	74.357	73.291	73.318	74.797
Weight (pounds)	196.294	195.941	195.925	211.659	199.538	198.207	208.955

[a] *Examples*: Nick Bonino, Colton Sissons, Barclay Goodrow
[b] *Examples*: Anze Kopitar, Jamie Benn, Tyler Seguin
[c] *Examples*: Sidney Crosby, Auston Matthews, Connor McDavid
[d] *Examples*: Tanner Jeannot, Ryan Reaves, Pat Maroon
[e] *Examples*: Adam Larsson, Rasmus Ristolainen, Radko Gudas
[f] *Examples*: Roman Josi, Victor Hedman, Cale Makar
[g] *Examples*: Ivan Provorov, Christopher Tanev, Brian Dumoulin

5   Comparing Player Salary

One use of the clusters is to compare similar players regarding their roles with respect to salary. We compared each player's cap hit to their ten nearest neighbors to determine how the player's cap hit compares to their peers. The definition of neighbor in this context is based on selecting ten players with whom a given player has the lowest Euclidean distance, where the distance is measured by considering the fuzzy cluster membership probabilities. Due to the very right-skewed distributions of cap hit a logarithmic transformation was used. After computing the difference in cap hit and distance for a pair of players, the difference is then divided by the player's own cap hit and then considered as the basis for determining if a player is underpaid or overpaid when considering the cap hit of their neighbors. A summary of the fifteen most underpaid and overpaid players, relative to their neighbors, per position can be seen in Table 3. In general, a negative value of average difference indicates that a player is earning less than similarly performing players, while a positive value suggests the opposite. The value should not be interpreted objectively to determine whether a player has a good or bad contract, but rather how their contract stands in relation to players whose role was similar during the 2021–2022 season.

The results indicate that the most overpaid players, relative to their role, are Oliver Ekman-Larsson, Sean Monahan, and Milan Lucic, while the players who are deemed to be most underpaid are Oliver Kylington, Trevor Zegras, and Mason Marchment. A shared attribute among many underpaid players is that they are still on their entry-level contract, which is the first contract they sign when entering the league. As such, their true value may not (yet) be seen in their contract. However, some of the players that are suggested to be underpaid have after the season signed more lucrative contracts, including e.g., Jason Robertson, Mason Marchment, Jack Hughes, and Adam Fox[4]. Moreover, some of the overpaid players have since signed smaller contracts (Anton Strålman), retired (Duncan Keith and P.K. Subban), or are no longer in the league (Alexander Radulov and Danny DeKeyser). Interestingly, players who had a more unique distribution of cluster membership degrees, such as Brady Tkachuk, were more difficult to evaluate, as they can be quite distant to their nearest neighbors. Consequently, they may be overrated by the model while in reality the contract is not as bad as the model describes.

6   Team Composition

Team composition can have a substantial impact on team performance [6]. Therefore, we also investigate if there are any patterns between player roles and team success for the given season. We first compute the minutes played for all players per team and retain the 18 players with the highest playing time. The choice of 18 players is based on the roster size in the NHL, where 20 players, of whom 18 are skaters and 2 goaltenders, are allowed to be used in any given game. Thus,

---

[4] https://www.capfriendly.com/transactions.

Table 3. Most underpaid and overpaid players, relative to players with similar cluster membership probabilities for each position.

(a) Underpaid defenders.

Rank	Player	Avg. Rel. Diff.
1	Oliver Kylington	−1.060
2	Evan Bouchard	−0.812
3	Adam Fox	−0.750
4	Adam Boqvist	−0.726
5	Erik Gustafsson	−0.688
6	Anthony DeAngelo	−0.663
7	Moritz Seider	−0.654
8	Bowen Byram	−0.636
9	Noah Dobson	−0.636
10	Alexandre Carrier	−0.584
11	Rasmus Sandin	−0.565
12	Kale Clague	−0.551
13	Calle Rosen	−0.548
14	Gabriel Carlsson	−0.541
15	Jaycob Megna	−0.536

(b) Overpaid defenders.

Rank	Player	Avg. Rel. Diff.
1	Oliver Ekman-Larsson	0.484
2	Esa Lindell	0.416
3	Ryan McDonagh	0.410
4	Marc-Edouard Vlasic	0.402
5	Jeff Petry	0.382
6	Anton Strålman	0.380
7	Nick Leddy	0.375
8	T.J. Brodie	0.374
9	Darnell Nurse	0.367
10	Danny DeKeyser	0.357
11	P.K. Subban	0.352
12	Duncan Keith	0.352
13	Tyler Myers	0.348
14	Rasmus Ristolainen	0.348
15	Ryan Pulock	0.345

(c) Underpaid forwards.

Rank	Player	Avg. Rel. Diff.
1	Trevor Zegras	−0.927
2	Mason Marchment	−0.889
3	Jason Robertson	−0.869
4	Joshua Norris	−0.837
5	Jack Hughes	−0.800
6	Matthew Boldy	−0.795
7	Anton Lundell	−0.779
8	Martin Necas	−0.759
9	Tim Stützle	−0.744
10	Michael Bunting	−0.717
11	Carter Verhaeghe	−0.715
12	Nathan Walker	−0.703
13	Nick Suzuki	−0.673
14	Cole Caufield	−0.672
15	Lucas Raymond	−0.655

(d) Overpaid forwards.

Rank	Player	Avg. Rel. Diff.
1	Sean Monahan	0.483
2	Milan Lucic	0.438
3	Brady Tkachuk	0.418
4	Jonathan Drouin	0.418
5	Antohy Beauvillier	0.397
6	Tyler Johnson	0.394
7	Jamie Benn	0.392
8	Kevin Hayes	0.387
9	Andrew Ladd	0.385
10	Alexander Radulov	0.374
11	Dustin Brown	0.373
12	Colton Sissons	0.371
13	Christian Dvorak	0.356
14	Nick Foligno	0.356
15	Niklas Bäckstrom	0.353

these 18 players can then represent a possible composition of players for any given team and game. Except for the San Jose Sharks (8D/10F) and the Florida Panthers (5D/13F), the team compositions either consisted of 7 defenders and 11 forwards or 6 defenders and 12 forwards. Next, for a given team we then sum the cluster probabilities among all players in each position group (defenders and forwards) to obtain an estimate of how many players they have in each role, which is then divided by the total number of players for the given position to find the proportion of roles each team has. Thus, the sum of all forward clusters sums to one and likewise for defenders. This is illustrated in Fig. 3, where a hierarchical clustering using Ward's linkage method and Euclidean distance groups the playoff and non-playoff teams by team composition.

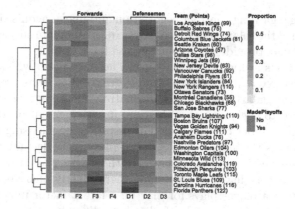

Fig. 3. Team composition and playoffs.

An observation from the clustering is that a distinction between playoff and non-playoff teams is apparent, as 14 out of 16 playoff teams were grouped together with the two exceptions being the New York Rangers and the Dallas Stars. Similarly, the Anaheim Ducks and Vegas Golden Knights, who both missed the playoffs, were clustered with the other playoff teams. In general, the playoff team cluster had a higher proportion of forwards from role F3, while the proportions of F1 and F2 were lower than the corresponding roles for the non-playoff cluster. There did not seem to be any noticeable differences between the two hierarchical clusters with respect to F4, as most teams had few players in this role. Among defenders, the playoff teams tended to have higher proportions of role D1 and fewer players of role D2 and D3. Conversely, D2 and D3 were more common among the non-playoff teams, which consequently implies a lower proportion of D1. For the incorrectly clustered teams some additional information may shed light on how they were clustered. In particular, by contrasting the Dallas Stars and Vegas Golden Knights we note a point differential of 4 in favor of Dallas, while Dallas scored 29 fewer goals than Vegas. This could indicate that Vegas was more offensively capable but less consistent. Both teams concede the same number of goals. For the New York Rangers the offensive capabilities were league average, as their goals scored ranked 16th out of 32 teams but they had 2nd fewest goals conceded, which can be attributed to their goaltender Igor Shesterkin who was voted the top goalie during the season. Finally, the Anaheim Ducks had an even distribution of roles and thus may be closer in distance to many teams.

7   Conclusion

In this paper we have proposed a novel method for quantifying player roles in ice hockey from a large set of performance indicators and player data using fuzzy c-means. We also investigated the application of comparative contract evaluation for the comparison of salary and player role, which can be used as a component in decision-making regarding contract negotiation and player acquisition. Moreover, an investigation of the relation between player roles and team success gave insight into what roles may provide additional success for a team.

Some limitations are worth mentioning. The data upon which this study is based is not bias-free and does not cover all events that occur in an ice hockey game. This is particularly evident for evaluating the defensive contribution of players. In regard to the contract evaluation, it is dependent on the chosen distance metric and number of neighbors. For instance, by choosing the maximum number of neighbors the league's highest paid players are deemed the most overrated. In addition, the highest paid players in the league cannot be underpaid, as there is nobody or very few paid more than them. Lastly, there is the possibility that the team that a player plays for may be a latent factor unaccounted for in this analysis, since a player's style of play may differ between teams and their performance may also be affected.

An extension of this work could be to include variables not available in the data used here that can further distinguish between player roles, e.g., passes and zone entries. Our method could easily be extended to capture these new variables. Additionally, by analyzing multiple seasons the results would also highlight changes in performance and role over a player's career. This method can also be generalized and applied to other leagues around the world, as the style of play may differ between leagues.

References

1. Aalbers, B., Van Haaren, J.: Distinguishing between roles of football players in play-by-play match event data. In: Brefeld, U., Davis, J., Van Haaren, J., Zimmermann, A. (eds.) MLSA 2018. LNCS, vol. 11330, pp. 31–41. Springer, Cham (2018). https://doi.org/10.1007/978-3-030-17274-9_3
2. Assent, I.: Clustering high dimensional data. Wiley Interdisc. Rev. Data Min. Knowl. Discov. **2**(4), 340–350 (2012). https://doi.org/10.1002/widm.1062
3. Bezdek, J.C.: Pattern Recognition With Fuzzy Objective Function Algorithms. Springer, New York (1981). https://doi.org/10.1007/978-1-4757-0450-1
4. Bezdek, J.C., Ehrlich, R., Full, W.: FCM: the fuzzy c-means clustering algorithm. Comput. Geosci. **10**(2–3), 191–203 (1984). https://doi.org/10.1016/0098-3004(84)90020-7
5. Campello, R.J., Hruschka, E.R.: A fuzzy extension of the silhouette width criterion for cluster analysis. Fuzzy Sets Syst. **157**(21), 2858–2875 (2006). https://doi.org/10.1016/j.fss.2006.07.006
6. Chan, T.C., Cho, J.A., Novati, D.C.: Quantifying the contribution of NHL player types to team performance. Interfaces **42**(2), 131–145 (2012). https://doi.org/10.1287/inte.1110.0612
7. Dave, R.N.: Validating fuzzy partitions obtained through c-shells clustering. Pattern Recogn. Lett. **17**(6), 613–623 (1996). https://doi.org/10.1016/0167-8655(96)00026-8
8. Dembele, D., Kastner, P.: Fuzzy C-means method for clustering microarray data. Bioinformatics **19**(8), 973–980 (2003). https://doi.org/10.1093/bioinformatics/btg119

9. Dunn, J.: A fuzzy relative of the isodata process and its use in detecting compact well-separated clusters. J. Cybern. **3**(3), 32–57 (1973). https://doi.org/10.1080/01969727308546046

10. Felmet, G.: Ice hockey. In: Krutsch, W., Mayr, H.O., Musahl, V., Della Villa, F., Tscholl, P.M., Jones, H. (eds.) Injury and Health Risk Management in Sports: A Guide to Decision Making, pp. 485–489. Springer, Heidelberg (2020). https://doi.org/10.1007/978-3-662-60752-7_74

11. Ferraro, M.B., Giordani, P.: A toolbox for fuzzy clustering using the R programming language. Fuzzy Sets Syst. **279**, 1–16 (2015). https://doi.org/10.1016/j.fss.2015.05.001

12. Glorfeld, L.W.: An improvement on Horn's parallel analysis methodology for selecting the correct number of factors to retain. Educ. Psychol. Measur. **55**(3), 377–393 (1995). https://doi.org/10.1177/0013164495055003002

13. Horn, J.L.: A rationale and test for the number of factors in factor analysis. Psychometrika **30**(2), 179–185 (1965). https://doi.org/10.1007/BF02289447

14. Lefebvre, J.S., Martin, L.J., Côté, J., Cowburn, I.: Investigating the process through which National Hockey League Player Development Coaches 'develop' athletes: an exploratory qualitative analysis. J. Appl. Sport Psychol. **34**(1), 47–66 (2022). https://doi.org/10.1080/10413200.2019.1688893

15. Miyamoto, S., Ichihashi, H., Honda, K.: Algorithms for Fuzzy Clustering. Springer, Heidelberg (2008). https://doi.org/10.1007/978-3-540-78737-2

16. Pakhira, M.K., Bandyopadhyay, S., Maulik, U.: Validity index for crisp and fuzzy clusters. Pattern Recogn. **37**(3), 487–501 (2004). https://doi.org/10.1016/j.patcog.2003.06.005

17. Peres-Neto, P.R., Jackson, D.A., Somers, K.M.: How many principal components? Stopping rules for determining the number of non-trivial axes revisited. Comput. Stat. Data Anal. **49**(4), 974–997 (2005). https://doi.org/10.1016/j.csda.2004.06.015

18. Rousseeuw, P.J.: Silhouettes: a graphical aid to the interpretation and validation of cluster analysis. J. Comput. Appl. Math. **20**, 53–65 (1987). https://doi.org/10.1016/0377-0427(87)90125-7

19. Sattari, A., Johansson, U., Wilderoth, E., Jakupovic, J., Larsson-Green, P.: The interpretable representation of football player roles based on passing/receiving patterns. In: Brefeld, U., Davis, J., Van Haaren, J., Zimmermann, A. (eds.) MLSA 2021. CCIS, vol. 1571, pp. 62–76. Springer, Cham (2022). https://doi.org/10.1007/978-3-031-02044-5_6

20. Schwämmle, V., Jensen, O.N.: A simple and fast method to determine the parameters for fuzzy c-means cluster analysis. Bioinformatics **26**(22), 2841–2848 (2010). https://doi.org/10.1093/bioinformatics/btq534

21. Vincent, C.B., Eastman, B.: Defining the style of play in the NHL: an application of cluster analysis. J. Quant. Anal. Sports **5**(1) (2009). https://doi.org/10.2202/1559-0410.1133

22. Vollman, R.: Hockey Abstract Presents... Stat Shot: The Ultimate Guide to Hockey Analytics. ECW Press (2016)

23. Wang, W., Zhang, Y.: On fuzzy cluster validity indices. Fuzzy Sets Syst. **158**(19), 2095–2117 (2007). https://doi.org/10.1016/j.fss.2007.03.004

24. Wierzchoń, S.T., Kłopotek, M.A.: Modern Algorithms of Cluster Analysis. Springer, Cham (2018). https://doi.org/10.1007/978-3-319-69308-8

Elite Rugby League Players' Signature Movement Patterns and Position Prediction

Victor Elijah Adeyemo[1,2,3,4](✉)(iD), Anna Palczewska[1](iD), Ben Jones[2,3,4,5,6](iD), and Dan Weaving[2](iD)

[1] School of Built Environment, Engineering and Computing, Leeds Beckett University, Leeds, UK
{v.adeyemo,a.palczewska}@leedsbeckett.ac.uk
[2] Carnegie School of Sport, Leeds Beckett University, Leeds, UK
{b.jones,d.a.weaving}@leedsbeckett.ac.uk
[3] England Performance Unit, Rugby Football League, Leeds, UK
[4] Leeds Rhinos Rugby League Club, Leeds, UK
[5] School of Science and Technology, University of New England, Armidale, Australia
[6] The University of Cape Town and the Sports Science Institute of South Africa, Cape Town, South Africa

Abstract. Although sports on-field activities occur sequentially, traditional performance indicators quantify players' activities without regard to their sequential nature. Nowadays, movement patterns are used to sequentially quantify players' activities to understand match demands on players. However, the specific behavioural (i.e., signature) movement patterns of rugby league players per playing position remain unknown and the prediction of rugby league players into all nine playing positions based on their movement patterns is largely unexplored. Hence, this study identified the signature movement patterns of elite rugby league players per position and revealed the contribution of movement patterns towards the prediction of players into positions during the 2019 and 2020 seasons. Varying numbers of signature movement patterns were identified across playing positions with centres having the highest number of signature patterns (i.e. 1241). Random Forest best predicted elite rugby league players' positions at 73.41% accuracy, 0.74 recall, and 0.73 f1-score and precision scores based on movement patterns relative frequency values and top contributing movement patterns were identified. Therefore, we recommend sports stakeholders recognize the signature and contributing movement pattern of players per playing position while making decisions regarding training programmes, talent identification and recruitment.

The authors would like to acknowledge The Rugby Football League (RFL) for the access to GPS data.

Keywords: Signature Movement Patterns · Rugby Football League ·
Players Position Prediction · Training Optimisation · Talent
Recruitment and Identification

1   Introduction

Sporting events [9] happen sequentially and players' completed activities (i.e.,
external load) during matches or training are collected in a time-series format.
However, external loads are widely quantified and analysed without regard to
the sequential nature of sporting events [4] through the use of either technical-
tactical indicators (expertly coded by video-notational analysts from match
videos) or physical indicators (collected via a micro-technology unit containing accelerometer, magnetometer and or gyroscope worn by players). Few studies [11,12] have now quantified external loads with respect to their sequential
nature of occurrences - player movement profiling. Player movement profiling [11]
involves quantifying players' external loads through the extraction of sequential
movement patterns (i.e., exact sequential on-field activities) to understand match
demands and uncover how external loads were accumulated towards replicating
match characteristics for training aspects.

Movement patterns are identified subsets of discrete movement activities
performed by players. Discrete movement sequences (for a player) are a set of
time-series concatenation of discretized velocity, acceleration and turning angle
values without periods of athlete's inactivity. The study [12] is the first to identify players' movement patterns from discrete movement sequences formulated
from Global Positioning System (GPS) data by developing a better and more
stable framework, called Sequential Movement Pattern-mining (SMP). An example of an extracted movement pattern is "NNNNN", (denoted as [Run-Neutral-
Straight] × 5 based on study [11] or denoted as [Sprint-Deceleration-Backwards]
× 5 based on study [12]).

In study [5], the SMP framework [12] was utilised to quantify the difference between three competition levels of the Rugby Football League based on
movement units obtained from decomposed movement patterns, through the use
of linear discriminant analysis algorithm. However, unique movement patterns
were not identified for each competition level which may be due to SMP framework [12] limitations of identifying a few movement patterns which must be the
longest common movement patterns within each of twenty-five clusters of similar
discrete movement sequences. This type of movement pattern contains omission
of adjacent movement activities and may not represent exact match characteristics required for training aspects. Additionally, other movement patterns that
are not the longest common subsequences but could be useful and of interest for
training aspects are discarded by the SMP framework.

The study [2] formulated and developed a sequential pattern mining algorithm as a solution to the SMP framework limitations. The developed algorithm,
l-length closed contiguous sequential pattern mining (LCCspm), was used to
extract user-defined lengths of frequent closed contiguous movement patterns

from sets of discrete movement sequences of elite rugby league players as well as frequent closed contiguous match events patterns performed by national team players that participated in the men's FIFA 2018 world cup. The algorithm was reported to extract a user-defined length of closed contiguous patterns faster, scaled better and used lesser memory than other existing related algorithms. More so, a large number of frequent player movement patterns and match-event patterns were reportedly discovered by LCCspm.

The study [3] quantified elite rugby league players' external loads via three distinct types of obtainable movement patterns, used the sets of extracted movement patterns as independent variables to classify rugby league players into two tactically distinct playing positions (i.e., hookers and wingers), and reported LCCspm algorithm [2] closed contiguous movement patterns as the best type of patterns for profiling players into playing positions. However, the specific behavioural (i.e., signature) movement patterns of rugby league players belonging to each position remain unknown and also the prediction of rugby league players into all nine playing positions based on their movement patterns is largely unexplored. Identifying the signature movement patterns and the classification of players into playing positions is important for training optimisation for the overall team and player performance improvement as well as for talent identification and recruitment among others. Therefore, this study aims to uncover the signature movement patterns of elite rugby league players for each nine playing positions and use movement patterns to predict the playing positions of elite rugby league players while investigating the contribution of movement patterns towards the prediction.

2   Method

2.1   GPS Data, Collection and Processing

The method for processing GPS data into discrete movement sequences as published [12] by was followed. Each movement unit and its encoded character is published on [12] page 165. Two seasons (2019 and 2020) worth of GPS data of 217 professional Rugby League players who participated in 338 fixtures were collected using the micro-sensor units including global positioning systems [12] (Optimeye S5, Catapult Sports, Melbourne, Australia) sampling at 10 Hz and was processed into sets of discrete movement sequences. This study only considered players who played at one fixed position throughout the seasons. The distribution of the players across playing positions was 31 centres, 8 Five-Eighths, 22 Full-Backs, 26 Half-Backs, 22 Hookers, 8 Loose-Forwards, 47 Prop-Forwards, 25 SecondRows and 28 Wingers. Collected GPS data were processed into a total of 4,640 sets of discrete movement sequences at the player-per-fixture level. This study got the approval of the University Ethics Committee and obtained written informed consent from the organisation representing the participants.

2.2 Signature Movement Patterns Mining

This study used the LCCspm [2] to extract a user-defined length of frequent closed contiguous patterns from sets of discrete movement sequences. The parameters of LCCspm were set to 20 (i.e., 2 s time frame), and the support was set to 5% (to include both low and high-frequency movement patterns), to extract movement patterns. For each playing position, signature movement patterns were derived by analysing extracted movement patterns to identify those performed only by players within the playing position. Afterwards, signature movement patterns of each position were visualised based on their frequency across all fixtures.

2.3 Playing Position Prediction and Feature Contribution

To predict the playing positions of players and investigate the contribution of movement patterns for the prediction, the union of all extracted movement patterns was computed and used as the set of independent variables to generate a dataset for classification modelling. An observation in the generated dataset represents a player per fixture. The dataset was populated with "relative frequency" values (i.e., the count of performed unique movement patterns divided by the total number of discrete movement sequences per match) or zeros. We refer to this data as "original" dataset.

Due to the class imbalance problem found in the original dataset and to investigate the influence of the total number of player-per-fixture observations toward position prediction, both oversampling of minority playing positions and undersampling of majority playing positions [6] were considered. The Synthetic Minority Oversampling TEchnique (SMOTE) method was applied to oversample seven minority playing positions and referred to the generated dataset as oversampled dataset. Prop-forward and Centre players have 898 and 779 observations respectively, which were not oversampled. Five-eighths, fullbacks and loose-forwards have 188, 378 and 230 observations, which were oversampled at 275%, 100% and 220%, generating 705, 756, and 736 SMOTE observations respectively. Half-backs, hookers, second-rows and wingers have 619, 499, 513, and 536 observations, which were oversampled at 15%, 50%, 50%, and 35%, generating 711, 748, 769 and 723 SMOTE observations respectively. Also, the Random Under-Sampler (RUS) method undersampled all classes except the minority playing positions (i.e., Five-Eighths) and referred to the generated dataset as the undersampled dataset. In total, three (i.e. original, over-sampled and under-sampled) datasets were developed as input for classification modelling. The original dataset has 4640 observations, the oversampled dataset has 6827 observations and the undersampled dataset has 1692 observations

This study utilized six (6) machine learning supervised algorithms for the classification of players into playing positions. These supervised machine learning methods were selected because they are based on different learning schemes. All classifiers were developed using the 10-fold cross-validation technique [1] and evaluated by accuracy and macro averages of precision, recall and f1-score. The selected algorithms are: Decision Tree, Gaussian Naive Bayes, Random Forest,

Logistic Regression, Multi-Layered Perceptron (MLP), and K-Nearest Neighbors. The default parameters for each algorithm were used except MLP whose hidden layer sizes were set to 1000, 500, 250, 125, 50 and 25. Also, SHapley Additive exPlanation (SHAP) values technique via "kernelExplainer" [7] was applied to identify the contribution of each unique movement pattern towards the classification of elite rugby league players into playing positions based on the most accurate classification model. The machine learning classification algorithms and SHAP value technique are all implemented in the Scikit-learn [10] and SHAP [8] python modules.

3 Results and Discussion

3.1 Signature Movement Patterns

Centres: 3,307 movement patterns were performed by centres, where only 1241 (approximately 37.5%) were uniquely performed. The number of times each of the 1241 movement patterns was performed by all centres varied from 1 to 365,692. The signature movement patterns performed by elite rugby league centres are visualised in Fig. 1a. An example is "eeeeeea" denoted as [Walk-Neutral-Straight] × 6 and Walk-Deceleration-Straight.

Five Eighths: 1,199 movement patterns were performed by five-eighths, where only 13 (approximately 1.08%) were uniquely performed. The number of times each of the 13 movement patterns was performed by all five-eighths varied from 6 to 56,405. The signature movement patterns performed by elite rugby league five-eighths are visualised in Fig. 1b. An example is "rqqqqqqq" denoted as Jog-Neutral-Acute-Change and [Jog-Neutral-Straight] × 7.

Full Backs: 1,561 movement patterns were performed by full-backs, where 122 (approximately 7.82%) were uniquely performed. The number of times each of the 122 movement patterns was performed by all full-backs varied from 1 to 96,574. The signature movement patterns performed by elite rugby league centres are visualised in Fig. 1c. An example is "yyyyzyyy" denoted as [Run-Deceleration-Straight] × 4, Run-Deceleration-Acute-Change and [Run-Deceleration-Straight] × 3.

Half Backs: 2,881 movement patterns were performed by half-backs, where only 612 (approximately 21.24%) were uniquely performed. The number of times each of the 612 movement patterns was performed by all half-backs varied from 1 to 169,958. The signature movement patterns performed by elite rugby league centres are visualised in Fig. 1d. An example is "eeeefeeeeeeeeee" denoted as [Walk-Neutral-Straight] × 4, Walk-Neutral-Acute-Change and [Walk-Neutral-Straight] × 9.

Hookers: 1,282 movement patterns were performed by hookers, where only 300 (approximately 23.4%) were uniquely performed. The number of times each of the 300 movement patterns was performed by all hookers varied from 1 to 12,604.

The signature movement patterns performed by elite rugby league hookers are visualised in Fig. 1e. An example is "vwvv" denoted as Jog-Acceleration-Acute-Change, Jog-Acceleration-Large-Change and [Jog-Acceleration-Acute-Change] × 2.

Loose Forwards: 1,177 movement patterns were performed by loose forwards, where only 13 (approximately 1.11%) were uniquely performed. The number of times each of the 13 movement patterns was performed by all loose-forwards varied from 4 to 374,428. The signature movement patterns performed by elite rugby league loose forwards are visualised in Fig. 1f. An example is "zznmm" denoted [Run-Deceleration-Acute-Change] × 2, Jog-Deceleration-Acute-Change and [Jog-Deceleration-Straight] × 2.

Prop Forwards: 2,712 movement patterns were performed by prop forwards, where only 771 (approximately 28.43%) were uniquely performed. The number of times each of the 771 movement patterns was performed by all prop-forwards varied from 1 to 145,249. The signature movement patterns performed by elite rugby league prop forwards are visualised in Fig. 1g. An example is "mmmmma" denoted as [Jog-Deceleration-Straight] × 5 and Walk-Deceleration-Straight.

Second Rows: 1,967 movement patterns were performed by second rows, where only 194 (approximately 9.86%) were uniquely performed. The number of times each of the 194 movement patterns was performed by all second rows varied from 1 to 115,168. The signature movement patterns performed by elite rugby league second rows are visualised in Fig. 1h. An example is "KKKKKLKK" denoted as [Sprint-Deceleration-Straight] × 5, Sprint-Deceleration-Acute-Change and [Sprint-Deceleration-Straight] × 2

Wingers: 3,174 movement patterns were performed by wingers, where only 1066 (approximately 33.59%) were uniquely performed. The number of times each of the 1,066 movement patterns was performed by all wingers varied from 1 to 28,830. The signature movement patterns performed by elite rugby league wingers are visualised in Fig. 1i. An example is "GGSSSSSSS" denoted as [Run-Acceleration-Straight] × 2 and [Sprint-Acceleration-Straight] × 7.

This study was able to identify signature movement patterns of elite rugby league for each playing position, using closed contiguous movement patterns, as opposed to the study [5] that did not identify signature movement patterns of elite rugby league players for each competition level, using longest common subsequence movement patterns.

3.2 Playing Position Prediction

It is noteworthy to point out that the default probability of correctly predicting the playing position of players per fixture among the nine positions is computed as (100/9) % i.e., 11.11%. The performance evaluation of all six (6) classifiers fitted on the original, oversampled and undersampled datasets were obtained (Table 1). A set of 7,167 movement patterns were obtained as the union of all

(a) Centres

(b) FiveEighths

(c) Full-Backs

(d) Half-Backs

(e) Hookers

(f) Loose Forwards

(g) Prop Forwards

(h) SecondRows

(i) Wingers

Fig. 1. Signature Movement Patterns of Elite RFL players per Playing Positions

Table 1. Prediction Accuracies of Elite RFL Playing Positions

Classifier	Precision	Recall	F1_Score	Sampling Method	Variables Value	Accuracy (%)
Decision Tree	0.32	0.31	0.31	N/A	Relative Frequency	33.99
Gaussian Naïve Bayes	0.24	0.16	0.1			10.41
Random Forest	0.53	0.43	0.44			51.9
Logistic Regression	0.53	0.45	0.46			53.53
MLP	0.51	0.49	0.49			53.79
5-NN	0.5	0.46	0.46			48.36
Decision Tree	0.09	0.09	0.09	Random Undersampler	Relative Frequency	9.1
Gaussian Naïve Bayes	0.11	0.12	0.07			11.58
Random Forest	0.1	0.1	0.1			10.17
Logistic Regression	0.12	0.13	0.12			12.41
MLP	0.1	0.12	0.07			11.64
5-NN	0.12	0.12	0.11			12.0
Decision Tree	0.46	0.46	0.46	SMOTE	Relative Frequency	45.51
Gaussian Naïve Bayes	0.38	0.23	0.18			22.09
Random Forest	**0.73**	**0.74**	**0.73**			**73.41**
Logistic Regression	0.6	0.61	0.6			60.37
MLP	0.73	0.73	0.73			72.85
5-NN	0.66	0.65	0.61			63.6

Table 2. Top-25 Contributing Movement Patterns for RFL Position Prediction

Ranking	Centres	Five Eighth	Full Backs	Half Backs	Hookers	Loose Forwards	Prop Forwards	Second Rows	Wingers
1	ij	HH	SS	ij	iij	ijj	ijj	HH	ijj
2	ijj	GH	jii	ii	ef	ij	HH	ijj	iij
3	jji	ijj	ij	iij	ij	iij	ij	ij	ij
4	iij	jii	HII	GH	iii	HH	jii	iij	ji
5	HH	ii	iij	ijj	ijj	iji	SS	GH	iji
6	ii	jjj	GH	jii	ii	GH	iij	iji	jjj
7	fb	HG	iii	HH	fb	jjj	GH	jii	HH
8	GH	ff	jji	jji	mq	ii	jji	ji	jii
9	ff	iij	ej	HG	iji	jii	iii	jji	SS
10	jii	iji	iji	jj	jjj	iii	iiij	mq	ab
11	ji	iii	iij	ji	HH	jji	iji	jj	GH
12	jjj	ji	mq	jjj	jji	ji	ji	ii	ff
13	jj	jji	ji	iii	GG	mq	jj	uv	vu
14	HG	ab	jj	jij	HG	no	uvv	fb	uv
15	fa	uuuu	ii	vuv	ji	ba	jjj	ej	ii
16	iiij	ij	uuu	iji	vuvv	uuu	ff	ef	jj
17	iii	vuuv	uuvu	iiij	uuvu	iiij	vuvvu	GG	fb
18	uv	bb	jjj	GG	ff	HG	bbb	iii	jji
19	jij	uv	vvuv	vvu	jii	vuuv	HG	no	uuuv
20	uuu	uuv	HGG	mq	SS	ff	eff	vvu	iii
21	iji	jj	vuv	GGG	ur	vuvv	ii	ff	uuuu
22	mq	qu	ff	uuu	qu	fb	HGG	iiii	uq
23	iu	jij	GGG	uu	jj	jj	mq	uvv	mq
24	vuuvu	GG	jf	bbb	ej	qq	ab	ab	vvu
25	ef	mq	efe	SS	vuv	vu	uvuuv	jij	no

extracted movement patterns across playing positions and it was used as independent variables for classification modelling.

The Logistic Regression classifier, fitted on the original dataset, had an accuracy of 53.53%, 0.53 precision, 0.45 recall and 0.46 F1-score for predicting players into nine RFL playing positions. However, the MLP classification model achieved a maximum accuracy of 53.79%, 0.49 recall and F1 score respectively and 0.51 precision score. Five of the six classification models achieved an accuracy higher than the default prediction probability except for the Gaussian Naive Bayes. The low performance of the Naive Bayes algorithm can be associated with its naive assumption of independent variables whereas the independent variables are high-dimensional and there maybe be a correlation among some.

The prediction of RFL players into playing positions, using the undersampled dataset, had a minimum accuracy of 9.1%, 0.09 precision, F1-score and recall scores as achieved by the Decision tree classifier. The maximum accuracy of 12.41%, precision and F1-score of 0.12 and recall of 0.13 was achieved by the Logistic Regression classifier. The prediction accuracies of all classifiers on the undersampled dataset were lower than the default prediction probability in two cases (Decision tree and Random Forest models).

The prediction of RFL players into playing positions, using the oversampled dataset, had a minimum accuracy of 22.09%, 0.38 precision, 0.23 recall and 0.18 F1-score as achieved by the Gaussian Naive Bayes classifier. The classifier with the maximum performance is Random Forest with an accuracy of 73.41%, 0.73 F1-score, 0.73 precision and 0.74 recall scores (Table 1). Four of the six classifiers had accuracies above 50% except for the Decision tree and Gaussian Naive Bayes classifiers. Decision tree low performance (i.e. underfitting) can also be attributed to a large number of independent variables as the classifier decision splits will be based on numerous variables.

A comparative analysis of the prediction models revealed the individual prediction accuracies of the classifiers were better on the original dataset and best on the oversampled dataset. For example, the Random Forest model had an accuracy of 51.9% on the original dataset, 10.17% accuracy on the undersampled dataset and 73.41% accuracy on the oversampled dataset. Additionally, this study's Random Forest 73.41% accuracy for predicting elite rugby league players into nine playing positions is higher than the classification accuracy of 70.1% reported by [13] for classifying elite junior Australian football players into midfield, defence, forwards or rucks positional groups using technical performance indicators.

SHAP values revealed the rank and contribution of each unique movement pattern. From Table 2, the top-25 most contributing movement patterns for the prediction of RFL players' varied across playing positions. This suggests that each unique movement pattern contributed more or less information depending on the rugby league players' playing positions. For example, the movement pattern "mq" is the twenty-second most contributing movement pattern for classifying players into the centres. However, it is the twenty-fifth and twentieth most contributing movement pattern for classifying players into the five-eighths and half-backs respectively. Additionally, there are featured contributing movement patterns(s) which are not present across playing positions, such as movement pattern "SS" featured by half-backs, prop-forward and wingers.

4   Conclusion and Future Works

Through the application of data mining and machine learning algorithms on sport-related big data (i.e. two seasons' worth of GPS data), this study conducted the first attempt to quantify players' external loads via movement patterns towards revealing the signature movements of each elite rugby league players' playing positions as well as predicting players' positions based on movement patterns. Signature movement patterns of each playing position were discovered which is essentially useful for training customisation, talent identification and performance assessment. Similarly, movement patterns can predict the playing position of rugby league players at 73% accuracy which may help with young-talent pathway development. An important future work for this study is the reduction of movement patterns used as independent variables for predicting players' positions via feature selection and to improve the overall prediction accuracy. In addition, the establishment of movement patterns for performance variability assessment is another important future work to be considered.

References

1. Adeyemo, V.E., Balogun, A.O., Mojeed, H.A., Akande, N.O., Adewole, K.S.: Ensemble-based logistic model trees for website phishing detection. In: Anbar, M., Abdullah, N., Manickam, S. (eds.) ACeS 2020. CCIS, vol. 1347, pp. 627–641. Springer, Singapore (2020). https://doi.org/10.1007/978-981-33-6835-4_41
2. Adeyemo, V.E., Palczewska, A., Jones, B.: LCCspm: l-length closed contiguous sequential patterns mining algorithm to find frequent athlete movement patterns from GPS. In: 2021 20th IEEE International Conference on Machine Learning and Applications (ICMLA), pp. 455–460. IEEE (2021)
3. Adeyemo, V.E., Palczewska, A., Jones, B., Weaving, D.: Identification of pattern mining algorithm for rugby league players positional groups separation based on movement patterns. arXiv preprint arXiv:2302.14058 (2023)
4. Chambers, R., Gabbett, T.J., Cole, M.H., Beard, A.: The use of wearable microsensors to quantify sport-specific movements. Sports Med. 45(7), 1065–1081 (2015). https://doi.org/10.1007/s40279-015-0332-9
5. Collins, N., White, R., Palczewska, A., Weaving, D., Dalton-Barron, N., Jones, B.: Moving beyond velocity derivatives; using global positioning system data to extract sequential movement patterns at different levels of rugby league match-play. Eur. J. Sport Sci. 23(2), 201–209 (2023)
6. Lemaître, G., Nogueira, F., Aridas, C.K.: Imbalanced-learn: a python toolbox to tackle the curse of imbalanced datasets in machine learning. J. Mach. Learn. Res. 18(1), 559–563 (2017)
7. Lundberg, S.M., Lee, S.I.: A unified approach to interpreting model predictions. In: Advances in Neural Information Processing Systems, vol. 30 (2017)

8. Lundberg, S.M., Lee, S.I.: A unified approach to interpreting model predictions. In: Guyon, I., et al. (eds.) Advances in Neural Information Processing Systems, vol. 30, pp. 4765–4774. Curran Associates, Inc. (2017). http://papers.nips.cc/paper/7062-a-unified-approach-to-interpreting-model-predictions.pdf

9. O'Donoghue, P.: An Introduction to Performance Analysis of Sport. Routledge, London (2014)

10. Pedregosa, F., et al.: Scikit-learn: machine learning in Python. J. Mach. Learn. Res. **12**, 2825–2830 (2011)

11. Sweeting, A.J., Aughey, R.J., Cormack, S.J., Morgan, S.: Discovering frequently recurring movement sequences in team-sport athlete spatiotemporal data. J. Sports Sci. **35**(24), 2439–2445 (2017). https://doi.org/10.1080/02640414.2016.1273536. pMID: 28282752

12. White, R., Palczewska, A., Weaving, D., Collins, N., Jones, B.: Sequential movement pattern-mining (SMP) in field-based team-sport: a framework for quantifying spatiotemporal data and improve training specificity? J. Sports Sci. **40**(2), 164–174 (2022)

13. Woods, C.T., Veale, J., Fransen, J., Robertson, S., Collier, N.F.: Classification of playing position in elite junior Australian football using technical skill indicators. J. Sports Sci. **3**(1), 97–103 (2018)

Boat Speed Prediction in SailGP

Benedek Zentai[1(✉)] and László Toka[1,2]

[1] Budapest University of Technology and Economics, Budapest, Hungary
benedek.zentai@edu.bme.hu
[2] ELKH-BME Cloud Applications Research Group, Budapest, Hungary
toka.laszlo@vik.bme.hu

Abstract. The significance of data analysis in high-performance sports has largely increased in recent years offering opportunities for further exploration using machine learning techniques. As a pioneer work in the academic community, our work showcases the power of data-driven approaches in enhancing performance and decision-making at high-performance sailing events. Specifically, we explore the application of data mining techniques on the dataset collected at a high-performance sailing event in Bermuda in 2021. By analyzing data from Race 4, the study aims to gain valuable insights into the relationship between variables such as wind speed, wind direction, foil usage, and daggerboard adjustments, and their impact on boat speed. Various prediction models, including Gradient Boosting, Random Forest, and a stacked model, were employed and evaluated using performance metrics like R2 score and mean squared error. The results demonstrate the models' ability to accurately predict boat speed. These findings can be utilized to refine race strategies, optimize sail and rudder settings, and improve overall performance in SailGP races. Future plans include collaboration with SailGP to work with larger datasets and integrate the models into live racing scenarios.

Keywords: Sailing analytics · boat speed · prediction

1 Introduction

SailGP [3] has emerged as a thrilling and revolutionary sailing championship that showcases the pinnacle of high-performance sailing. One of the most captivating aspects of SailGP is the sheer speed and adrenaline experienced by the boats as they harness the power of the wind and glide above the water's surface using foiling technology. Foiling, a groundbreaking innovation, allows the boats to achieve remarkable speeds and push the boundaries of what was once thought possible in sailing. By shedding light on the intricate relationship between boat speed and the various influencing factors, this project aims to contribute to the broader knowledge and understanding of high-performance sailing. The findings and predictive models derived from this project hold the potential to aid sailors, teams, and race strategists in making informed decisions and optimizing their

U. Brefeld et al. (Eds.): MLSA 2023, CCIS 2035, pp. 155–164, 2024.
https://doi.org/10.1007/978-3-031-53833-9_13

performance on the water. As the world of sailing continues to embrace data-driven approaches, this project serves as a stepping stone towards leveraging the power of data analysis in unlocking the secrets to success in SailGP and other high-stakes sailing competitions.

In conducting a thorough review of the state-of-the-art literature in the field of sailing analytics, it became evident that there is a significant gap in research specifically focused on SailGP. Despite the growing interest in data-driven approaches and analytics in various sports, including sailing [7], there is a dearth of information and studies specifically addressing sailing analytics within the context of SailGP. This absence of literature indicates an untapped potential for exploring and leveraging the power of data analysis in the realm of high-performance sailing. The lack of available research in sailing analytics for SailGP suggests an opportunity to pioneer innovative approaches and methodologies tailored to this unique sailing competition.

Although specific information about the data mining process employed by the teams in SailGP is not readily available, it can be assumed that data mining plays a crucial role in enhancing their performance [1,2,8].

2   Background

In the context of SailGP, several key terminologies play a vital role in understanding the dynamics of the sport. Foiling refers to the technique of raising the catamaran's hulls out of the water using hydrofoils, which are positioned beneath each hull. These hydrofoils, commonly known as daggerboards, provide lift and stability to the boat. Additionally, foils can also be present on the rudders, which are horizontal fins located at the stern of each hull. These rudder foils significantly contribute to the overall lift and control of the catamaran, amplifying its maneuverability and maximizing its speed on the water.

Regarding the sails, the boats are equipped with innovative wingsails, which are designed to resemble the wings of an aircraft. These wingsails are crucial to the foiling technique and provide stability and aerodynamic efficiency to harness the wind's power effectively. The innovative design of SailGP boats enables them to achieve remarkable speeds, soaring above the water at exhilarating velocities. This technology, combined with the skillful navigation of the sailors, unlocks a new level of performance and competitiveness in the world of sailing.

3   Data Set

Through the use of advanced sensors and onboard data collection systems, teams gather vast amounts of data during training sessions and races. The SailGP dataset we used in this project provides a comprehensive and detailed record of a single race, spanning approximately 12 min. What makes this dataset particularly valuable is the fact that it captures data at a granularity of one record per second, offering a high-resolution view of the race dynamics and performance. With nearly 60 features available, encompassing various aspects of boat speed, wind speed, rudder, daggerboard, jib (headsail), and other critical components, the dataset offers a wealth of numerical information for analysis and modeling. However, there are also non-numeric features present, including boat names and maneuver labels. It is worth noting that the data has a high temporal resolution.

However, obtaining a dataset of this complexity presented significant challenges due to the strict confidentiality surrounding SailGP data. As the information is considered highly sensitive and confidential, gaining access to such a dataset required extensive effort and collaboration. To overcome this obstacle, several email communications were initiated with the top teams involved in SailGP, seeking their assistance and cooperation in acquiring the necessary data. The process involved establishing trust, explaining the project objectives, and assuring the teams of the utmost confidentiality and data protection. Through persistent communication and the cooperation of the teams, access to this intricate and valuable dataset was ultimately secured. The complexity and sensitivity of the data within the SailGP dataset make it a rarity in the field of sailing analytics.

The inclusion of various units of measurement, such as degrees and knots, further adds to the intricacy of the dataset. The diverse nature of the features and the high temporal resolution provide a unique opportunity to gain deep insights into the race dynamics, team performance, and the impact of different components on the overall outcome. By successfully navigating the challenges associated with data confidentiality and secrecy, we have been able to leverage the richness of the SailGP dataset, allowing for detailed analysis, modeling, and valuable insights into the intricacies of high-performance sailing.

This dataset includes data from the Bermuda event in 2021, specifically Race 4 which took place on the second day of the event [9]. During this race, all the boats were competing to secure a spot in the final, where the top three teams from that weekend's event would face off.

4   Boat Speed Analysis

The components influencing boat speed are multifaceted and interconnected. Wind plays a crucial role, as teams must strategically harness its power to propel the boat forward. Efficient foiling techniques, where the boat is lifted out of the water by hydrofoils, can significantly increase speed by reducing drag. The optimal flying height of the boat, achieved through precise control of the foils, is critical to maximizing performance. The set of the daggerboard and the rudder directly affects the boat's stability and maneuverability. Adjusting these components allows sailors to optimize lift, resistance, and control, enabling them to navigate challenging racecourses effectively. Sails, such as the wingsail and jib, are pivotal in capturing wind energy and converting it into forward motion. The crew's position onboard also plays a vital role in boat speed, as their weight distribution can impact stability and balance (Fig. 1).

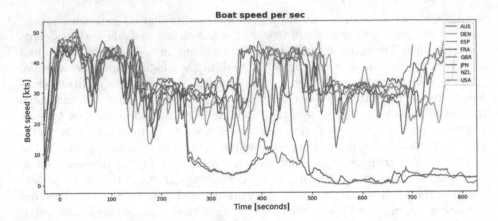

Fig. 1. This figure depicts the boat speed of each team recorded throughout the duration of the race. The data collection begins at T-30 s, and it is evident from the chart that every team endeavors to maximize their speed leading up to the start. Notably, during this phase and the initial leg, the teams exhibit their highest speeds, with team GBR reaching a remarkable 50.0 knots (92.6 km/h). The chart also reveals slight drops in speed during maneuvers and discernible variations in speed during upwind and downwind sections. It is worth noting that in this race, both team JPN and team USA encountered a collision during the first upwind leg, resulting in their withdrawal from the race.

Analyzing these components collectively provides valuable insights into how teams can enhance their boat speed. By leveraging data mining and machine learning techniques, patterns can be identified, and predictive models can be developed to optimize performance. This analysis enables teams to make data-driven decisions regarding sail trim, foil settings, crew positioning, and overall race strategy, ultimately giving them a competitive edge in the fast-paced and dynamic world of SailGP.

4.1   Unveiling the Key Component

The feature importance analysis offers valuable insights into the relative significance of different features within our boat speed regression model. We used random forest and gradient boosting regressor models to calculate feature importance, which is determined by the algorithms themselves, and subsequently, they are ranked based on their relative significance in predicting boat speed. These results shed light on the contributions of each feature to the model's predictive performance, allowing us to prioritize and focus on the most influential factors.

Among the features examined, the most influential feature was found to be ANGLE_DB_RAKE_LIM_DEG, with an importance score of 0.696855. This indicates that variations in the rake angle of the daggerboard have the most substantial impact on boat speed prediction. The rake angle is measured by assessing the inclination of the daggerboard in relation to the boat's hull. The measurement is taken at the leading edge or trailing edge of the daggerboard using specialized instruments or sensors. The rake angle is adjusted by either moving the daggerboard forwards or backwards, or by adjusting the angle of the daggerboard relative to the boat's hull. The daggerboard rake angle plays a crucial role in controlling the lift and drag forces acting on the boat, thereby directly influencing its speed and maneuverability [10].

Similarly, the feature that represents the angle of the rudder obtained a relatively high importance score of 0.114463. This suggests that differences in the rudder angle contribute significantly to boat speed variations. Precise and coordinated rudder adjustments can optimize the boat's trajectory and minimize drag, resulting in improved speed.

On the other hand, specific features indicating the average angle of the rudder and the cant angle of the daggerboard in a specific context exhibited lower importance scores of 0.034179 and 0.004883, and 0.001960, respectively. Cant refers to the angle at which the daggerboard is tilted or angled sideways from the vertical axis of the boat. While these features may have a lesser impact individually, they still contribute to the overall predictive performance of the model, albeit to a lesser extent.

The obtained feature importance results emphasize the importance of considering specific aspects of boat design and control mechanisms in predicting boat speed accurately. The prominence of features related to the daggerboard, platform length, and rudder adjustments underscores their critical role in optimizing performance. The final regression model was refined by removing irrelevant features. These findings provide valuable insights for understanding the factors that influence boat speed and can guide future efforts in performance enhancement and optimization within the context of sailing competitions like SailGP.

4.2   Random Forest Model

Random Forest regression is particularly well-suited for handling high-dimensional data and capturing complex relationships between features [5]. It can effectively handle both categorical and continuous variables, making it suitable for diverse datasets commonly found in boat speed prediction tasks. This ensemble approach helps to improve the robustness and accuracy of the model by combining multiple decision trees to make predictions. The random forest regression model employed in this project yielded promising results, demonstrating its effectiveness. The reported results are obtained using TimeSeriesSplit, a specialized form of cross-validation, tailored for datasets where the temporal order of the data is crucial [6]. TimeSeriesSplit ensures that during cross-validation the training and testing sets maintain the temporal sequence of the data, preventing any data leakage and preserving the integrity of the time series structure, and reflects the performance on the test sets. The model achieved an impressive R2 score of 0.94, indicating that approximately 94% of the variance in boat speed can be explained by the selected features. This high R2 score suggests a strong correlation between the predicted boat speed and the actual values.

Additionally, the mean squared error (MSE) for the random forest regression model was calculated to be 4.5. A lower MSE value indicates better model performance, as it represents reduced prediction errors. The MSE of 4.5 suggests that, on average, the predicted boat speed deviates by approximately 2.1 knots from the true values (Fig. 2).

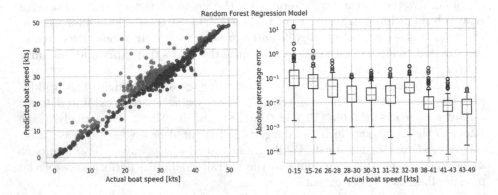

Fig. 2. This scatter plot provides a visual comparison between the actual boat speeds and the predicted boat speeds from the meta-model. The points on the plot are colored differently, indicating overestimation (red points) or correct/underestimation (blue points). The plot of the random forest regression reveals a concentration of predicted boat speeds around 30 knots (55.6 km/h). Notably, there is a tendency for overestimation within the range of 25 knots (46.3 km/h) to 30 knots (55.6 km/h). This observation suggests that the model tends to predict slightly higher boat speeds within this particular range. (Color figure online)

4.3   Gradient Boosted Model

The decision to utilize a gradient boosted regression model for predicting boat speed in this project is based on several advantageous characteristics of this particular modeling technique. Gradient boosting is known for its ability to handle complex relationships and capture non-linear patterns in the data [4]. This is particularly relevant in the context of boat speed prediction, as the factors influencing speed can exhibit intricate and non-linear dynamics. Furthermore, gradient boosted models are robust against overfitting and can effectively handle high-dimensional feature spaces. The employed XGBoost model demonstrated exceptional performance in predicting boat speed. The XGBoost model is based on the concept of boosting, which combines the predictions of multiple weak learners, such as decision trees, to create a strong predictive model. With an impressive R2 score of 0.95, the model successfully explains the variance in boat speed based on the selected features. The gradient boosted regression model attained a mean squared error (MSE) of 4.3, which quantifies the average squared disparity between the predicted and actual boat speeds (Fig. 3).

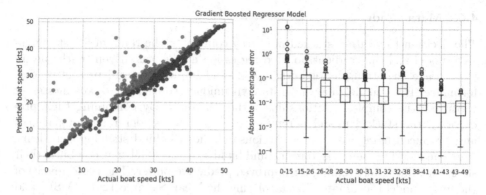

Fig. 3. The model exhibits a lower mean squared error (MSE), indicating a reduced deviation between the predicted and actual boat speeds. Notably, the plot demonstrates improved accuracy in the higher speed ranges, particularly for boat speeds exceeding 40 knots (74 km/h). This observation suggests that the model's predictions align closely with the actual boat speeds in these higher ranges, indicating a higher level of precision and accuracy in those predictions.

4.4   Benchmark

Benchmarking allows us to evaluate models against a predefined standard or reference point. In this case, the naive baseline model served as a starting point for comparison, representing a simplistic approach without extensive optimization. This naive model reached an R2 score of 0.92. The naive baseline models utilized in this project involved using regression models without any form of hyperparameter tuning or model optimization. Our models, on the other hand, leveraged cross-validation to systematically fine-tune the model's hyperparameters, optimizing its predictive capabilities.

The higher R2 score obtained by the hyperparameter-tuned models (0.94 and 0.95) indicates improved ability to explain the variability in boat speed based on the selected features. It suggests that these models capture more of the underlying patterns and relationships in the data, leading to more accurate predictions. The optimized hyperparameters enable the model to adapt better to the nuances of the dataset, resulting in improved performance.

Furthermore, the use of a variation of k-fold cross-validation in our models helps mitigate overfitting by evaluating the model's performance on multiple subsets of the data. This technique ensures that the model's performance is not overly influenced by a specific training-test split, enhancing its generalization capabilities.

In conclusion, our regression models, incorporating TimeSeriesSplit, outperform the naive baseline model by achieving a higher R2 score. The optimization and robust evaluation provided by the hyperparameter tuning process contribute to the improved performance of the model, making it a preferred choice for predicting boat speed in this project.

4.5 Meta Model

The decision to create a stacked model by combining the random forest regression model and the gradient boosted regression model was driven by the desire to leverage the strengths of both models and improve overall predictive performance. Each model may have its own unique strengths and weaknesses in capturing the complex relationships within the data. By combining their predictions, the stacked model potentially captured a broader range of patterns and produced more accurate predictions. The idea behind stacking is to learn from the individual models' outputs and build a meta-model that combines their strengths, ultimately aiming for improved predictive power. The performance of the meta-model is evaluated by calculating the Mean Squared Error (MSE) and R2 score, which provide insights into the accuracy and goodness-of-fit of the model (Fig. 4).

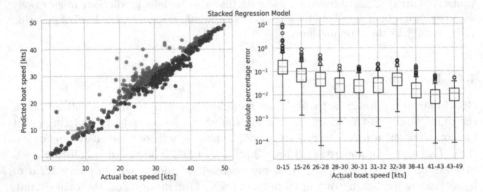

Fig. 4. The plot reveals the effectiveness of predicting boat speed, particularly in the higher speed ranges of 30+ knots (55.6 km/h). Moreover, the stacked model exhibits a lower deviation, indicating its ability to make precise predictions with reduced errors. However, it's worth noting that there is a tendency for overestimation around 30 knots (55.6 km/h) across all of the models, suggesting a potential area for further refinement.

The obtained results reveal important information about the effectiveness of the meta-model. The calculated MSE value of 3.2 indicates the average squared difference between the predicted boat speeds and the actual boat speeds. Lower MSE values suggest better prediction accuracy, and in this case, the achieved MSE implies relatively small prediction errors.

Furthermore, the R2 score of 0.97 indicates the proportion of the variance in the boat speeds that can be explained by the meta-model. A high R2 score close to 1 signifies a strong relationship between the predicted and actual values. In this case, the R2 score of 0.97 suggests that the meta-model captures a substantial portion of the boat speed variability.

5   Conclusion

SailGP stands at the forefront of a rapidly evolving and highly competitive sailing landscape. This dynamic sport is characterized by its cutting-edge technology, intense competition, and a strong reliance on data-driven strategies. As SailGP continues to develop and push the boundaries of what is possible in sailing, the role of analytics and data mining becomes increasingly vital. It is worth noting that, within the research community, our work represents a pioneering effort in exploring the realm of data mining in the context of SailGP. By delving into this uncharted territory, we aim to shed light on the untapped potential of leveraging data to gain insights and unlock performance gains in this exhilarating sport.

Overall, the results indicate that the stacked regression model, incorporating the predictions from RF and GBM models, along with the meta-model, yields promising outcomes in predicting boat speeds. The relatively low MSE and high R2 score suggest that the model captures and explains a significant portion of the boat speed variations. These findings indicate the potential practical utility of the model in estimating boat speeds accurately and its value in optimizing performance in the context of sailboat racing.

The teams' integration of data analytics to optimize their boats' performance showcases the increasing significance of data-driven decision-making within the realm of competitive sailing. In SailGP, where the margins between victory and defeat are often razor-thin, harnessing the power of data becomes crucial for gaining a competitive edge.

Looking ahead, an exciting opportunity lies in the collaboration with SailGP, which will grant access to further datasets and potentially real-time racing data. By working closely with SailGP, we aim to expand our predictive models to encompass a wider range of scenarios and to obtain more accurate predictions during live racing events.

Acknowledgement. We would like to express our sincere gratitude to the providers of the valuable dataset used in this project. Their contribution has been instrumental in enabling us to conduct our research and derive meaningful insights. We are thankful for their generosity and commitment to advancing knowledge in this domain.

Project no. 2021-1.2.4-TÉT-2021-00053 has been implemented with the support provided by the Ministry of Culture and Innovation of Hungary from the National Research, Development and Innovation Fund, financed under the 2021-1.2.4-TÉT funding scheme.

References

1. Oracle cloud infrastructure. https://www.oracle.com/customers/sailgp/. Accessed 01 June 2023
2. Sailgp. https://sailgp.com/news/nobu-katori-joins-japan/. Accessed 01 June 2023
3. Sailgp homepage. https://sailgp.com/. Accessed 01 June 2023
4. Sklearn gradient boosting regression. https://bit.ly/3YoA6ch. Accessed 01 June 2023

5. Sklearn random forest regressor. https://bit.ly/3Kgkd1p. Accessed 01 June 2023
6. Sklearn time series split. https://bit.ly/3QdXYNv. Accessed 01 June 2023
7. Flying across the sea, propelled by AI (2021). https://www.mckinsey.com/capabilities/mckinsey-digital/how-we-help-clients/flying-across-the-sea-propelled-by-ai. Accessed 01 June 2023
8. Oracle Help Center (2021). https://docs.oracle.com/en/solutions/sailgp-on-oci/index.html. Accessed 01 June 2023
9. Sailgp, bermuda results (2021). https://sailgp.com/news/bermuda-season-2-results/. Accessed 01 June 2023
10. Ridley, J.: Sail GP: how do supercharged racing yachts go so fast? An engineer explains (2019). https://theconversation.com/sail-gp-how-do-supercharged-racing-yachts-go-so-fast-an-engineer-explains-121902. Accessed 01 June 2023

Individual Sports

Exploring Table Tennis Analytics: Domination, Expected Score and Shot Diversity

Gabin Calmet[1,2], Aymeric Eradès[1,2], and Romain Vuillemot[1,2(✉)]

[1] École Centrale de Lyon, Ecully, France
romain.vuillemot@ec-lyon.fr
[2] LIRIS CNRS UMR 5205, Ecully, France

Abstract. Detailed sports data, including fine-grained player, ball positions, and action types, is becoming increasingly available thanks to advancements in sensor and video tracking technologies. In this study, we explore the potential of utilizing such data in table tennis to analyze player superiority, scoring opportunities, and creativity. Our approach involves adapting existing metrics by incorporating additional attributes provided by the detailed data, such as player zones and shot angles. Furthermore, we present a methodology for visualizing all metrics simultaneously during a single set, enabling a comprehensive assessment of their significance. We expect this approach to help for developing, comparing, and applying a broader range of metrics to table tennis and other racket sports. To facilitate further research and the benchmarking of novel metrics, we have made our code and dataset available as an open-source project.

Keywords: Sports Analytics · Table Tennis · Visual Analysis

1 Introduction

A new generation of detailed sports data is emerging for sports analysis in general, including racket sports that require more precise analysis. A flagship example is the TTNet [13] video tracking system, which enables real-time identification of players and ball positions. This level of detail represents a paradigm shift, as tracking data [8] of this kind is typically under-explored in such sports. Meanwhile, a plethora of advanced tools are beginning to leverage this data, such as iTTvis [13], which is aimed at experts to explore game sequences and discover tactics. Other approaches also focus on sequence analysis to visually explore frequent patterns [3], using an a-cyclic graph to represent all points in a match, and extract tactics. TIVEE [2] leverages shot types, player positions, and shuttle trajectory and speed to find correlations between strokes, aiding in the discovery of tactics. TacticFlow [12] utilizes multivariate events in racket sports to mine frequent patterns and detect how these patterns change over time. Tac-Miner [11] allows users to analyze, explore, and compare tactics of multiple matches based on three consecutive strokes. All of these works share the commonality of being driven by the availability of detailed tracking data.

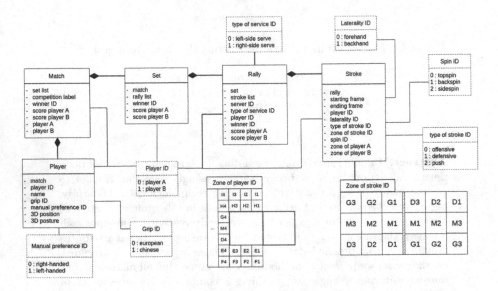

Fig. 1. Example of an extended table tennis detailed data model (from [3]). It includes additional metadata (e. g., players' names, score and winner) with advanced strokes types, players and ball rebound zones. It also takes into account continuous player positions and ball position (that we haven't yet collected).

We hypothesize that such detailed data provide deeper games analysis, and thus need to be anticipated. Figure 1 illustrates a detailed table tennis data model that captures all data currently available (mostly meta and event-based data). In this work, we use a combination of event-based data and video tracking data, on a 2D space. Such data can be collected with regular technical skills using a blend of computer vision, deep learning and manual annotation tools. It extends the format previously used in [3] but with finer grained players position, orientation and ball rebound position. Some researches have been led to collect such data automatically. [6] uses Twin convolutional neural networks with 3D convolutions on RGB data and optical flow to classify strokes in table tennis. [5] shows the importance of optical flow and human detection algorithms to improve action detection. [9] uses a CNN layer inspired by optical flow algorithms for action recognition without having to compute optical flow. And TTNet [13] is a multi-task convolution-based neural network to collect positions and stroke events data simultaneously. Additional data could be collected, such as the 3D position of players as well as ball effects, but this requires more work on video detection. We discuss this part in the last section of this paper.

To illustrate our analysis in this paper, we use the following scenario from an international table tennis game: Lebrun, the French champion, against Zhendong, the world champion and number one player in the world, in the quarterfinal match during WTT[1] Championship in Macao, 2023. In this match, Lebrun wins 3 sets to 2. They took turns winning the sets. It was a really close game, and Lebrun won the decider 11–9 by touching the edge of the table. During this match, our experts noticed that Lebrun was very strong when attacking from the left side of the table. Usually, he would win the point just after his attack, often down the line with his backhand. If we focus on the first set, we can see that Lebrun's domination decreased after the second point, while he didn't execute these shots. However, after his domination increased again, these shots began to be more and more common. Moreover, we noticed that during an important moment (7–4 for Zhendong), he manages to score twice using these shots, and this made him take the lead of the set. We may suppose that this is an important feature of his game plan. In the first set, we found 4 points won by Lebrun when he makes these strokes (indicated by the red vertical lines in Fig. 2):

- **Point A** (1–0) Lebrun serves, Zhendong pushes on the left side of Lebrun's table, then Lebrun attacks down the line with his forehand and wins the point.
- **Point B** (4–7) Zhendong serves, Lebrun pushes short on Zhendong's forehand, who pushes long on the left side of Lebrun's table. Lebrun attacks with his forehand on the left side of Zhendong's table.
- **Point C** (5–7) Lebrun serves short on Zhendong's forehand, who pushes long on the left side of Lebrun's table. Lebrun attacks with his backhand down the line.
- **Point D** (9–7) Lebrun serves long on Zhendong's backhand, who attacks on Lebrun's left side of the table. Lebrun counters with his backhand and wins the point after a few shots.

We derived a series of high level questions from this game analysis, as a way to address more general tasks analysts often conduct when processing table tennis data:

1. Why is a particular point effective during a game?
2. What is the effect of shots diversity?
3. What shots combination are the most efficient?
4. What are strokes difference between players?
5. How a stroke can win you a point?
6. Can we classify players by their playing style?

To address these questions, we first selected a *domination metric* commonly used in adversarial sports or games to measure the advantage held by a player and designed it to capture both local efficiency for each shot and global trends.

---

[1] World Table Tennis, a commercial organization that runs table tennis tournaments.

We then used another metric often used in soccer matches by bookmakers to assess the reliability of the match outcome: *Expected Goals* [7]. This metric calculates the probability that a scoring opportunity will result in a goal, providing insight into whether the winning team had the most dangerous scoring opportunities or not. Finally, we included a last metric that captures creativity in the choice of shots techniques, based on a shot similarity distance.

We have released our benchmark code and datasets (collected and augmented) in a public GitHub repository[2].

2   Domination Analysis in Table Tennis

Analyzing the pressure or domination is popular in team sports. In general, it is an umbrella term that encompasses all the ways to prevent the opposite team to develop an attack [1]. There is always an objective component of the domination that is calculated at a given moment without depending on the past. But most games and sports requires physical, technical and mental capacities that can't be objectively quantified without depending on the past. In racket sports, usually more fragmented than team sports that have long, continuous actions, but also that have high scoring opportunities, there is a need to re-define this notion to account for those characteristics. In such context with two opponents, we define it broadly as follows:

Definition 1 (Domination).   *A situation in which a player (or a team) consistently outperforms their opponents and maintains a significant advantage.*

We used various data from Fig. 1 (scores, positions of both players, zone of rebound, type of stroke, laterality) to define the domination function $D(t)$ normalized between -1 and 1 to indicate which team dominates. At the beginning of the match, no team dominates, in other words $D(0) = 0$. As domination usually relies on many factors (e. g., endurance, precision, self-confidence, power, speed, trajectory prediction, agility, decision-making, strategy, to name a few) we will therefore consider multiple types of domination: **score**, **physical** and **mental**. However, we know that three functions won't be enough to analyze every aspect of a table tennis match, this definition is an initial approach that inevitably contains many limitations.

- **Score domination** is calculated using the current scores at a given instant. It is highly reliable because the scores are what the winner is declared on at the end of the match, and because they are considered an absolute truth during the game. In this case, we consider that the score domination is proportional to the winning chances of player A, $P_{a,b}$ (see Appendix A for detailed definition). The value of $P_{a,b}$ between 0 and 1 is then linearly re-scaled between -1 and 1 to give us the score domination $S_d(t)$.

---

[2] https://github.com/centralelyon/table-tennis-analytics.

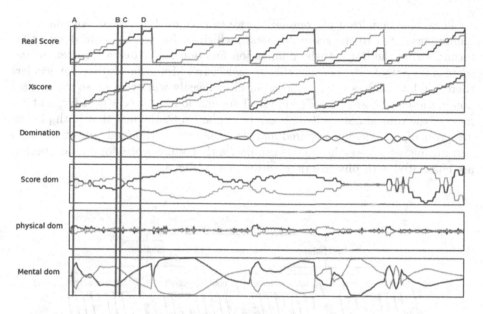

Fig. 2. Detailed metrics during the first set of a match between Lebrun and Zhendong at the WTT Championships in Macao, China in 2023. Red vertical lines the 4 points during the first set we focused on. (Color figure online)

– **Physical domination** in table tennis is supposedly based on three factors: endurance, aggression and playing angle. At each stroke, we calculate the distance $d_X(t)$ covered by each player, the playing angle $a(t)$ and we update also their respective rate of offensive shots $r_X(t)$. We then combine the three contributions to get the full physical domination function (see Appendix A for further explanation):

$$P_h(t) = \frac{1}{3}\left(a(t) + d(t) + r(t)\right)$$

– **Mental domination** in table tennis is difficult to quantify because it depends a lot on the players and on the context of the match. However, we assume that certain mental characteristics are found in a majority of cases [14]. Our model takes into account defeat anxiety $l(t)$, self-confidence $c(t)$ and the stress of long rallies $s(t)$ (see Appendix A for detailed definition). We combine those three factors to get the mental domination function:

$$M(t) = \frac{1}{3}\left(l(t) + c(t) + s(t)\right)$$

– **Global domination.** On a larger scale, the three types of domination are also combined to obtain the global domination function:

$$D(t) = 0.4S_c(t) + 0.3P_h(t) + 0.3M(t)$$

From this definition of domination, we can see on Fig. 2 that domination is highly correlated to the score difference, which is due to the score domination term. During the last set, the domination function fluctuates a lot because the score is very tight, and because this set is decisive. Moreover, during the decider, there is a lot of stress because both player can easily win or loose, so the mental domination is also at stake. The physical domination is not very decisive, and it's most of the time almost null. This can be explained by the fact that both players are probably physically prepared and that they are authorized to rest between and during sets. Nevertheless, we can notice that some score domination period are correlated with physical domination peaks (Fig. 3).

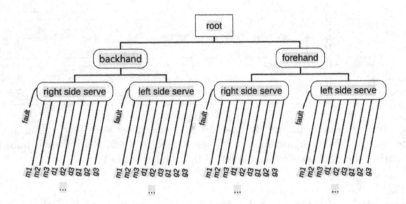

Fig. 3. Theoretical structure of the Playing Patterns Trees (PPT) that enumerates all shot attributes combination.

3   Expected Score (XScore) in Table Tennis

We have developed a second metric that draws inspiration from Expected Goals (often referred to as ExpG or XG) in soccer [4,7]. The objective of this metric is to predict the outcome of a point based solely on the first three strokes. By consistently applying this prediction to all points in a set, we can construct an **expected score (XScore)** that indicates the logical winner of the set. We accomplish this by exploring a tree that represents all possible three-stroke playing patterns and calculating a winning probability based on the statistics of the branch in which each **expected point** is situated, and defined as:

Definition 2 (Expected Points). *A statistical metric to estimate the probability of winning a point based on various factors such as player skill, shot quality, and opponent performance.*

To construct the similarities between the games, we build a Playing Patterns Trees (**PPT**) described by those simple rules:

1. The children of a zone node or of the root are laterality nodes: **backhand** and **forehand**
2. The children of a laterality node are type nodes: **right side** and **left side** for services and **offensive**, **push** and **defensive** for the others strokes.
3. The children of a type node are zone nodes according to the zone of rebound of the ball (**d1, d2, d3, m1, m2, m3, g1, g2, g3**. It also has a child named **fault** if the rally ends there.

Each node stores the probability that the sequence results in a win. Theoretically, the PPT up to the third stroke contains 62, 651 nodes, but in reality, many of them are never explored because they represent unlikely sequences. For instance, after an offensive stroke, it is unlikely to find a short zone of rebound like d1, m1, or g1. Actually, the trees that are built on several real match analyses haven't more than 2, 000 nodes. We have built our PPT from the analysis of 9 simulated matches, augmented from 3 different set annotated manually.

This metric is particularly interesting because it allows us to introduce the concept of chance (or unlikely success) and its analysis can explain certain subtleties of mental domination. As Fig. 2 suggests, the expected score respects the global match outcome 3–2 for Lebrun. However, the set winners are not always the same as expected. The third set is particularly interesting because Lebrun wins by a wide margin and dominated during the whole set. But the expected score is totally different: he is expected to lose by a wide margin. This can be explained by the fact that he just lost the previous set and needs now to be careful. Moreover, Zhendong just came back to a draw and may be less concentrated: he still plays aggressively, which means he has occasions but commits mistakes. The fourth set is similar, both players are very close in terms of expected score, but Lebrun loses by a wide margin, as Zhendong did in the previous set: he just won the previous set, he is less concentrated, and he makes mistakes. This is an important feature that could be useful for the understanding of mental domination.

An important remark is that this metric isn't used to point the finger at players who are lucky; it is used to show how luck can sometimes work in a player's favor to gain a mental advantage. Moreover, what we call 'luck' is only those sequences that are statistically losing and still result in a win. It is quite possible that a precise refinement of the quality of the stroke will be undetectable in our analysis and will allow a losing sequence to become a win. For instance, this metric doesn't quite work with players that are extremely creative, like Lebrun. This leads us to our last metric.

4   Shots Diversity in Table Tennis

Being able to vary playing patterns during a match is one of the keys to victory in table tennis. A player who always responds in the same way to a sequence is bound to lose in the long term, even if their technique is perfect. However, it is well known that humans are particularly bad at creating randomness, especially when things are going fast and when the mind is in automatic mode. Therefore, analyzing the variation of playing patterns during a set should be an interesting way to look at the mental domination.

Definition 3 (Shots Diversity). *Variety of shots and techniques employed by a player during a match, including variations in racket side, placement, and shot selection.*

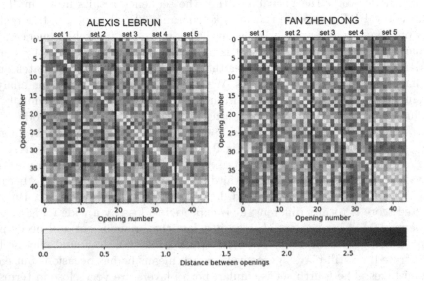

Fig. 4. Distance matrix between openings of the match between Lebrun and Zhendong at the WTT Championships in Macao, 2023. At the beginning Lebrun doesn't vary much, probably to start with his strength and take the lead. Only then, he starts to change to keep surprising his opponent with new openings. During the first set, Zhendong started to lose when Lebrun started to vary openings. The most interesting analysis is from the last set. We can see that Zhendong didn't change a lot of opening during this set (white square). We can suppose that he noticed that these tactics were efficient, and he wanted to take the lead at the beginning of it. But Lebrun adapted to this and managed to come back. Then, Zhendong never tried to change pattern and lost the match. This may reflect a mental fatigue of Zhendong (maybe with the stress he wanted to stay with something familiar to him, or maybe he wasn't lucid enough to take the decision to change of opening).

In a previous paper [3], we saw that some players tend to serve in the same way, while they did not lose a point after such a serve. Here, we are going further in the sense that we explore more strokes into the rally, and because we create a metric representing the distance between two openings. By collecting the three first strokes of every rally of a match, we can calculate similarities between sequences.

An opening U is defined as a list of nodes of the PPT that are successively one of the children of the previous node. The first element of an opening is always the root of the PPT. The distance between two openings, U and V, of the same length n, is defined as:

$$D(U, V) = \sum_{i=1}^{n} (n - i) \cdot d(U_i, V_i) \tag{1}$$

with

- $d(U_i, V_i) = 0$ if $U_i = V_i$,
- $d(U_i, V_i) = 1$ if $U_i \neq V_i$ and if U_i and V_i are laterality nodes or type nodes,
- $d(U_i, V_i) = M_{j,k}$, if U_i and V_i are zone nodes, where M is the zones' adjacency matrix and where j and k are respectively the indices for the zones U_i and V_i in M.

For a given list of openings $M = (M_i)_{i \in [0,m]}$, we can build the distance matrix defined as $Dist(M) = (D(M_i, M_j))_{i,j \in [0,m]^2}$. A feature worth attention on Fig. 4 is the similarity of consecutive sequences, that appears as white squares on the diagonals of both matrix. Because of the temporal aspect of this figure, we can see Zhendong tends to vary less in his opening at the end of the match, and this can be a sign of a mental fatigue.

5   Discussion, Limits and Perspectives

In this work, we adapted three metrics that relied upon detailed table tennis data that we collected and augmented to analyze a specific game. It showed that these metrics already enabled a general analysis of the game, as well as particular key moments. In particular, metrics that account for a global context (e. g., domination) enabled to provide more nuance to hypothesize on players' strategic decisions. For instance, we showed a player can become more conservative in their technical choices when dominated to reduce the chance of errors, as we have seen in the last set of our game.

The main limitation of our work is the volume of data used for analysis, which remains limited to a single game (despite we collected and released data for multiple games). The reason is that table tennis is an adversarial sport, so only comparable situations can be compared, as players adapt their behavior against players with similar styles (which was one of our early questions). Another limitation is that we currently communicated and analyzed the metrics separately, while there is an opportunity to combine them. Furthermore, although we collected tracking data with detailed position, we only operated on aggregation by zone to capture strategic choices and filter out noise. Position data presents an opportunity for designing novel metrics. We anticipate the development of more continuous metrics based on ball position and players' body, such as spatial occupation [10].

As we have released our code and datasets (both collected and augmented) as an open-source project, we hope it will foster research to develop and compare new metrics. We also plan to update these datasets with even more detailed data, including better 3D pose estimation, ball spin effects, and trajectories.

A   Appendix

A.1   Definition of the Winning Probability $P_{a,b}$

Considering the scores being a for player A, and b for player B, we define the probability for A to win the next point by $p = \frac{a}{a+b}$.

Then we can calculate the winning probability of A knowing the scores (noted $P_{a,b}$) by using the following recursive formula,

$$P_{a,b} = pP_{a+1,b} + (1-p)P_{a,b+1} = \frac{1}{a+b}\left(aP_{a+1,b} + bP_{a,b+1}\right)$$

and by applying those limit conditions:

- If $a \geq 11$ and $b < a - 1$, therefore $P_{a,b} = 1$,
- If $b \geq 11$ and $a < b - 1$, therefore $P_{a,b} = 0$,
- If $a = b$, therefore $P_{a,b} = 0.5$.

Because of the quite extreme winning probabilities that we encounter for low scores, we added another condition to complete the model:

- If $a + b < 5$, therefore $P_{a,b} = 0.5$ (Fig. 5).

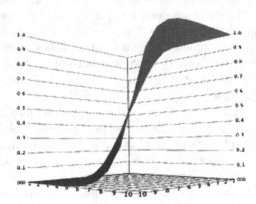

Fig. 5. Winning probability $P_{a,b}$ (vertical axis) as a function of the scores a and b (horizontal axes)

For the winning probability of a match, the same process is applied, taking into account the probability to win the current set.

A.2   Definition of the Three Factors of Physical Domination

We can extract domination function for the endurance and aggressiveness values:

$$- \; d(t) = \frac{d_B(t) - d_A(t)}{d_A(t) + d_B(t)} \text{ for the domination of endurance,}$$

$$- \; r(t) = \frac{r_A(t) - r_B(t)}{r_A(t) + r_B(t)} \text{ for the domination of aggressiveness}$$

The playing angle measures if the receiver of the ball is physically put in trouble by the one who sent it. Given A and B the position of the players, and C the rebound point of the ball, the playing angle depends on the scalar product $\alpha = \overrightarrow{AC} \cdot \overrightarrow{CB}$ which is 1 when the receiver is not in trouble (points are aligned) and -1 in the worst case. Thus, the playing angle is defined as:

$$a(t) = \begin{cases} \dfrac{\alpha - 1}{2}, & \text{if A receives the ball} \\[2mm] \dfrac{1 - \alpha}{2}, & \text{if B receives the ball} \end{cases}$$

so that $a(t) = 1$ if B is in trouble (meaning that A dominates) and $a(t) = -1$ if it is the opposite.

A.3   Definition of the Three Factors of Mental Domination

If a player is close to defeat or is caught by the score, his anxiety about losing increases. If a player makes several winning shots in a row, his self-confidence increases, but if he makes a lot of mistakes in a row, he loses his self-confidence. And each time a rally takes place, the losing player's stress increases by an amount proportional to the length of the rally. We get ourselves three functions ($l_X(t)$ for loss anxiety, $c_X(t)$ for self-confidence, and $s_X(t)$ for stress) for each player (A and B). We first combine them two by two to get three functions between -1 and 1:

$$- \; l(t) = \frac{l_B(t) - l_A(t)}{l_A(t) + l_B(t)} \text{ for the domination of loss anxiety}$$

$$- \; c(t) = \frac{c_A(t) - c_B(t)}{c_A(t) + c_B(t)} \text{ for the domination of self-confidence,}$$

$$- \; s(t) = \frac{s_B(t) - s_A(t)}{s_A(t) + s_B(t)} \text{ for the domination of stress of long rally.}$$

These definitions are highly debatable, as we consider the relationship between the player and the context as unidirectional: the context of the match impacts the player mental state. We know that this is not necessary the case, some player may have the ability to self-regulate and boost his self-confidence, which impacts the game in return. However, table tennis is known to be a highly stressful sport where mental characteristics of players can vary a lot. We tried to build this mental domination metric, with advice from experts and elite table tennis players.

References

1. Andrienko, G., et al.: Visual analysis of pressure in football. Data Min. Knowl. Disc. **31**(6), 1793–1839 (2017). https://doi.org/10.1007/s10618-017-0513-2
2. Chu, X., et al.: TIVEE: visual exploration and explanation of badminton tactics in immersive visualizations. IEEE Trans. Vis. Comput. Graph. **28**(1), 118–128 (2021)
3. Duluard, P., Li, X., Plantevit, M., Robardet, C., Vuillemot, R.: Discovering and visualizing tactics in a table tennis game based on subgroup discovery. In: Brefeld, U., Davis, J., Van Haaren, J., Zimmermann, A. (eds.) MLSA 2022. CCIS, vol. 1783, pp. 101–112. Springer, Cham (2023). https://doi.org/10.1007/978-3-031-27527-2_8
4. Green, S.: Assessing the performance of premier leauge goalscorers. OptaPro Blog (2012). https://www.statsperform.com/resource/assessing-the-performance-of-premier-league-goalscorers/
5. Jhuang, H., Gall, J., Zuffi, S., Schmid, C., Black, M.J.: Towards understanding action recognition. In: 2013 IEEE International Conference on Computer Vision, pp. 3192–3199. IEEE, Sydney (2013). https://doi.org/10.1109/ICCV.2013.396. http://ieeexplore.ieee.org/document/6751508/
6. Martin, P.E., Benois-Pineau, J., Peteri, R., Morlier, J.: 3D attention mechanism for fine-grained classification of table tennis strokes using a Twin Spatio-Temporal Convolutional Neural Networks. In: 2020 25th International Conference on Pattern Recognition (ICPR), pp. 6019–6026. IEEE, Milan (2021). https://doi.org/10.1109/ICPR48806.2021.9412742. https://ieeexplore.ieee.org/document/9412742/
7. Mead, J., O'Hare, A., McMenemy, P.: Expected goals in football: improving model performance and demonstrating value. PLoS ONE **18**(4), e0282295 (2023)
8. Perin, C., Vuillemot, R., Stolper, C.D., Stasko, J.T., Wood, J., Carpendale, S.: State of the art of sports data visualization. In: Computer Graphics Forum (EuroVis 2018), vol. 37, no. 3, pp. 663–686 (2018). https://doi.org/10.1111/cgf.13447. https://onlinelibrary.wiley.com/doi/abs/10.1111/cgf.13447
9. Piergiovanni, A., Ryoo, M.S.: Representation flow for action recognition. In: 2019 IEEE/CVF Conference on Computer Vision and Pattern Recognition (CVPR), pp. 9937–9945. IEEE, Long Beach (2019). https://doi.org/10.1109/CVPR.2019.01018. https://ieeexplore.ieee.org/document/8953712/
10. Rolland, G., Vuillemot, R., Bos, W.J., Rivière, N.: Characterization of space and time-dependence of 3-point shots in basketball. In: MIT Sloan Sports Analytics Conference (2020)
11. Wang, J., Wu, J., Cao, A., Zhou, Z., Zhang, H., Wu, Y.: Tac-miner: visual tactic mining for multiple table tennis matches. IEEE Trans. Vis. Comput. Graph. **27**(6), 2770–2782 (2021). https://doi.org/10.1109/TVCG.2021.3074576. https://ieeexplore.ieee.org/document/9411869
12. Wu, J., Liu, D., Guo, Z., Xu, Q., Wu, Y.: TacticFlow: visual analytics of ever-changing tactics in racket sports. IEEE Trans. Vis. Comput. Graph. **28**, 835–845 (2022). https://doi.org/10.1109/TVCG.2021.3114832. https://ieeexplore.ieee.org/document/9552436
13. Wu, Y., et al.: iTTVis: interactive visualization of table tennis data. IEEE Trans. Vis. Comput. Graph. **24**(1), 709–718 (2017)
14. Zhu, Y., Naikar, R.: Predicting tennis serve directions with machine learning. In: Brefeld, U., Davis, J., Van Haaren, J., Zimmermann, A. (eds.) MLSA 2022. CCIS, vol. 1783, pp. 89–100. Springer, Cham (2023). https://doi.org/10.1007/978-3-031-27527-2_7

Performance Measurement 2.0: Towards a Data-Driven Cyclist Specialization Evaluation

Bram Janssens[1,2,3]($\boxtimes$) (iD) and Matthias Bogaert[1,2] (iD)

[1] Department of Marketing, Innovation, and Organization, Ghent University, Tweekerkenstr. 2, 9000 Ghent, Belgium
bram.janssens@ugent.be
[2] FlandersMake@UGent–corelab CVAMO, Ghent, Belgium
[3] Research Foundation Flanders, Brussels, Belgium

Abstract. Current cycling analytics solutions do not account for either the raced course profile or the level of the competition. Therefore, this paper suggests a two-stage approach which initially clusters races into coherent clusters based upon both elevation and road surface type. Subsequently, underlying skill levels are determined per cluster through the observed race results. Our results indicate that the methodology results into clusters which match the commonly known specializations in road cycling. The ranking methodology results into skill ratings which enable the identification of specialization and can be used in other downstream tasks.

Keywords: Cycling Analytics · Performance Evaluation · Unsupervised Learning

1 Introduction

The field of professional cycling has seen major changes in recent years. In the last couple of decades, the sport has shifted to appeal to a wider range of regions and nationalities (Van Reeth, 2016). This shift has also resulted in many new innovations being introduced in the sport, including the use of data analytics techniques, colloquially known as cycling analytics. These innovations have created large value in the sport, where racing is now more data-driven, with riders racing based upon their known strengths and weaknesses as measured through their power profiles.

While descriptive techniques, such as measuring threshold power, are deeply embedded in the field, a different story is observed for predictive techniques. This type of approach was only recently introduced in the field (Hilmkil et al, 2018; Kataoka & Gray, 2018), which could allow for even deeper tactical advantages as team managers and riders could now start anticipating future behavior. Initial approaches were mainly based upon riders from within one team, as teams typically have much richer information on their own riders (e.g., detailed power outputs, and training regimes) compared to riders who compete for rival teams. However, researchers quickly realized the potential in estimating future performances of athletes across teams, which allowed for race outcome

U. Brefeld et al. (Eds.): MLSA 2023, CCIS 2035, pp. 179–190, 2024.
https://doi.org/10.1007/978-3-031-53833-9_15

estimation (Kholkine et al., 2020; Kholkine et al., 2021), and future talent identification (Van Bulck, Vande Weghe & Goossens, 2021; Janssens, Bogaert & Maton, 2022). Unfortunately, these applications need to work with publicly available data as performances need to be compared across athletes and teams. This entails that current solutions primarily focus on eventual race results, as they give detailed information on the eventual outcome of a highly competitive race. These individual race results are then simply aggregated (Van Bulck et al., 2021), grouped manually (Janssens et al., 2022), or linked in a race-by-race method (Kholkine et al., 2021).

This completely disregards several aspects of the competitiveness typically observed in professional cycling. Race profile type heavily influences which riders are the a priori race favorites, with heavier athletes typically thriving more on flatter terrain compared to their lightweight colleagues who generally thrive in mountainous terrain. In contrast to other racing sports, cycling is heavily influenced by in-race dynamics and tactics. This means that one cannot directly measure performance through absolute values such as race time. Therefore, current solutions look at riders finishing places. However, some races see very different starting fields across the years, which means that a third place in a certain edition could be a stronger performance than a win in another year. Notably, this was recently discussed by cycling observers, who debated on whether Geraint Thomas performed higher during the 2022 Tour (where he finished third) compared to his victorious 2018 edition (Ozols, 2022).

Ideally, performance measurement, which is currently used as dependent variable for several studies, should account for race profile and level of competition. Therefore, this study sets out to formulate a methodology to determine who does so. Specifically, we propose a two-stage process. In the first step, the races are clustered by information on both course elevation and ridden surface types. Semi-supervised constrained clustering is shown to outperform traditional unsupervised clustering techniques by leveraging community expertise on race similarity. After races are clustered into coherent groups, the second step ranks the performance of each rider per cluster. The Bayesian TrueSkill algorithm is used for this purpose, a novelty in the field of cycling analytics and multi-entrant sports competitions as a whole. This ranking algorithm has several interesting properties such as the capability to account for multiple participants (i.e., more than two) and the fact that it values performance relative to the level of the competition, this as opposed to traditional points systems. Our results show that trustworthy rankings are outputted when performance is quantified on an individual level rather than on the team level.

2 Literature Review

Wearable sensors (e.g., heart rate monitors, power sensors) have revolutionized the field of professional cycling. The quintessential role these detailed data points play in the current professional cycling industry inspired many data mining researchers to develop automated tools who enable value estimates without the need of all possible sensors (e.g., Hilmkil et al.; Kataoka & Gray, 2018; de Leeuw et al., 2022). Recently, these systems have also reached subfields of the sports such as track cycling (Steyaert, De Bock & Verstockt, 2022), and cyclocross (De Bock & Verstockt, 2021).

These methods are extremely valuable for stakeholders from within teams. However, they do not allow for insights across teams. To know which athlete is most likely to succeed in winning a certain race we would need to have fitness level estimates across all participating teams, which teams of course are not willing to share. Moreover, teams often do not even want to share 'less sensitive' unhandled data such as power outputs and heart rate responses, with athletes often hiding this type of information on platforms such as Strava. Therefore, we can observe a trend where researchers who are interested in comparing athletes across teams use less fine-grained data sources due to availability reasons.

This is typically observed in race outcome prediction research. In this field, researchers try to accurately estimate the most likely outcome of individual races. Initial developments were made by Kholkine et al. (2020) who develop a model to predict the outcome of the Tour of Flanders, where the authors handpick several races as being the most informative races to look at previous performances. The fact that these races need to be selected indicates a grouping of race specializations. Generally speaking, grand tour performances have limited information towards predicting the outcome of several classics races such as the Tour of Flanders. Rather, information needs to be searched in more closely linked races as the ones selected by the authors. However, handpicking similar races seems a tedious task when dealing with the thousands of races which are being raced on the professional calendar across seasons. This is even further complicated by the fact that not all riders compete in all races, as also indicated by a high number of missing values in the study. Moreover, the study also highlights how performance is currently hard to measure in professional cycling, with the ordered predicted relative time used as dependent feature. Time differences in cycling are typically relatively small compared to the total raced time, and heavily influenced by race tactics, and the level of the other participants. These issues are alleviated to a certain degree in Kholkine et al. (2021). Their method is generalized to include six classics and the authors acknowledge the importance of 'relative' performances by adopting a learn-to-rank approach. However, relevant races are still handpicked, and overall historic performance is calculated by points scored, which does not account for the level of competition. Another major field of research is talent identification, where researchers use machine learning methods to automatically detect which prospects show the greatest potential. Interestingly, similar observations to the limitations of the race outcome prediction studies can be made. Both Van Bulck et al. (2021) and Janssens et al. (2022) use future points scored as the dependent variable in their predictive set-up. This feature, however, is inevitably flawed as it does not account for the level of the competition. Moreover, the issue of race-to-race relevance remains. To limit this issue, Van Bulck et al. (2021) group races based upon CQ ranking labels: sprints, mountain stages, time trials, general classification, and hilly, with the latter being a rest category of races which are unlabeled on CQ. The large hill category, as well as the lack of a typical category such as cobbled races, already indicates a limitation in this data source. Janssens et al. (2022) follow a manual approach, which manually groups together several races into eight homogenous categories. Once again this method is hard to extrapolate to a system which tries to evaluate performance across all races.

A recurring story in recent literature clearly is the lack of a performance evaluation method which (without the use of sensor data) is capable of fairly evaluating individual performances based upon the typical characteristics of professional cycling. Therefore, this study develops a performance evaluation methodology which incorporates both the type of racecourse as well as the level of the competition.

3 Methodology

3.1 Data

Several aspects of the racecourse influence the riders which are the a priori favorites of the races. Perhaps the most well-known aspect is elevation, with the physical demands required for flat sprint stages (Menaspà et al., 2015) differing heavily from those required in mountain climbs (Lucia, Joyos & Chicharro, 2000). This translates into a range of rider specialties which excel based upon the elevation changes which are encountered during the race. Detailed information on racecourse elevation is, however, not directly available on popular data sources such as ProCyclingStats (Kholkine et al., 2020) or CQ Ranking (Van Bulck et al., 2021). Rather, we use a community-based website[1] which discusses races in detail, and also shares detailed information about the racecourse, which fans can then use to spot riders during the race or to ride the course themselves during recreational rides. The website offers the potential to download the course as a GPX (GPS eXchange Format) file. A web scraper was built to retrieve all race profiles which were available on the website during Spring 2022. The GPS data in the GPX file are stored in the form of the sequence of the GPS points forming the GPS track as used for navigation. Geographical coordinates in the GPX file are supplemented with the data concerning elevation above sea level, which allows for calculating metrics related to course elevation.

However, elevation is not the sole specialization determinant in professional cycling. Road cycling is raced on public roads, which may vary heavily. When roads get smaller, positioning becomes more important as the narrow roads hinder moving through the peloton. Bad positioning has several disadvantages such as inability to respond to attacks at the front, or sudden shifts in time differences due to further narrowing of the road which may results in time differences of tens of seconds between the first and last riders of the same group, which can be extremely detrimental in a sport which is often decides by differences of seconds. This is even further complicated by road surfaces such as unpaved sections or cobble sections. It is clear that these aspects should be accounted for. However, obtaining structured information on these aspects can be hard, and may explain why this is currently unaccounted for in academic research. Therefore, we suggest using the Komoot application[2], which is an application directed at people who participate in outdoor sports such as running, hiking, and cycling. The application allows for detailed route creation which users can use to explore the outdoors. One of the features is that it calculates statistics about the surface and road type. This information was retrieved by building a web scraper which automatically uploaded all GPX files

---

[1] https://www.la-flamme-rouge.eu/.

[2] https://www.komoot.com/discover.

from the previous step into the application, which then calculated and stored this for every course in our data set.

Besides racecourse information, it is also essential to have information on actual results. Results were scraped from ProCyclingStats, a popular website which stores information on professional cycling results, which has been popular in previous research (Kholkine et al., 2020; Kholkine et al., 2021; Van Bulck et al., 2021; Janssens & Bogaert, 2022; Janssens et al., 2022; Baron et al., 2023). Each race which was present on La Flamme Rouge was searched on the website, and results were stored.

3.2 Clustering

Much domain knowledge is present within the field of professional cycling. This means that fans and professionals are capable of grouping very similar races together. This could indicate that grouping of similar races could be done manually. However, the scalability to do so for thousands of races is limited. A natural solution lays in the deployment of clustering algorithms. However, such an approach would completely disregard all the domain knowledge in the field. Wagstaff et al. (2001) propose the use of a Constrained K-means algorithm which imposes constraints on which races should be clustered together and which races may not be clustered together. Using these constraints the observations are assigned to the cluster centers, which results into different eventual cluster centers. The algorithm takes a dataset D (i.e., the races in this case), a list of must-link constraints $Con_= \subseteq D \times D$, and a list of cannot-link constraints $Con_{\neq} \subseteq D \times D$. Accordingly, we have created a list of constraints $Con = Con_= \cup Con_{\neq}$.

Besides Constrained K-means, we also benchmark several clustering algorithms which are fitted without constraints to check and validate whether the constrained app-roach improves the clustering performance: K-Means (Sculley, 2010), Affinity Propaga-tion (Frey & Dueck, 2007), Mean Shift (Comaniciu & Meer, 2002), Spectral Clustering (Shi & Malik, 2000), Hierarchical Clustering with Ward's Linkage (Ward, 1963), Hier-archical Clustering: Average Linkage (Sneath & Sokal, 1973), DBSCAN (Ester et al., 1996), OPTICS (Schubert & Gertz, 2018), BIRCH (Zhang, Ramakrishnan & Livny, 1996), and Gaussian Mixture Model-Based (Raftery & Dean, 2006). If the number of clusters was required, this was evaluated between 3 and 9 as a limited number of race types seems to be reflecting the limited number of specialties observed in earlier research (e.g., Menaspà et al, 2012; Janssens et al., 2022) as well as a more convenient practical use afterwards (i.e., too many categories could hinder decision making). Each clustering outcome was externally validated against a test set, which was labeled simultaneously with list of constraints Con. The test set contains 100 unique race combinations, which have been labeled as must-link or cannot-link. The test set has no overlap with the list of constraints Con to ensure no possible data leakage.

3.3 Performance Ranking

Performance value in competitive sports is heavily influenced by the strength of the opponent. A soccer team's victory can only be valued to the level of the opposing team. When Germany beat fellow favorite Brazil with 7-1 in the semi-finals of the 2014 FIFA World Cup, this was considered big news. However, their larger 9-0 victory over Liechtenstein in November 2021 gained little international attention. It is clear that performance should be regarded as relative to the level of competition. To enable athletes and other stakeholders to estimate the level of the competitors, ranking systems are used across several sports. In cycling, (team) ranking is used to define which teams are allowed to compete in the most important races on the calendar, known as the WorldTour. However, performance is not calculated relative to the skill of the competition, but based on a classification system in which top-level races have more points on offer than lower-level races. This has resulted in heavy critique on the system (e.g., Hood, 2022). Directly using this flawed system for an objective athlete evaluation system would also result in a skewed evaluation with athletes who compete a lot in low-competition races being overvalued. Rather, we should adopt an algorithm which accounts for the level of the competition. Herbrich et al. (2006) propose the TrueSkill ranking method. This Bayesian approach is able to model multi-entrant competitions, and can infer individual skills from team results. This methodology is ideally suited for the multi-entrant race environment as observed in professional cycling. The authors achieve this increased complexity by assuming a population of n athletes: $\{1, \ldots, n\}$ who are assigned to k teams which compete in a match. Team assignments A_j are defined so that each athlete can only compete for one team: $A_j \subset \{1, \ldots, n\}$, $with A_j \bigcap A_l = \varnothing\ if\ j \neq l$. These observed outcome of the competition these teams compete in, is then defined as $r = (r_1, \ldots, r_k) \in \{1, \ldots, k\}$, the observed ranking of these teams. They model game outcome (i.e., ranking) probability based upon the skills s of the participating players and the vector of team assignments A: $P(r|s, A)$. When deploying Bayes' rule this results in the following formula of the posterior skill distribution:

$$P(s|r, A) = \frac{P(r|s, A)P(s)}{P(r|A)}$$

We are interested in $P(s)$, which is a Gaussian distribution which is defined as follows: $P(s) = \prod_{i=1}^{n} P(s_i) = \prod_{i=1}^{n} N(\mu_i, \sigma_i^2)$. It is these skill ratings μ_i and rating deviations σ_i^2 which will define the overall rating. The final skill rating is determined by $\mu_i - 15\sigma_i$. This to penalize for uncertainty, as otherwise inexperienced athletes with some good starting results may directly jump to the top rankings. However, their definition requires a link between hidden individual skills and observed team performances. They conceptualize individual performance p_i as an outcome which is driven by the true underlying skill level s_i: $p_i \sim N(s_i, \beta^2)$. Team performance t_j is then the sum of all team members' individual performance, with the observed r defined through the differences in $t_j\ \forall j \in \{1, \ldots, k\}$. Cycling is a unique sport in the sense that it can be considered a hybrid between a team sport and an individual sport. As already mentioned above, this has implications on how one can define team assignments A and observed ranking r. One could assign each individual rider to either their sponsor team (e.g., Julian Alaphilippe to Soudal-Quick-Step) or to their own personal 'team' (e.g., Julian Alaphilippe to Julian Alaphilippe). It is feasible to see value in each approach: while a team-focused approach might undervalue individual performances, an individual approach might ignore any work carried out by teammates. Therefore, we will compare both approaches. Moreover, the team-focused approach also raises the issue of how to aggregate the (individual) official results to a team-level ranking. One could either look at the best result per team, or at the overall average ranking of the team. Accordingly, we will compare three approaches: (1) the original individual rankings, disregarding team formation, (2) first rider per team rankings, and (3) average ranking per team. As it is hard to establish a ground truth about which rider's skill should be ranked above another rider's, we will compare the outcomes of the three methods based upon some example cases.

4   Results

Table 1. Internal Validation Results: Percentage of elements represented in largest cluster on entire dataset. Each clustering algorithm is represented in a row. If the number of clusters was set, columns represent setting.

	3	4	5	6	7	8	9
K-Means	45.35%	39.90%	38.33%	36.97%	28.53%	24.73%	17.62%
Affinity Propagation							5.75%
Mean Shift							95.61‰
Spectral Clustering	76.73%	54.86%	52.54%	39.87%	39.88%	39.76%	40.46%
Ward	55.25%	41.66%	36.44%	36.41%	36.41%	36.41%	36.36%
Agglomerative Clustering	99.94%	99.90%	99.86%	99.86%	99.84%	99.84%	99.79%
DBSCAN							100.00%
OPTICS							99.39%
BIRCH	55.26%	55.26%	55.23%	55.18%	36.63%	36.63%	36.63%
Gaussian Mixture	71.49%	30.31%	42.56%	32.39%	30.55%	28.70%	26.88%
Constrained K-Means	97.97%	38.68%	39.63%	40.81%	32.05%	37.96%	31.81%

Table 2. External Validation Results: Percentage of elements correctly classified on test set. Each clustering algorithm is represented on a row. If number of clusters was set, columns represent setting. Best performance underlined and in bold.

	3	4	5	6	7	8	9
K-Means	81	76	75	75	77	76	77
Affinity Propagation							54
Spectral Clustering	77	77	77	79	80	81	81
Ward	72	74	76	76	76	76	76
BIRCH	81	80	80	80	77	77	77
Gaussian Mixture	66	68	60	62	64	66	65
Constrained K-Means	81	54	79	77	72	82	**84**

Table 1 depicts the percentage of observations which are assigned to the largest cluster. It is clear that many algorithms (i.e., Mean Shift, Agglomorative Clustering, DBSCAN, and BIRCH) have the tendency to put almost all observations into the same cluster. Such outcomes counterargue with prior knowledge (i.e., specialization across races) and are not informative. Accordingly, they are not included in Table 2, which depicts the number of correctly clustered or separated observation pairs of the clustering algorithms on the labeled test set (N = 100). Constrained K-means with K = 9 has the best performance on the test set (i.e., 84/100 correctly linked/separated). Only a few clustering algorithms achieve accuracies competitive with this algorithm, most notably K-Means, and Spectral Clustering. However, they are all outperformed by the Constrained K-Means algorithm, which correctly links 84 out of 100 instances in the test set, while also resulting into an insightful grouping of races, with the largest cluster which only includes around 30% of races. This is also confirmed when inspecting the resulting clusters and assigned races. When going through the various clusters, they seem to form coherent specialization clusters: time trials, cobble races, short races, sprint races, mountain stages, hilly races, hilly races & cobbled races, races with off-road sections, and short sprint stages. The inclusion of cobbled races and races with off-road sections clearly shows the added value of including surface type in the clustering analysis.

Remarkably, maximal performance is obtained with the maximal number of possible clusters as feasible within our methodological set-up. This could suggest that the true number of clusters is even higher. To check this, we performed a small robustness check where we allowed the number of clusters to be higher (i.e., up to 20) for the most-performant algorithm (i.e., constrained clustering). Figure 1 depicts the results of this analysis. The results clearly depict an ideal performance of K = 9, which is only matched at a very high number of clusters. These clusters (i.e., K = 19) proofed less humanly interpretable compared to our suggested number, as they agreed on most clustered pairs, while the approach with the higher number of clusters tended to group small niche groups of races together, which would also be uninformative to our ranking approach.

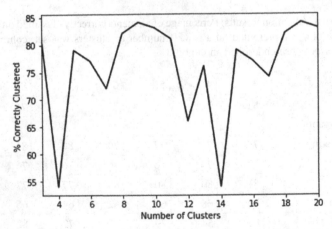

Fig. 1. Influence Number of Clusters (K) on Clustering Performance

The results of the three TrueSkill ranking methodologies are reported in Table 3. We interpret the results on the mountain stage cluster, as teammates can still offer large advantages during these types of stages while stochastic effects (i.e., luck or race tactics) have limited effects, resulting in more coherent rankings across races (i.e., ranking being more directly linked to underlying skill level). This way, we should be able to interpret the methods' performances despite the absence of an objective ground truth. The top-10 ranked riders for each method are reported. The mean team method is heavily outperformed by the other two methods, with Emerson Santos being the suggested top rider, which evidently is a worse suggestion than two-time Tour de France winner Tadej Pogačar. The best rider team method results into some useful top-ranked riders, however, the top-5 contains riders who very few observers would put in their top-5 of the period 2017-early 2022 compared to the individual method (e.g., Alejandro Osorio, Óscar Sevilla).

Table 3. Top-5 Rankings Using All Three TrueSkill Methods on Mountain Stage Cluster

Individual Method	Best Rider Team Method	Mean Result Team Method
POGAČAR Tadej	POGAČAR Tadej	SANTOS Emerson
BARDET Romain	LÓPEZ Miguel Ángel	POELS Wout
ROGLIČ Primož	OSORIO Alejandro	SEVILLA Óscar
QUINTANA Nairo	QUINTANA Nairo	MUÑOZ Daniel
BERNAL Egan	SEVILLA Óscar	MUGISHA Samuel

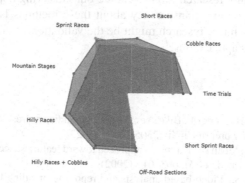

Fig. 2. Depiction Tim Merlier (green), Mathieu van der Poel (purple), and Wout van Aert (red) scores across the various clusters. (Color figure online)

The individual method results into fair rider evaluations across the various clusters. Consider Fig. 2. The figure compares the scores of the riders Tim Merlier (green), Mathieu van der Poel (purple), and Wout van Aert (red) across the 9 detected clusters. Note how all riders have the lowest possible score on the short sprint race cluster, as they have not performed in this race category (typically lower-level races). The figure suggests that Tim Merlier is the best sprinter, but that van Aert and van der Poel perform better at the other specialization clusters. Interestingly, the results also suggest that van Aert outperforms van der Poel on all other clusters besides the cobbled races, and that the difference between the two is the largest for mountain stages and time trials. All these observations match the expectations fans and followers may have upfront. Moreover, these specialization scores could also be used as features in other downstream tasks such as race outcome prediction or talent identification.

5 Conclusion

This study assesses the feasibility of a combined cluster-ranking method to come up with a reliable rankings of rider performance. Semi-supervised constrained clustering is shown to outperform traditional unsupervised clustering techniques while only using a limited number of human-labeled observations. The study also introduces the TrueSkill algorithm to the field of cycling. Despite it being an extension to popular one-on-one ranking methods often used in sports analytics, such as the ELO rating system, its application in sports settings is uncommon. We demonstrate that using individual race results translates to much better rankings compared to team-based performances.

Future research might focus on the relationship between label set size and constrained clustering performance, as while already outperforming other methods, theoretically this performance should only increase with enlarged labeled set size. Unfortunately, the creation of such a dataset is a cumbersome process which is heavily influenced by the labeler's own prejudices. Moreover, some fan accounts have also shown early methodologies which focus on the grouping of related races. Unfortunately, limited information is provided on to how these groupings are created, which makes comparative analysis difficult. Future research might validate our clustering approach compared to these approaches once more transparency about these methods is provided. Another interesting avenue for future research might be the validation of this methodology as a step in other analytics applications.

References

Baron, E., Janssens, B., Bogaert, M.: Bike2Vec: vector embedding representations of road cycling riders and races. arXiv preprint arXiv:2305.10471 (2023)

Comaniciu, D., Meer, P.: Mean shift: a robust approach toward feature space analysis. IEEE Trans. Pattern Anal. Mach. Intell. **24**(5), 603–619 (2002)

De Bock, J., Verstockt, S.: Video-based analysis and reporting of riding behavior in cyclocross segments. Sensors **21**(22), 7619 (2021)

de Leeuw, A.W., Heijboer, M., Verdonck, T., Knobbe, A., Latré, S.: Exploiting sensor data in professional road cycling: personalized data-driven approach for frequent fitness monitoring. Data Min. Knowl. Discov. 1–29 (2022)

Ester, M., Kriegel, H.P., Sander, J., Xu, X.: A density-based algorithm for discovering clusters in large spatial databases with noise. In: KDD, vol. 96, no. 34, pp. 226–231 (1996)

Frey, B.J., Dueck, D.: Clustering by passing messages between data points. Science **315**(5814), 972–976 (2007)

Herbrich, R., Minka, T., Graepel, T.: TrueSkill™: a Bayesian skill rating system. In: Advances in Neural Information Processing Systems, vol. 19 (2006)

Hilmkil, A., Ivarsson, O., Johansson, M., Kuylenstierna, D., van Erp, T.: Towards machine learning on data from professional cyclists. CoRR abs/1808.00198 (2018)

Hood, A.: Former UCI president questions WorldTour relegation/promotion: 'why change if it's working well?' (2022). https://www.velonews.com/news/former-uci-president-questions-worldtour-relegation-promotion/. Accessed 8 Dec 2022

Janssens, B., Bogaert, M.: Imputation of non-participated race results. In: Brefeld, U., Davis, J., Van Haaren, J., Zimmermann, A. (eds.) MLSA 2021. CCIS, vol. 1571, pp. 155–166. Springer, Cham (2022). https://doi.org/10.1007/978-3-031-02044-5_13

Janssens, B., Bogaert, M., Maton, M.: Predicting the next Pogačar: a data analytical approach to detect young professional cycling talents. Ann. Oper. Res. 1–32 (2022)

Kataoka, Y., Gray, P.: Real-time power performance prediction in tour de France. In: Brefeld, U., Davis, J., Van Haaren, J., Zimmermann, A. (eds.) MLSA 2018. LNCS, vol. 11330, pp. 121–130. Springer, Cham (2019). https://doi.org/10.1007/978-3-030-17274-9_10

Kholkine, L., De Schepper, T., Verdonck, T., Latré, S.: A machine learning approach for road cycling race performance prediction. In: Brefeld, U., Davis, J., Van Haaren, J., Zimmermann, A. (eds.) MLSA 2020. CCIS, vol. 1324, pp. 103–112. Springer, Cham (2020). https://doi.org/10.1007/978-3-030-64912-8_9

Kholkine, L., et al.: A learn-to-rank approach for predicting road cycling race outcomes. Front. Sports Active Living 3 (2021)

Lucia, A., Joyos, H., Chicharro, J.L.: Physiological response to professional road cycling: climbers vs. time trialists. Int. J. Sports Med. 21(07), 505–512 (2000)

Menaspà, P., Rampinini, E., Bosio, A., Carlomagno, D., Riggio, M., Sassi, A.: Physiological and anthropometric characteristics of junior cyclists of different specialties and performance levels. Scand. J. Med. Sci. Sports 22(3), 392–398 (2012)

Menaspà, P., Quod, M., Martin, D.T., Peiffer, J.J., Abbiss, C.R.: Physical demands of sprinting in professional road cycling. Int. J. Sports Med. 36(13), 1058–1062 (2015)

Ozols, K.: Geraint Thomas was Stronger in the Tour de France 2022 compared to his 2018 Victory (2022). https://lanternerouge.com.au/2022/11/07/geraint-thomas-was-stronger-in-the-tour-de-france-2022-compared-to-his-2018-victory/. Accessed 2 Dec 2022

Raftery, A.E., Dean, N.: Variable selection for model-based clustering. J. Am. Stat. Assoc. 101(473), 168–178 (2006)

Schubert, E., Gertz, M.: Improving the cluster structure extracted from optics plots. In: LWDA (2018)

Sculley, D.: Web-scale k-means clustering. In: Proceedings of the 19th International Conference on World Wide Web, pp. 1177–1178 (2010)

Shi, J., Malik, J.: Normalized cuts and image segmentation. IEEE Trans. Pattern Anal. Mach. Intell. 22(8), 888–905 (2000)

Sneath, P.H., Sokal, R.R.: Numerical taxonomy. The principles and practice of numerical classification (1973)

Steyaert, M., De Bock, J., Verstockt, S.: Sensor-based performance monitoring in track cycling. In: Brefeld, U., Davis, J., Van Haaren, J., Zimmermann, A. (eds.) MLSA 2021. CCIS, vol. 1571, pp. 167–177. Springer, Cham (2022). https://doi.org/10.1007/978-3-031-02044-5_14

Suzuki, A.K., Salasar, L.E.B., Leite, J.G., Louzada-Neto, F.: A Bayesian approach for predicting match outcomes: the 2006 (association) football world cup. J. Oper. Res. Soc. 61(10), 1530–1539 (2010)

Van Bulck, D., Vande Weghe, A., Goossens, D.: Result-based talent identification in road cycling: discovering the next Eddy Merckx. Ann. Oper. Res. 1–18 (2021)

Reeth, D.: Globalization in professional road cycling. In: Van Reeth, D., Larson, D.J. (eds.) The economics of professional road cycling. SEMP, vol. 11, pp. 165–205. Springer, Cham (2016). https://doi.org/10.1007/978-3-319-22312-4_9

Wagstaff, K., Cardie, C., Rogers, S., Schrödl, S.: Constrained k-means clustering with background knowledge. In: ICML, vol. 1, pp. 577–584 (2001)

Ward Jr., J.H.: Hierarchical grouping to optimize an objective function. J. Am. Stat. Assoc. **58**(301), 236–244 (1963)

Zhang, T., Ramakrishnan, R., Livny, M.: BIRCH: an efficient data clustering method for very large databases. ACM SIGMOD Rec. **25**(2), 103–114 (1996)

Exploiting Clustering for Sports Data Analysis: A Study of Public and Real-World Datasets

Vanessa Meyer[✉][iD], Ahmed Al-Ghezi[✉][iD], and Lena Wiese[✉][iD]

Institute of Computer Science, Goethe University Frankfurt, Robert-Mayer-Str. 10, 60325 Frankfurt am Main, Germany
v.meyer@em.uni-frankfurt.de, {alghezi,lwiese}@cs.uni-frankfurt.de

Abstract. Clustering as a data mining method has significant importance in data analysis. To achieve the goal of identifying prototypical features in sports data, this paper focuses on well-known clustering methods applied to publicly available data from the field of sports and activities, as well as a real-world dataset representing multi-domain measurements about professional athletes. Difficulties of the wide range of preprocessing methods as well as clustering methods are highlighted in this paper. In addition, the selected data sets are critically reviewed.

Keywords: Sports Analytics · Clustering · Multidisciplinary Sports Data

1 Introduction

Data mining methods are increasingly being used to analyze data. Thus, these methods are also becoming more important for analyzing sports data to provide training recommendations to athletes based on their data [5]. Finding prototypical features in sports data using clustering techniques and the associated methods for preprocessing the data is the goal of this paper. To achieve this goal, two sports data sets are used: First, the public Body Performance data set [4] was used in the development whereas the real-world data set of the *in:prove* project is used as a validation use case.

In this paper we hence make the following contributions: The mentioned data sets are preprocessed accordingly before clustering, where different variants and combinations are tested. Furthermore, the following well-known clustering methods are used: K-Means, Hierarchical Clustering, Density-Based Spatial Clustering of Applications with Noise (DBSCAN), Affinity propagation, Mean-shift and Balanced Iterative Reducing and Clustering using Hierarchies (BIRCH). By choosing different clustering methods and preprocessing methods, differences between methods and the resulting influence on the clustering results are clarified.

U. Brefeld et al. (Eds.): MLSA 2023, CCIS 2035, pp. 191–201, 2024.
https://doi.org/10.1007/978-3-031-53833-9_16

Our research focuses on understanding how these clustering algorithms perform on distinct types of sport-related data sets. By comparing the effectiveness of the clustering algorithms on two distinct data sets, we can draw more conclusions about the applicability of the algorithms and methods used.

2   Related Work

One of the basic methods of data mining is clustering. Clustering belongs to the unsupervised methods [9]. Several approaches apply clustering to sports-related data (as surveyed in the following) without however providing the comprehensive comparison as we do in this paper.

For mixed data, the authors present a robust fuzzy clustering model in [2]. In addition, noise clusters are used, and a weighting system is used for mixed attribute to obtain feature sets relevant for clustering. The authors present a simulation study and an empirical application. For this purpose, data from football players are considered, which are grouped based on their performance and position. The clustering algorithm the authors present proves effective for finding clusters that remained hidden without the multi-attribute approach [2].

In [6], a clustering algorithm is developed based on the Delaunay method. The authors group heat maps of football games into average formations of players and use hierarchical clustering to subdivide the average formations. In the resulting clusters, the players' configurations are different. Thus, according to the authors, typical transition patterns of formations of a team can be extracted.

To make better decisions for training, data collected with the help of wearable devices from athletes of an NCAA Division 1 American football team are grouped using K-Means clustering in [11]. The average playing demands of the athletes were determined to form appropriate training groups. According to the authors, the results are similar to traditional groupings for American Football training.

In [12], motivational profiles of young college athletes are found with the help of clustering. To do this, the athletes filled out questionnaires that were used to assess their motivation indices. According to the authors, four clusters were found to be meaningful. This could serve as a support for coaches to develop intervention programs regarding the motivational needs of their athletes.

3   Clustering Comparison

In this chapter, we first describe the public Body Performance data set. The Body Performance data set contains twelve features and 13393 data points. The features include a binary attribute called *gender*, as well as numeric attributes such as *age*, *weight_kg*, *height_cm*, *body fat_%*, blood pressure values *diastolic* and *systolic*, as well as measures of athletic activities such as *sit-ups counts*, *gripForce*, *sit and bend forward_cm*, and *broad jump_cm*. Furthermore, there is a categorical attribute called *class*, which is not considered further as it is a target variable. In future studies, external cluster validation indices could be used since the use of *class* provides a ground truth label.

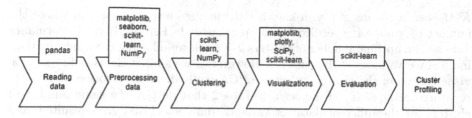

Fig. 1. Representation of our process with associated Python libraries

We now discuss our process; Fig. 1 shows the sequence of methods applied, as well as associated Python libraries. After preprocessing, clustering divides the data into groups. Subsequently, the resulting clusters are evaluated using internal cluster indices. In the following, the cluster results of the different clustering methods are described. Clustering was applied to three different variants of the Body Performance data set resulting from the three preprocessing pipelines sketched in Table 1. A comparison of the clusters formed by applying k-means, hierarchical clustering and BIRCH to the first variant of the Body Performance data is visualized with Principal Component Analysis (PCA) in Fig. 2.

Table 1. Three versions of preprocessing pipelines for body performance data

	Version 1	Version 2	Version 3
Missing Values	No	No	No
Outlier Removal	Yes	Yes	Yes
Feature Selection	Pearson Correlation	PCA	No
Scaling	MinMaxScaler	StandardScaler	MinMaxScaler

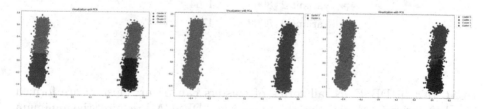

Fig. 2. Visualization with PCA of the resulting k-means (left), hierarchical (middle) and BIRCH (right) clusters of the first data set variant.

K-Means: K-Means is a well-known partitioning clustering method where the number of groups is specified by the parameter k. For the Body Performance data set, an optimal number of clusters $k = 4$ was found using the Elbow method in all three variants of the data set. However, if we look at the two-dimensional visualization of the clusters using the PCA method, we tend to see two clearly separated groups. It can be seen in Table 2 that despite the same number of clusters for the different data set variants, different cluster sizes resulted, and thus different preprocessing pipelines resulted in different clusters.

Table 2. Overview of the sizes of resulting k-means clusters for each data set variant

Data Set	Cluster 0	Cluster 1	Cluster 2	Cluster 3
Variant 1	2607	5395	1901	2822
Variant 2	3290	4619	2948	1868
Variant 3	2557	5445	1844	2879

Hierarchical Clustering: We use the agglomerative approach, in which clusters are combined. To determine a suitable number of clusters for hierarchical clustering, we first formed dendrograms. Color-coded subgraphs of the dendrograms were used to determine the number of clusters: two clusters were formed for each of the variants. Table 3 shows the cluster sizes of the different data set variants of the hierarchical clustering method.

Table 3. Overview of the sizes of resulting hierarchical clusters for each data set variant

Data Set	Cluster 0	Cluster 1
Variant 1	8002	4723
Variant 2	8061	4664
Variant 3	8002	4723

DBSCAN: In DBSCAN, all forms of clusters can occur: clusters are formed based on regions with high density. In addition, DBSCAN requires the minimum number of neighboring points and the distance between neighboring points and a core sample as parameters [10]. For the Body Performance data set, DBSCAN formed two clusters for each variant. In doing so, Variant 2 had some data points marked as noise which is also included in Table 4. Variants 1 and 3, on the other hand, received clusters of the same size as in hierarchical clustering.

Table 4. Overview of the sizes of resulting DBSCAN clusters for each data set variant

Data Set	Noise	Cluster 0	Cluster 1
Variant 1	–	8002	4723
Variant 2	1319	7420	3986
Variant 3	–	8002	4723

Affinity Propagation: Affinity Propagation (AP) forms clusters by exchanging messages between data points. The message exchange reveals whether one data point is a match for the other data point. Up to convergence, the suitability is updated based on responses to values of other pairs [10]. Due to its complexity and the many data objects in the Body Performance data set, Affinity Propagation could not be applied to the full data. For this reason a smaller sample of the data set is generated, including 100 random data points. Table 5 shows an overview of the cluster sizes per data set variant. Notably, AP finds much more clusters than other methods.

Table 5. Overview of the sizes of resulting Affinity Propagation clusters

Data Set	Cl. 0	Cl. 1	Cl. 2	Cl. 3	Cl. 4	Cl. 5	Cl. 6
Variant 1	19	18	13	28	22	–	–
Variant 2	14	21	15	13	9	9	19
Variant 3	12	25	4	9	14	22	14

Mean-Shift: Among the center-based clustering methods is Mean-shift. Candidate centers are determined by mean values of data points in a region and updated. In a post-processing phase, candidates are filtered to remove near-duplicates to form the cluster centers [10]. Again, the cluster sizes differ (see Table 6). Yet, for the third variant of the body performance data set, Mean-Shift results corresponds to the results of hierarchical clustering and DBSCAN.

Table 6. Overview of the resulting Mean-Shift clusters for each data set variant

Data Set	Cluster 0	Cluster 1	Cluster 2
Variant 1	8002	2727	1996
Variant 2	7732	4993	–
Variant 3	8002	4723	–

BIRCH: The BIRCH algorithm builds a Cluster Feature Tree (CFT). The data points are packed into so-called Cluster Feature (CF) nodes [10]. The resulting clusters of the body performance variants are also different (see Table 7). In the two-dimensional visualizations with the PCA method, it is also clear that clusters formed with BIRCH overlap more than clusters formed by other algorithms.

Table 7. Overview of the resulting BIRCH clusters for each data set variant

Data Set	Cluster 0	Cluster 1	Cluster 2	Cluster 3
Variant 1	5618	2145	2384	2578
Variant 2	5992	3478	1994	1261
Variant 3	3262	3552	4740	1171

Cluster Validation Indices: Table 8 shows cluster validation scores of the respective data set variants and clustering algorithms to determine the goodness of the clusters: Silhouette Coefficient, Calinski-Harabasz Score and Davies Bouldin Score were used to calculate the validation scores.

To provide a comprehensive understanding of the results, we will present the cluster validation indices in more detail.

Cluster validation indices are often used to evaluate cluster results. Internal cluster validation indices like the above-mentioned scores evaluate cluster results based on information found in the data itself. In general, these metrics are used to evaluate clusters for compactness, i.e., the density of data points within a cluster, and separability, i.e., the distance between two clusters [7,8].

For the silhouette coefficient, a higher score indicates better defined clusters. The silhouette coefficient is calculated for each data point in the data set by taking the average distance between one data point and all other data points in the same cluster and calculating the average distance between the data point and all other data points in the closest cluster [10]. For multiple data points The silhouette coefficient is calculated by taking the average of the individual silhouette coefficients of data points. Its values range from -1 to 1. A silhouette coefficient of zero indicates overlapping clusters, while higher values represent denser and better separated clusters. It is important to note that the silhouette coefficient has a drawback: It tends to compute higher values for convex clusters. Non-convex clusters, which can be found in DBSCAN, may have a lower silhouette coefficient [10].

The Calinski-Harabasz index is another evaluation method. Similar to the silhouette coefficient, a higher value indicates better defined clusters. The index represents the ratio of the sum of dispersion between clusters and the dispersion within clusters. An advantage of the Calinski-Harabasz index is its fast calculation. However, similar to the silhouette coefficient, it also has the disadvantage that the values are higher for convex clusters. This may mean that non-convex clusters, such as those that may occur in DBSCAN, have lower Calinski-Harabasz index values [10].

In contrast to the Silhouette coefficient and the Calinski-Harabasz index, a lower Davies-Bouldin index indicates that the clusters of a model are better separated from each other. The index indicates the average similarity, where this similarity is the comparison of the distance between clusters with the size of the clusters. A value close to zero stand for better partitioning, with zero being the best value. An advantage of the Davies-Bouldin index is that it is easier to calculate compared to the silhouette coefficient. In addition, only pointwise distances are used in the calculation, and the index is based solely on the sizes and features of the data set. However, the Davies-Bouldin index also has the disadvantage that the values for convex clusters are higher than for non-convex clusters [10].

According to the indices for the Body Performance data set, DBSCAN and Hierarchical Clustering with data set variant 1 provide the best cluster results. The clusters formed in this process consist of two well-separated groups, which can also be seen in the two-dimensional visualizations. If we examine the Body Performance data, we observe that the data was clustered by gender. This highlights that clustering methods may not provide meaningful results when not excluding categorical or binary attribute types like the gender attribute. One possibility is to remove the gender feature from the data set. However, in addition to gender, age and the performance features, the data set contains only a few physiological features (height, weight, body fat, diastolic and systolic) which can be dependent on gender and age. Therefore, this data set is useful for testing purposes, but a data set that provides more physiological features would be desirable for cluster analysis.

Table 8. Cluster validation indices for each cluster algorithm and data set variant

Algorithm	CVI	Variant 1	Variant 2	Variant 3
K-means	SC	0.4110	0.4206	0.3224
	CH	14710.2149	15712.3319	9809.0281
	DB	0.9744	0.8695	1.2407
Hierarchical	SC	0.5410	0.5128	0.4876
	CH	17908.5849	16327.5031	14628.0959
	DB	0.7762	0.7589	0.8700
DBSCAN	SC	0.5410	0.4353	0.4876
	CH	17908.5849	6880.5246	14628.0959
	DB	0.7762	2.2385	0.8700
Affinity Propagation	SC	0.3402	0.3732	0.2204
	CH	107.9007	118.1503	49.4514
	DB	1.1333	0.8626	1.4335
Mean-Shift	SC	0.4855	0.5154	0.4876
	CH	12662.8634	16957.4042	14628.0959
	DB	0.8465	0.7626	0.8700
BIRCH	SC	0.3935	0.4015	0.2790
	CH	13946.9398	13528.6883	8865.8700
	DB	1.0066	0.8307	1.3273

4   Evaluation on Real-World Data Set

We consider in this section the in:prove data set[1]. It is a multi-disciplinary sport data set that is being dynamically collected from about 600 professional athletes. It also represents more than 100 measurement parameters categorized as personal and body measurements, performance, training, physiology, cognition, and sociology. Those diverse and dense measurements sketch a training profile for each athlete. We collect another type of evaluation that is the competitions data. These data sketch the performance of the athletes in real world competitions. In this paper, we will concentrate on a subset of data from approximately 50 basketball athletes for whom we already have a competition evaluations metric (that is, their "ranking"). We aim to discover how well those competition points cluster with the performance and cognition data of the same athletes. The performance measurements provide quantitative assessments of an athlete's behaviors, captured through specific performance measurement devices. Since we have many measurements within the performance space, our first step was to find the features that show the best clustering results within the performance space itself. For this, we iteratively ran the BIRCH clustering algorithm on the competition evaluation feature combined with all of the performance features and selected the best combination. To evaluate a clustering run, we use an average between Silhouette Score and Calinski-Harabasz Index. In this context, the best performing features were:

- **LPI Hand.** Laterality Preference Inventory value for hands.
- **LPI Auge.** Laterality Preference Inventory value for eyes.
- **LPI Ohr.** Laterality Preference Inventory value for ear.
- **Inhi RT Hand.** Inhibition reaction time of the hands.

The results of clustering the above features with the competitions evaluation are shown in Table 9. AffinityPropagation gives the best indexes (CVI) results in Table 9. However, it produces too many small clusters. Both K-Means and AgglomerativeClustering algorithms offer the best compromise between cluster separation and definition. They have comparable performance and provide a reasonable balance between cohesion (as indicated by the Silhouette score) and separation (as indicated by the Davies-Bouldin score). MeanShift and BIRCH could be considered as alternatives, with specific trade-offs in terms of cluster definition and separation.

Next, we considered the correlation between the cognition and the competition data. The cognition measurements record athletes' responses to carefully designed tests, providing a temporal assessment of their cognitive abilities. We applied the same iterative method to identify the best performing features in the clustering process for the combinations of both the competition and cognition features. In this context, those features were:

- **D2r BZO SW.** The time required to workout the test (the main measurement in this test).

---

[1] https://inprove.info.

- **CF P6 switchcost.** Cognitive Flexibility: Average time to click the next tile without a mistake. This measurement is specific to the sixth puzzle (out of the seven puzzles conducted in the test).

To state more context about the above two measurements, we briefly mention the tests that they belong to:

- **D2** [1]. The d2 Test of Attention is an assessment tool designed to evaluate both selective and sustained attention, as well as the speed of visual scanning. This is typically a written exercise that instructs participants to mark out each instance of the letter "d" that is encircled by a pair of marks in any configuration, whether above or below. The task is made challenging by the inclusion of distractor elements that closely resemble the target stimulus, such as a "p" accompanied by two marks or a "d" with either one or three marks.
- **CF** [3]. The Youmans Cognitive Flexibility Assessment is a puzzle-based task aimed at assessing an individual's capacity to swiftly alternate between distinct mental frameworks. It involves participants using a mouse to traverse a labyrinth of tiles, each possessing a unique shape, shape color, and background color. Movement from one tile to another is allowed whenever any one of these three attributes is identical on two neighboring tiles.

We performed the clustering of the above two cognition measurements with the competition measurement, and state the index (CVI) results in Table 10. K-means produced the best clustering results with 3 clearly identified clusters as given by the Calinski-Harabasz score of 42.82. Moreover, the clustering structure was very good as given by the Silhouette score of 0.63. These metrics are added to a Davies-Bouldin score of 0.53 indicates good separation between the clusters. The BIRCH algorithm also performed very well with a Silhouette score of 0.64, which is the second-highest. The Calinski-Harabasz score is lower than K-Means but still suggests reasonably well-defined clusters. The Davies-Bouldin score of 0.47 is also quite good, indicating well-separated clusters. In the third step, we aimed to find if the correlation relationship holds between all the selected features of cognition, performance as well as the competition. In this context, we implemented the six algorithms on the given features and stated the indexes results in Table 11. Considering those results, we see that the correlation relationship still holds in the combined features. That can be observed in the Mean Shift which performs fairly well. The Silhouette score of 0.36 is good and suggests that the clusters are cohesive. The Calinski-Harabasz score of 16.15 suggests more well-defined clusters compared to K-means and DBSCAN. The Davies-Bouldin score of 0.69 is relatively low, suggesting reasonably well-separated clusters.

Despite the identifiable clusters, there is generally a decreased quality in the resulting clusters of combined features compared to the case when considering the competitions feature with either the performance or the cognition features (Tables 10 and 9). This could arise from the general curse of dimensionality in the clustering algorithms. However, one way to interpret this from the application point of view is that sports experts need to consider grouping the given tests in cognition or performance alone for better correlation with the sports results in real competitions.

Table 9. Clustering indexes of performance and competition features with number of clusters

Algorithm	Silhouette	Calinski-Harabasz	Davies-Bouldin	#Clusters
K-means	0.42	21.61	0.90	2
DBSCAN	0.10	4.22	2.86	4
AffinityPropagation	0.48	32.79	0.72	10
MeanShift	0.38	24.92	1.03	3
BIRCH	0.42	11.22	0.74	2
Aggl. Clustering	0.42	21.61	0.90	2

Table 10. Clustering indexes of cognition and competition features with number of clusters

Algorithm	Silhouette	Calinski-Har.	Davies-B.	#Clusters
K-means	0.63	42.82	0.53	3
DBSCAN	0.48	10.78	1.50	4
Affinity Propagation	0.60	592.47	0.22	23
Mean Shift	0.22	18.61	1.12	5
BIRCH	0.64	31.89	0.47	3
Aggl. Clustering	0.77	26.94	0.14	2

Table 11. Clustering indexes of performance, cognition and competition features

Algorithm	Silhouette	Calinski-Har.	Davies-B.	#clusters
K-means	0.34	13.92	1.13	2
DBSCAN	−0.13	0.91	2.48	2
Affinity Propagation	0.44	39.41	0.64	10
Mean Shift	0.37	16.16	0.70	4
BIRCH	0.44	10.60	0.61	3
Aggl. Clustering	0.33	13.61	0.98	2

5   Conclusion

We presented an implementation and comparative evaluation of clustering algorithms on sports data sets. This paper provides a comprehensive evaluation based on several cluster validation indexes (CVIs).

Based on the tables described, it can already be seen that the groupings can differ greatly depending on the clustering algorithm and data set variant (i.e., preprocessing), as well as the selected parameters. Therefore, before applying a clustering procedure and preparing the data, it is important to determine a context to be studied using clustering. The publicly available Body Performance data set was used for testing purposes to learn about the behavior of different clustering methods. Our validation on a real-world dataset confirms the observations on the publicly available dataset.

The general purpose of our platform is to be able to assign athletes to a cluster based on their individual features and provide individual training recommendations to improve performance. Hence in future work we will apply our implementation to larger data sets and extend our platform. Additionally, various alternative clustering algorithms, such as spectral clustering, as well as other preprocessing and evaluation methods can be applied to the sports-related data sets in future work to investigate whether they lead to even better cluster results.

Acknowledgements. This project was funded with research funds from the Bundesinstitut für Sport-wissenschaften based on a decision of Deutscher Bundestag (Project Number: ZMI4-081901/21-25).

References

1. Brickenkamp, R., Schmidt-Atzert, L., Liepmann, D.: Test d2-Revision: Aufmerksamkeits-und Konzentrationstest. Hogrefe, Göttingen (2010)
2. D'Urso, P., De Giovanni, L., Vitale, V.: A robust method for clustering football players with mixed attributes. Ann. Oper. Res. 1–28 (2022)
3. Figueroa, I., Youmans, R., Shaw, T.: Cognitive flexibility and sustained attention. In: Proceedings of the Human Factors and Ergonomics Society Annual Meeting, vol. 58, pp. 954–958 (2014). https://doi.org/10.1177/1541931214581200
4. Kaggle: Body Performance Dataset. https://www.kaggle.com/datasets/kukuroo3/body-performance-data?resource=download. Accessed 05 Mar 2023
5. Li, X., Chen, X., Guo, L., Rochester, C.A.: Application of big data analysis techniques in sports training and physical fitness analysis. Hindawi Wirel. Commun. Mob. Comput. **2022**, Article ID 3741087 (2022)
6. Narizuka, T., Yamazaki, Y.: Clustering algorithm for formations in football games. Sci. Rep. **9**(1), 1–8 (2019)
7. Rendón, E., Abundez, I., Arizmendi, A., Quiroz, E.M.: Internal versus external cluster validation indexes. Int. J. Comput. Commun. **5**(1), 27–34 (2011)
8. Rendón, E., et al.: A comparison of internal and external cluster validation indexes. In: Proceedings of the 2011 American Conference, San Francisco, CA, USA, vol. 29, pp. 1–10 (2011)
9. Rokach, L., Maimon, O.: Data Mining and Knowledge Discovery Handbook. Springer, New York (2005). https://doi.org/10.1007/b107408
10. Scikit Learn: Clustering. https://scikit-learn.org/stable/modules/clustering.html#. Accessed 05 Mar 2023
11. Shelly, Z., Burch, R.F., Tian, W., Strawderman, L., Piroli, A., Bichey, C.: Using K-means clustering to create training groups for elite American football student-athletes based on game demands. Int. J. Kinesiol. Sports Sci. **8**(2), 47–63 (2020)
12. Zason Chian, L.K., John Wang, C.K.: Motivational profiles of junior college athletes: a cluster analysis. J. Appl. Sport Psychol. **20**(2), 137–156 (2008)

Author Index

U. Brefeld et al. (Eds.): MLSA 2023, CCIS 2035, pp. 203–204, 2024.
https://doi.org/10.1007/978-3-031-53833-9

Printed in the United States
by Baker & Taylor Publisher Services